Data Acquisition and Analysis in Geoinformatics

NIPA® GENX ELECTRONIC RESOURCES & SOLUTIONS P. LTD.
New Delhi-110 034

About the Author

Dr. Adikant Pradhan completed under graduate and post-graduate in Agriculture from Indira Gandhi Krishi Vishwavidyalaya, Raipur and then joined as a scientist in All India Coordinated Research Project on Small Millets in 2003 and worked for 13 years in millet research with landform study and natural resource management for diverse form of crop and management aspects. Looking to the real time management of resources in research new dimension of modern tools like remote sensing, GIS and GPS based data analysis and finalizing programmes; meanwhile working on GIS and remote sensing he developed resource map of more than 500 villages of the region for better management of natural resource available in the rainfed area. For the next five years he served as Chief Scientist dealing in rainfed agriculture under All India Coordinated Research Project on Dryland Agriculture at S.G. College of Agriculture & Research Station, IGKV, Jagdalpur, again village level resource conservation of land and water resources have been successfully done. By using remote sensing technique and image processing all watersheds were delineated at micro level to plan for 500 to 700 hectares land of confined villages and delivered the findings to state and district level planning. For working in tribal and remote area he received ICAR-Fakhruddin Ali Ahmed Award-2019 for outstanding research in tribal farming system as team leader where digital planning and application of remote sensing was widely used within time frame and faster way. Digital mapping also expanded while working in All India Coordinated Research Project on Integrated Farming at Krishi Vigyan Kendra where he studied the local waterbody mapping and irrigation water distribution system for efficient and useful utilization due to proper aerial photometry and developed digital maps.

He has over two decades of experience in teaching, research and extension with present and future prospect of rural agriculture. Dr. Pradhan has more than 50 scientific papers numerous international and national repute journals he also published 5 books and various articles on recent technologies to minimize the labour cost as well as time saving phenomenon. Under his supervision more than 20 Master students and 5 Ph. D. students have got degrees. Presently he is deeply involved in research of small level map of soil, land, topography and waterbody through drone technology and satellite imageries at micro level planning.

Data Acquisition and Analysis in Geoinformatics

Adikant Pradhan
Chief Scientist, AICRP-IFS
Department of Agronomy
Indira Gandhi Krishi Vishwavidyalaya
Krishak Nagar, Jora, Raipur (C.G.) 492012

NIPA® GENX ELECTRONIC RESOURCES & SOLUTIONS P. LTD.
New Delhi-110 034

NIPA® GENX ELECTRONIC
RESOURCES & SOLUTIONS P. LTD.

101,103, Vikas Surya Plaza, CU Block
L.S.C. Market, Pitam Pura, New Delhi-110 034
Ph : +91 11 27341616, 27341717, 27341718
E-mail: newindiapublishingagency@gmail.com
Web: www.nipabooks.com

For customer assistance, please contact
Phone: + 91-11-27 34 17 17
Fax: + 91-11- 27 34 16 16
E-Mail: feedbacks@nipabooks.com

ISBN: 978-93-94490-56-7

Composed and Designed by NIPA®.

Preface

This book is primarily designed to be used in the purpose of introduction and application of remote sensing techniques in agriculture and allied fields and as a reference for burgeoning number of practitioners who frequently use geo-spatial information and their analysis. Remote sensing, geographic information system (GIS) and global positioning system (GPS) are widely expanding tools in gripping world on finger tips, academic and professional settings where book will be useful in understanding basics and their applications with advance world. Rather writing book marginally oriented toward the business of learners and researchers of ecology, forestry, geography, geology, water management, landforms related to agricultural study, regional planning of natural resources etc. might be approached through studying the book. In gist, anyone involved in geospatial technology for data acquisition and analysis will find this book to be a valuable text and reference.

15 years of live field experience has been documented in the book with day to day change in remote sensing and GIS technology that have also been compiled for easy understanding of the users. The book covers basic work for planning and execution with emphasis laid on digital systems and analysis techniques specially as an applications of resource management in fields. Hence, the chapter matter contained herein ranges from the principles of geospatial interpretation and digital information from the earth and environment to operation and application of imageries and satellite data perfectly. Aerial photography, drone technology, image processing, satellite systems, cartography with old and new techniques, digital terrain analysis set new dimensions of geo-informatics are may be a vital in this book.

This book might serve as text as well as reference in helping various online remote sensing courses; it offers recent courses designed under graduate and post graduate studies. I have tried to cover basic concepts of geo-informatics and application in the chapters to provide space for all level of readers.

Thanks are due to my parents and family members for their understanding and support. I also extend my gratitude to honourable Vice Chancellor Dr. Girish Chandel, IGKV, Raipur for his cooperation and enthusiasts in shaping and structuring this book.

Author

Contents

1

Geographical Information System

Digital Technologies

In modern days, many informations receive through electronic media with instant connecting by satellite based information on social, economical, environmental etc. the informations are coded with feasible electronic encrypt and delivered to people. Similarly remote sensing, GIS (Geographical Information System) and GPS (Global Positioning System) also serve world for better understanding the ground reality along with reducing cost of operation, transforming data through electronic webs easily. In earlier phase, ground related information was not easily obtained because all kind of work had been done manually using analog maps of earth; even map draw was done by drafting from totposheet or hand maps, no interface of analog and digital world.

Remote sensing technology basically works on earth's information with ground truth conjucting spatial features made vival at present world, wide range of satellites has been launched and set on air to collect each and every information available on earth with change under scale. A large number of people already use better way for interpretation and developing models to predict upcoming event and also for monitoring these all events happening in the world. Demography, settlement, land use, land cover, resource mapping etc. are vital segment of remote sensing. Remote sensing includes GIS to process data as per need for proper interpretation and same time locations are tagged place search with maximum accuracy.

A Geographic Information System (GIS) integrates hardware, software, and data for capturing, managing, analyzing, and displaying all forms of geographically referenced information. GIS also allows the integration of these data sets for deriving meaningful information with output of the information derivatives in map format or tabular format.

A GIS can be viewed in three ways

1. **Database:** A GIS is a unique kind of database of the world - a geo graphic database. This contains Information System for Geography.

Basically, GIS expresses on a structure from database that details geographic terms.

2. **Map:** The GIS is package of smart map representation in maps and related views display features and relationship of features. Maps having geographic information may be drawn and used as windows of database to get queries, analysis and editing the information.
3. **Model:** A GIS is a transformer tool for a set of information that produces new geographic datasets from present datasets. The geoprocessing function obtains information from database/data sets, involves analytic function and give results in new form of datasets. The above three views always provides complete information on land resource, water resource and morphology.

Geographical Information System (GIS)

Geographical Information System (GIS) involves software, hardware and off course data to capture image, analysis and display of every forms of geographical information which is always geo-referred. GIS also helps in integration the data sets for getting meaningful information either in map or tabular format.

System of information and virtual arena make capable to receive information in the form of data about physical and even cultural features of the worlds in solving research issues i.e., instant retrieve of realistic data. Present advance technologies have forereached to an increased use of computer and information in place of manual process in every aspect of spatial data management. These information systems possess data in analog on about the phenomenon of the realistic world and are able to design, manipulate, contain and use that spatial data more speedy as compared to manual methods with storing longer in digital forms. Data itself be important and accentuate value as it is progressively used from data to information and knowledge, GIS is a software technology in this area. Especially GIS are then used to perform the planning work as spatial analysis functions. This whole progress can perform faster and allows modifying easily under analysis approach alongwith virtual assessment.

GIS may be defined as an integrations of system of hardware and software associated with some procedures and men involved in analysis which together helps in capture, store, manage, manipulate, analyze, model and display of reference data.

In precise, geographical information system support to create maps that integrate information, visualize prospect, solve difficult problems with the powerful ideas and design effective solutions just like never before we had the experience. Geographical analysis and making map are old work, but existence of GIS done quickly than those old manual methods. It may be said as helping tools in decision making process.

Data Models

Real world geographical variation can be converted into discrete outputs which is completed through this data models and it represents the connection between the real world geographical data and computer software in displaying the features. Therefore, people can represent in convenient forms with easy accessible. There are two types of data models, one is vector and another raster means change in form may be comfortable with software as raster or vector. Three different geometric classes of data often encounter in both the models, and dimensional polygon gives information of area and perimeter measurement.

Raster Model

Basically raster type representation of data contain geographic information. Cell sets located by coordinate is used, the individual cell is independently addresses with the value of attribute and each has a single value with location corresponding information. Fundamentally one set of cell associated value is known layer.

Vector Model

Generally vector data include lines and points representing their clear cut "x" and "y" coordinates to know the locations. Discrete features are designed by connecting line segments that area is delineated by set of line segments. Even vector data require less space for storage and outputs are appreciable. Measurement of area or perimeters is accurate and editing work is faster and comfortable as raster model.

Layers and Coverage

For access data it is commonly needed on the basis of more classes of feature with result in applying several schemes in which all data of specific level of classes like rivers, road, vegetation types etc. are categorized into layers and more number of layers create coverage layerings that shows several things in separate forms. Either it can be seen singly or in group to view compressive features. Conceptually layer is formed including both vector and raster models. The layers are arranged in different combination with each other to create new layers which is a expression of the individual one. Each layer's characteristic within GIS based layer is about all locations with each layers it may be called to a single aerial cell or area which might be a polygon surrounded by lines in vector system, or a grid cell in a raster system. The grids represent particular aspects of image. Although it is possible to have multiple attribute for each region.

GIS itself a abbreviations of Geographical Information System that includes three words: geography, information and System, all these words together pronounced for developing map and related in formations.

Geographic: It is obvious in acquiring data from earth which is about 90% collected being associated to some location in space.

Information: Information not in that meaning to acquire spelling words, facie information includes digital forms for better interpretation of mapping. The attributing data extends in spatial and non-spatial form with various degrees of magnitudes.

System: System works in scientific manner to draw meaningful conclusion using tools. It follows some set of sequence for seamless operations, Roger Ragra developed this concept first, and further many generational changes took place afterwards with present advance techniques to be well in favour of human beings. GIS, presently wider Forms of utilization curbs data acquired and processing through GIS by inputs, storage, manipulations analysis representation, and retrieval of executing data tool.

Philosophy of GIS

In universal contest, each country has their own dynamic vision in developmental activities targeting people of the country and present word is fast and furious with expectation of finger guided technologies which can not fulfill without modern technologies. GIS may be answer of this philosophy to acquire data from earth coordinating geo-reference after data collected from satellite. Working with GIS data can be processed according our requirement as end users. There are types of question evolve in this philosophy of GIS.

Locations includes latitude and longitude as cross point of place along with elevation, condition of location: soil types, slope, pH, rain etc. may be a part of condition, trend analysis, pattern with temporal or spatial even both can be a focus of studies. Now-a-day, projection of existing situation in future time scale with probability modeling to arrange future short fall or unexpected issue at present.

Components of GIS

Hardware: Computer hardware is a collective term used to describe any of the physical components of an analog or digital computer. The term *hardware* distinguishes the tangible aspects of a computing device from software, which consists of written instructions that tell physical components what to do. Internal and external components are categorized as computer hardware may be stored either storage system. Internal components include such as the motherboard, central processing unit (CPU), random access memory (RAM), hard drive, optical drive, heat sink, power supply, transistors, chips, graphics processing unit (GPU), network interface card (NIC) and Universal Serial Bus (USB) ports. These components jointly process or store the instructions delivered by operating system (OS).

Software: Software, instructions that direct a computer what to do. Software involves the whole set of programs, procedures, and routines combined with the operation of a computer system. The term was used to differentiate the instructions from hardware *i.e.,* the physical components of a computer system. A set of instructions that directs a computer's hardware to perform a task is called a program, or software program.

Data: These are characteristics or information, usually numerical, that are collected through observation. In a technical term, *data* is a set of values belongs to qualitative or quantitative variables about persons or objects, while a datum (singular of *data*) is a single value of a single variable.

People: A user is a person who utilizes a computer or network service. ***Users*** of computer systems and software products generally lack the technical expertise required to fully understand how they work.

Method: A procedure or process for attaining an object as systematic procedure, technique, or mode of inquiry employed by or proper to a particular discipline.

Data Types in GIS

Data means collection of information either in digital or analog forms but GIS requires different kinds of data to process in proper manner with accurate conclusion. GIS accepts following types of data:

i) **Map data**: The features related to geography for drawing maps of different levels in software as well as hard form. Map data give details about present or earlier condition as data has been processed in certain time period.

ii) **Attribute data**: Basically each data processed in GIS is generated Information in tabular form simultaneously, map develops separately on GIS platforms. Whatever information is draw in GIS through lines, points and polygons with their dimension and every connecting information are atributes.

iii) **Image data**: Generally, image shows visual effects to maps while drawing lines, points and polygons over image in pdf, JEPG, Tiff etc. formats. Image is analyzed based on visual colour to separate polygons for mapping. Further drawing polygons and lines are calculated an GIS platforms to draw conclusions.

Input Data

Data are important input to sum GIS for calculating map information in different forms which are highly variables with use and purpose. Basically, data divide into two types:

i) Dissect data and

ii) Digital data, direct data includes vectorization and rasterization, Major source of data are an analog, aerial photography, satellite based data and reports.

Geo-referencing

Geo-graphical position is real representation of ground position by crossing lines each other where latitude and longitude meet at the points. This point is known as geo-referred position with various projections Systems. A projected coordinate system like Universal Transverse Mercator (UTM), Albers Equal Area, or Robinson, all of which (other map projection models) provide various mechanisms to project maps of the earth's spherical surface onto a two-dimensional Cartesian coordinate plane. All spatial data is created in coordinate system, whether it is points, lines, polygons, rasters, or annotation. The coordinates hence it can be specified in many different ways, such as decimal degrees, feet, meters, or kilometers; even any form of measurement can be used as a coordinate system. Identifying this measurement system is very first step in choosing a coordinate system which displays data in correct position under ArcGIS.

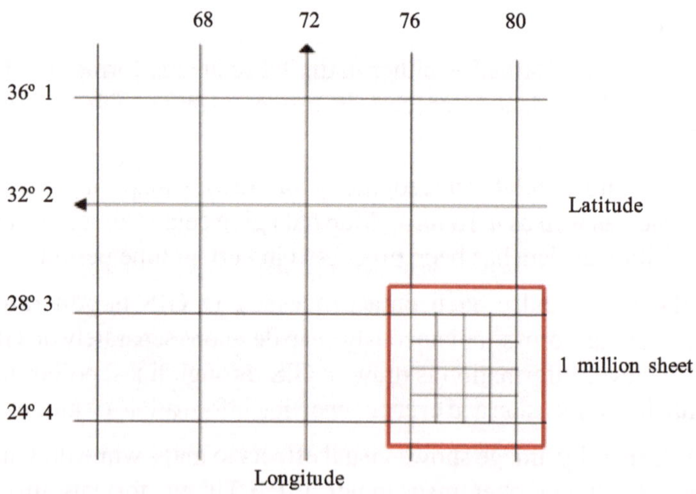

The geo-referencing technique fits the map for realistic position as it is to work on GIS platform with different objectives framing a reasonable conclusion, and important with resolution.

Manual Digitalizing

Manual tracing of lines to input shape point coordinating map is desirable polygons. Manual process of digitalization involves different features needed in points, lines and polygons showing shapes details on maps, Fallowing digitalization techniques are in further process:

Feature	Shape	Digitalization	Coordinate inputs
1. Point	•	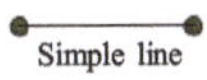 Simple line	X, y
2. Line	——	 Complex line	$X_1, Y_1, \ldots\ldots X_2, Y_2$
3. Polygon			$X_1 Y_1, \ldots X_2, Y_2 \ldots X_n, Y_n$

Editing Data

All the information related to drawing features on GIS format needs essential editing with skillful space matching otherwise mismatch can give error measurement after drawning manually for counting points, lines and polygons place and areas.

Few digitalizing errors includes some common errors while editing the maps and the errors involves nodes, arc, table, gap, overshoot, spike, duplicate, disconnected etc.

	Types of node	Symbol
a) Node	1. Dangling	
	2. Pseudo	
b) Arc	1. Dangling arc	
	2. Overshoot	
	3. Under shoot	
c) Label	1. Missing lab: gap	
	2. Overshoot	
	3. Spike	
	4. Duplicate	
	5. Disconnect	

Data Resonation

Data always represent basic unit of editing tools like points, line, polygon and surface; point would not have any dimension because of position denoted under this representation, line generally expresses connectivity among points and represent contour line, polygon separation; polygon represent various dimensional shapes which can measured with a well referred maps surface giving some support in study of surface features.

Principal Function of GIS

Data capture: Capturization of data in the form of scanned features, aerial photographs and paper maps are used for manual digitalization. Sometimes data in number and figures also considered as capturing data for drawing different kinds of maps.

Database management and update: Up-to-date available to users is prime goal of data management either through storing of or retrieval at a time after processing with editing as per needs of users. Data management models are already available in different software related to GIS with longer storability.

Geographic analysis: Base map provide basic information to us for using further more extra information if needed that also accounts valuable informations though integration of various components and conversion of geographical inputs in useable form results integrated output with perfect conversion.

Presenting results: Objective of thematic mapping decides the way of presentation, orientation and projection of a wrap, the theme expresses relativity of one way is on prime focus in GIS platforms, Soil map delineated into 2-4 or more layers can be drawn in single projection with showing geo-referred logs and preparation of boundary along the side of soil colour, texture, clay content etc.

Topology

Topology is defined as parts of something are organized arrangement of connected with each others. Further this definition explains the GIS platforms that guide with different objects under one of these mapping. Topology is basically executed in three ways:

i) Adjacency

ii) Containment

iii) Connectivity

The adjacent polygons are connected by some of overlapped lines differentiation of the connecting polygons. Containment is a form of topology in which one polygon contains same perforations inside polygon by demarcating area or marks. Connectivity is another kind of topology contacts some feature in special way to show relationship with directional arrow or movement in a map.

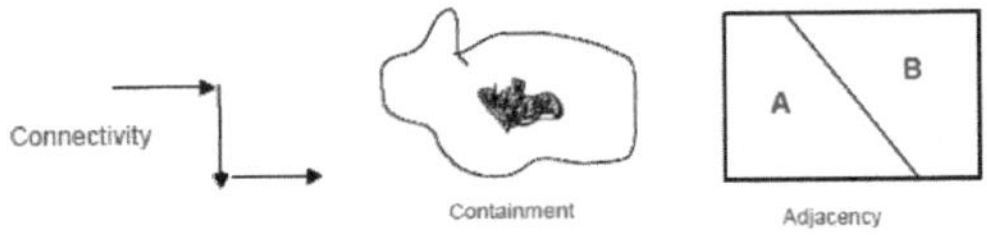

Data Structure Types

Map is a last outputs of whole process involved in development of map and data is primary requirement in the work development in which data are structured as per designed or theme, after arrangement of data in required structure gives basic information on expected models. The fundamental structural units in a model are:

Vector: The process of notarization involves various tools like point, line and polygon together forms a model on geo-referred geography of earth surface. These all are important editing tools on ground truth and digitalization of raster with certain measured scales.

Raster: Hard form of data can be converted into digital form through scanning of snaps further the raster is taken in drawing by vector tools extracting information from the raster to be used in particular purpose. Image or mat size cell means grids crosses in checker board pattern at particular vertical and horizontal dimension of lines; grid size is same that remains same in pixel count of simple and clear images of real world.

TIN (Triangular Irregular Networks): TIN is a reorientation of a continuous surface consisting entire triangular facets used mainly as Discrete Global Grid basically in elevation modeling. Three dimensional visualizations are readily created by rendering of the triangular facets.

Vector Data model: Model includes points, simple line, complex line (node vector), single polygon and connected polygon are major features in vectors data model which draws ever raster to obtain perfect mapping. Generally these tools are used for vectorization i.e. Point, Simple line, Complex lines, Simple polygon and Connected polygon.

Raster data model: Raster may be a remote sensing data or images or imageries contain some sensible data to be obtained a perfect digitalization. The model is hard in form for any modification that is the reason; the raster is subjected to conversion into vector for easy modification with desirable outputs.

Principle of GIS

GIS is an integrated assembly of hardware and software of computer, geographic data and individual designed to efficiently acquire, store, manipulate, retrieve, analyze, display and report all types of geographically reference information gathers towards a particular set of purposes (Burrough, 1986). GIS stores both temporal and a spatial data. The geo-coded spatial data define an object that has an orientation and relationship with other objects in two or three-dimensional space, also known as topological data and stores in topological database. On the other hand, attribute data are stored in a relational database that describes the objects in detail. GIS links these two databases by manipulating one-to-one relationship between records of object of location in the topological database and records of the object attribute in relational database by using end-user defined common identification index or code.

Principal Functions of GIS

- **Data capture:** The data are principally obtained from manual digitization and scanning of aerial photographs, paper maps and existing digital data sets.
- **Database update and management:** After data collecting and integration, the GIS provides facilities, which can store and maintain data.
- **Geographic analysis:** Data integration and conversion are only a part of the input phase in GIS. That is required next in the ability to interpret and analyze the collected information quantitatively and qualitatively.
- **Presenting results:** One of the most exciting aspects of GIS technology is the variety of the ways in which the information can be presented once it is processed by GIS.

Data Models in GIS

There are three basic data models that GIS uses are vector, raster and TIN.

Vector: Geographical phenomenon is represented by vector data with points, lines and polygons, in which points are pairs in x and y coordinates, lines represent a set of period coordinates that show a shape. The polygons are also set of coordinates pairs explicating boundaries that enclose areas. Usually coordinates are in pairs of x and y or in triplets of x, y and z.

Raster: Raster is basically known as a dataset of raster *i.e.* image which is simplest form and grid (matric) of cells. Individual cells contains with height, and is a part of the entire area represented by raster. The dimension can be changed as larger or smaller with compulsory to represent the area which forms within the area. As smaller the cell size, details of area will be more. But greater the number of cells, it takes more time to progress.

Triangulated Irregular Network (TIN): It represents a surface combining a set of continuous and non-overlapping tringle. The surface is shown by plane within each triangle. Mass points represent a set of points framing triangles.

Geographic Data Representation

A geographical data can be represented by points, lines, area and continues surfaces in GIS. A geographical data come in three basic forms *i.e.,* map data, attribute data and image data. A GIS can be seen in three ways *i.e.* Database view, Map view and Model view.

2

Global Positioning System

GPS stands for Global Positioning System, basically Navstar GPS is a radio based space aviation system developed by United state government which was operated by United State Air Force. It provides geographic location and time related information to GPS receivers under global navigation satellite from anywhere of earth where unobstructed line of sight to 4 or more GPS satellite co-ordinate (Anonymous, 2018). Even GPS not required any user for transmitting data, with working independently on any telephonic or internet receivers; through these technologies we can enhance usefulness of the GPS location based information. The GPS serves as critical positioning capacity to various fields like army operation, civil aviation, and commercial scope to wider scope in around world.

United State Department of Defence launched project in 1973 for getting information but it was fully operated in 1995 and was allowed for civilians in 1980s onwards. Advancement in technology and ever increasing demands over existing opened the path to have led in offset to advancing the GPS and important for next Generation Operational Control System (Anonymous, 2017). The development accelerated by the announcement from Vice President AI Gore and White House initiated the changes in 1998. It was modernized and authorized in upscaling GPS III by U.S. congress.

Apart from GPS, other systems are used or continuous developed, because of U.S. government selectively denied accessing to the system during happening of the Indian military in the Kargil War in 1999, or degraded the service at any time. BLONASS (Russian Global Navigation Satellite System) was created contemporary with GPS, but it was suffered from insufficient coverage of the globe till mid-2000s (Anonymous, 2011). For making more satellites available and enabling positions get fixed quickly and correctly within two metres GLONASS may be added to GPS (Anonymous, 2018). In European Union, Galileo Positioning system, BeiDou navigation satellite system, NAVIC of India and Quasi-Zenith satellite system of Japan also developed.

GPS (Global Positioning System) is a popular technology which provides non-equal accuracy and conformability for navigation, survey and data capturing.

The characteristic of GPS is providing regular three-dimensional positioning 24x7 throughout the world. This character also permits us for determining horizontal as well as vertical changes at spatial and temporal basis (Kalpan, 1996, Segall and Devis, 1977). The technology looks to be the users of GPS in mapping and geodetic positioning. The data collection, surveying and mapping can be done by application of GPS tremendously.

History

The first launch of GPS project was done in 1973 in United States to solve the problems related to navigation systems (Shrivastava, 2014) had limitations, by integration of ideas from many predecessors, including a classified engineering design from 1960s. Defense department of US created the system that originally involved 24 satellites. In beginning it was developed to facilitate for United States Military and been operated in 1995. Although, it was permitted to access for civilian use in 1980s onwards.

The GPS system follows partly on ground-based radio navigation systems, which includes LORAN and the Decca Navigator, designed in 1940s, and used by Royal Navy of Britain during World War II. It was proposed a test of general relativity detecting slows timing in a heavy gravitational field by accurate atomic clocks of orbit inside artificial satellites. Specific and relativity product work on the task of clock on the GPS satellites would be seen by the earth's observers to run fraction of second (38 microseconds) faster per day than the clocks on the earth. The calculating data 10 km per day was refined for correction on GPS (Kriening and Torsten, 2019).

GPS (Global Positioning System) is one kind of space-based Global Navigation Satellite System (GNSS) provides feasible location and time information in any weather and in anywhere on or near the earth under unobstructed line of sight to four or more GPS satellites, which maintained by United States Government and easily accessible by anyone with GPS receiver. US Department of Defense (USDoD) created and originally 24 satellites is run, which was established in 1973 to overcome the limitations of easier navigation systems. The system was established in 1973 to solve the limitations had in navigation system.

Basic Concept of GPS

Basically GPS conceptualized on time and known places specialized with satellites, the satellites contain strong stable atomic clocks which synchronized with each other even ground clocks. Drift from actual time on ground is corrected daily as maintenance of time therefore satellite locations are obtained with high precision. Clock is attached with GPS receivers but they are less precise and stable. The satellite of GPS regularly transmits information in the form of data from their current time and position. One GPS receiver monitors many satellites and validates equations for determining the precise position of the receiver and its deviation from true time. Minimum four satellites should be in a single view of the receiver to compute four clock and deviation from time of satellite.

The position of a place on earth has it self own identity with unique referencing of latitude and longitude, even altitude too, which are proper identity of the place. This uniqueness is sometime called geo-tagging.

Precise timing and signal sent by GPS satellites over the earth ground position is calculated a GPS receiver. Every satellite frequently transmits information which includes the time with message, the ephemeries (Precise orbital information), system condition and crude orbits of all GPS satellites like almanac.

The receivers use the information to determine the transmit time of every message and computes the distal position of each satellite, and the distances of satellites located in sparse position are used in possible helps of trilateration, on which algorithm is adopted for computing the position of the receiver, then the position is displayed possibly with a moving map and geo-references (latitude, longitude and elevation) might be included. Derived information like direction and speed is shown by many GPS units as change in position is also calculated.

Three satellites might seem enough to solve for position since space has three dimensions and a position near the Earth's surface can be assumed. However, even a very small clock error multiplied by the very large speed of light, the speed at which satellite signals propagate results in a large positional error.

It is a reason the receivers use either few or more satellite to time of location and time of receivers. Most of GPS applications hide effectively the very accurate computed time which later use only in location. Finger count specialized GPS does utilize the time, these include time transfer, timing of traffic signal and synchronize cell phone based station.

The GPS uses asterism (constellation) of 24 satellites, in regular manner orbiting earth and system (computer) to calculate position for earth location, and the satellite is based on ranging of the satellite, which means measuring distance from a group of satellites in space determine the position on earth. The system can be grouped into five fundamental steps to understand basis of GPS:

- For triangulation, GPS calculates the distance using time of travel of radio information by the distance of travelling.
- GPS always contains highly accurate clock to measure the time of travelling.

- Distance of satellite in space is known, then it needs to know the satellite's position after once knowing distance.
- As the GPS signal passing through the ionosphere and atmosphere of earth, delay in signal is common owing to hindrance in the way of incidence.

Triangonometric approach is used by the GPS for calculating the positions, GPS satellites are so away from earth but their orbits are very predictable and every satellite is set with precisely synchronized atomic clock.

Components of GPS

The GPS comprises the components, are divided into three major components as named below:

1. Control Segment
2. Space Segment
3. User Segment

Control Segment

It consists of monitoring stations which provides as link up installations, and above capacity of transmitting data to the satellites, involving separate ephemerides (as satellite positioning function of time), clock corrections and other broadcast information. All the GPS signal are tracked by monitoring their orbits. Even meteorological data are too collected at monitoring stations with permission of the most accurate analysis of tropospheric delays of GPS signals. The monitoring station collects satellite tracking data are subjected to transmit to master control station for further use and processing, in which processing includes computing satellites ephemerides and correction of satellite clock.

Space Segment

Constellation of 24 earth orbiting NAVASTAR satellites are consisted of space segment; these satellites are arranged in 6 orbital planes with four satellites per plane placed equally in 60° away from equator and inclined at 55° from equatorial plane positions. They locate for orbiting at elevation near about 12000 miles each alongwith orbital periods of 12 sidereal hours (determined from or by stars) or either proximately one half of earth's periods, 12 hours of fixed 3 dimension position. Further, block of satellites is called Block IIR and they improve reliability and have a capacity ranging in between satellites with increasing orbital accuracy. Every satellite contains 4 defined standards, and have microprocessor or board to limit own-monitoring and processing data. Trusters are well equipped with satellites may be used to modify and manage their orbits.

User Segment

Earth based GPS receivers are involved in user segment working smoothly and receivers basically depend on size and complexity, even basic design is so simple. The receivers are mainly comprised of antenna, radio signal microprocessor, pre-amplifier, display and control device, power supply and data recording unit. The first performance of GPS receiver decodes the timing signals from visible satellite and computes own longitude, latitude and elevation; and time being calculation of the distance which is regular process and update the position every second as a result of receiver display device, the receiver display device possesses data capture capabilities and storing with receiver logging unit.

GPS Positioning Types

Global positioning system deals with basically two different kinds of global positioning systems (GPS) as given below:

1. Absolute positioning: always this positioning system relies on a single receiver station, and also known as "stand alone GPS" due to unlike differential positioning and ranging is preferred precisely between receiver station and satellite, not with ground based reference station which help in computing error corrections. In consequences, derived positions are subject to not mitigated errors inherent position of satellite in absolute mode.
2. Differential positioning: Sometimes this is called relative positioning of GPS which processes the triangulation principles, next with a second receiver of known referred place. To determine the point relative to the defined place of the earth surface, setting requires mustering error-correction message from reference receiver. The established control point and reference station is being often worked by differential-mode positioning, is set on control, triangulated position and coordinate points under differential positioning. This allows rectifying by correction factor to be calculated and applied on other moving GPS units of same area and time series.

Inherent Sources of Errors

- Errors related to noise contains data to location not accurate upto few meters, are caused by receiver noise and random pseudo noise.
- Other one is bias errors resulted from addition of specific available signals. S/A amounts degrade signal intentionally to nearly two standard deviations of the potential resolution of C/A code which means it ranges from 30m to about 100m. Different S/A codes are generated by all NAVSTAR satellites and this is a cause of changing low frequency bias. On other hands, it includes clock inaccuracies, if the bias left uncorrected by ground control

can be in minor error like upto one meter. In consideration to atmospheric dynamics has over 10 meter errors with tropospheric factors *i.e.* changes in air temperature, pressure of barometer and humidity for one meter or less. Upto 10 meter, delay is possible due to upper atmosphere aberrations in ionosphere. Sub-meter belongs to multipath bias errors in range, are commonly unavoidable and is result of interference of signals with reflectance of waves of near-receiver, or other physical hindrance in line of sight between SVs and receiver.

- Blunders: this may be resulted as systematic errors from the mistakes of any user including non-corrected geodetic datum is selected problems in software, failurity of receiver or control segment faults. Positional solution inaccuracies are occurred by computer or human error from one meter to more than two orders commanded with greater magnitude.

GPS applications: Most unique and significant features of globe positioning systems is availability of positioning signal for users all over the world at any point or period of time. Large and wide range of different community can use the multiple applications with fully functionally GPS from surveying, mapping, valid results and data capturing by navigating to GPS. GPS becoming a part of various technology utilized in modern days.

Surveying and Mapping

The more precision of GPS equips phase measurements with proper adjustment algorithms and serves a strong means for several aspects for survey and mapping. By Differential Global Positioning System methods can be used accurately and timely.

i) **Weed/crop survey:** Most of the cases, similar weed flora are identified and documented which further creates huge confusion due to wide area denoted in documentation and later researchers do not connect that places perfectly so they can review the present status of the identified weeds or crops in particular site. If mapping is done on the basis of geo-reference definitely links the coordinating point to compare present status alongwith demarcation. Hence, GPS can nicely be utilized to recognize the specific zone and specific flora.

ii) **Soil-water engineering:** Now it is popularly used in geo-tagging, but still under wider use, because some of area or locality has not been covered due to lack of knowledge and experts on GPS. Robust amount may save if such arrangement is made over the location of construction points. Natural stream of any watershed gets diverted or drying or depletion of water flow can be tagged using temporal change and planner can execute the remedy measures.

Navigation

Monitoring with GPS can save time countless in the field. Any object/feature can be located up to one hundred meters simply by scaling coordinates from a map even under water observation, using waypoints, and reaching directly to the site.

Predecessors

When the Soviet Union launched the first artificial satellite in 1957, two American physicists, William Guier and George Weiffenbach, at Johns Hopkins University's Applied Physics Laboratory (APL) decided to monitor its radio transmissions (Anonymous, 2018). Within hours they realized that, because of the Doppler effect, it could pinpoint where the satellite was along its orbit. The Director of the APL gave them access to their UNIVAC to do the heavy calculations needed.

The Deputy Director of the APL, Frank McCluse enquired Guier and Weiffenbach to investigate the inverse problem-pinning points of location that of the satellite given (Navy was developing the submarine-launched Polaris missile, which needed them to know the submarine's location at the time). This led them and APL to develop the TRANSIT system (Anonymous, 2018). In 1959, ARPA (renamed DARPA in 1972) also played a role in TRANSIT (*National Research Council* U.S., 1995), *O'Leary et al.* (2009) and *Butterly* (2018).

Emblem of the 50th Space Wing

TRANSIT was first satellite navigation system used by US Navy successfully in 1960 (Anonymous, 2014). It used a constellation of five satellites and could provide a navigational fix approximately once per hour. In 1967, the U.S. Navy developed the Timation satellite, which proved the feasibility of placing accurate clocks in space through GPS.

The ground-based OMEGA navigation system on phase comparison of signal transmission from pairs of stations in 1970s (*Guier, and Weiffenbach,* 1997), been the first worldwide radio navigation system. Limitations of these systems drove the need for a more universal navigation solution with greater accuracy.

Precise navigation would enable United States ballistic missile submarines to get an accurate fix of their positions before they launched their SLBMs (*Johnson,* 2010). The USAF, with two thirds of the nuclear triad, also had requirements for a more accurate and reliable navigation system. The Navy and Air Force were under developing of their own technologies solving were faced essentially the same issue. To increase the survivability of ICBMs, there was a project to use portable launch platforms (comparable to the Russian SS-24 and SS-25) and so the need to fix the launch position had similarity as the SLBM situation.

Air Force proposed one radio based navigation system popularly known as MOSAIC (Mobile System for Accurate ICBM Control) which was compulsary in 3-dimension LORAN in 1960. Afterwards in 1963 project 57 was worked and it was conceptualized GPS as new technology. In same year existed the project 621B, had many attributes which can be seen in GPS now.

The information received in updated through Navy TRANSIT system was slow for operation in high speed Air Force, but Naval Research Laboratory continued the improvements with satellite possesses time navigation, was first launched in 1967 and third one in 1974 for carrying atomic clock in orbit, (Catherine Alexandrow, 2008). An important earlier GPS existed from other branch of US Military in 1964, US Army orbited first SECOR (Sequential Collation Range) satellite for geodetic surveying (DARPA, 2011). This system includes the ground based transmitters from certain locations that could send signal in orbit contained satellite transponder. A 4th ground based station might use later the signals to fix the location precisely. And last SECOR satellite was launched in the year 1969 (Howell, 2013).

After a decade, in beginning years of GPS the common people use surveying with GPS becames one of the first fields to take the opportunities of new technology due to benefits of signal from the advance technology rather depending on less complete GPS constellation years before the declaration of operation. The GPS system may be thought of as an improvement of SECOR system where other surface based transmitters to be transferred into orbit.

The event like Korean Air Lines flight 007, a Boeing 747 with 269 people were shot down in 1983 after entering in restricted area of USSR airspace (SECOR, Chronology, 2010). Another civilian utilization of GPS was issued by President Ronald Reagan in the areas of Sakhalin and Meneron Islands as directive making GPS would be freely available for common people, once it was sufficiently developed. In February 14th 1989, first Block II satellite was launched and 24th satellite was also launched in 1994 (MX Deployment Reconsidered, 2013). This time GPS was costed about 5 billion USD not including the cost of the user equipment but they included cost of satellite launches (Dick *et al.*, 2007).

In beginning, the highest quality signal was reserved for using in military and intentional purpose, degraded signal was for civilian use as selective availability. As the President changed and Bill Clinton became president of USA changed the use signing a policy to turn selective availability off in May 1st 2000 for providing the same level of accuracy among civilians. The use directive was provided by secretary of Defense US William Perry, due to widely spreading of differential GPS services in improving civilian use with accuracy and eliminate the advantage of military. However, US Military was actively developing to deny GPS services to significant adversaries based on region (Russell Rip and Hasik, 2002).

Since from beginning, US has implemented many improvement on GPS services involving new signals for people use and enhanced accuracy and integrity while maintaining compatibility with existing GPS tools. New dimension of satellite system is being initiated by US Defense Department. The requirement of military, people and commercial market is fulfilled by Department of Defense through a series of satellites. In 2005, high FAA class, high quality and SPS (Standard Positioning Services) were connected with GPS receivers which provide horizontal accuracy of better than 3.00 m (Hegarty and Eric., 2008), even factors like receiver quality and atmosphere factors decrease the accuracy.

GPS is developed and operated by US government as their own resource of nation, Actually Interagency GPS Executive Board (IGEB) takes care the policy issues since 1996 to 2004, later the need was felt for joint committee National Space Based Positioning, Navigation and Time Executive Committee (TEC) which was formed by directive of president to advise and coordinate Federal Department and agencies on this matter and related issue of GPS (John and Klobuchar, 2017). This executive committee is jointly chaired by Deputy Secretary, Defense and Transportation, extending with membership equipment rank officials from different specified departments (State, commerce and Homeland Security, Joint Chief Staff and NASA). In this venture, participating from components of executive office of president as observers and liaison between executive committee and chairman participates in the set up.

US Defense department is regulated by law to maintain a standard Positioning Service as per Federal radio navigation plan standard position service signal in specified manner, which will be available on regular and worldwide basis. This developed measures to escape hostile use of GPS along with rising without unwanted disrupting or substandard use among civilian.

Table. List of GPS satellites with Timeline and modernization

Block	launch Period	Satellite launches				Currently in orbit and healthy
		Success	Failure	In preparation	Planned	
I	1978–1985	10	1	0	0	0
II	1989–1990	9	0	0	0	0
IIA	1990–1997	19	0	0	0	0
IIR	1997–2004	12	1	0	0	12
IIR-M	2005–2009	8	0	0	0	7
IIF	2010–2016	12	0	0	0	12
IIIA	From 2017	0	0	0	12	0
IIIB	—	0	0	0	8	0
IIIC	—	0	0	0	16	0
Total	70	2	0	36	31	

(*last update:* March 9, 2016) 8 satellites from Block IIA are placed in reserve, USA-203 from Block IIR-M is unhealthy For a more complete list.

Detailed Description of GPS

Every GPS has the functional work of broadcasting a signal that possesses carrier wave with modulation which further includes:

- The sequence of ones and zeroes as a pseudorandom code that is familiar to the receiver. A receiver generates vision by aligning time and simultaneously receiver also measures code version, TOA (Time of Arrival) of certain point in code sequence, known as epoch, can be present in the receiver clock time scale.
- Time of transmission (TOT) of the code epoch in time scale of GPS and satellite position included in a message at the time of receiving data.

Conceptually the receiver scales up the TOAs as per its own clock of four satellite signal, both from TOAs and TOTs, the receiver creates four TOF (Time of Flight) values, which may be closely equivalent to receiver satellite ranges. TOFs help in computation of receiver for three dimensional position and clock variation from 4 TOFs.

User Satellite Geometry

It is not usually formed clearly in processing of receiver, measurement geometry is defined by conceptual time differences of arrival (TDOAs) and a multilateration

(Hyperboloid of revolution) is corresponded by each TDOA. Hyperboloid axis is formed by two satellites in line connection and receiver is commonly located at certain point, three hyperboloids really intersect each other (Modernized GPS satellite, 2005).

Receiver in Continuous Operation

As above mentioned about receiver's representative start up situation and more number of receivers have a task algorithm which is sometimes called a "Tracker", this combines a group of satellite measurements gathered at different times in effect, carry over the advantages of reality and successive receiver locations are often closed to each other. After processing a couple of measurements, the tracker expects the receiver position corresponding to further next set of measurement of satellites. The new measurements are gathered, the receiver utilizes priority based on scheme to integrate new measurements with prediction of tracker. Often it is expected a tracker can improve position and time of accuracy, discard bad measurements, estimate direction and speed of receiver.

The main limitation of a tracker is that differed in speed or direction may be calculated with a delay, the derived direction can be inaccurate with distance passed between two consecutive measurement of position which drops near or below the random error of measured position. Generally GPS units use Doppler shift measurement of signals collected to compute velocity (Johnson Bobbie, 2009). Advanced navigation systems use extra sensors as compass or inertial system of navigation to support GPS.

Non-navigation Application

In identical representative operation of GPS as a navigator, atleast four or more satellites must be visible to get proper and accurate result output of navigation equation which results the position of receiver with differentiating the time placed by receiver on-board desk and true time of days, by this process eliminating the requirement for a more precise and probably impractical designed information on receiver based clock. By the application of cellular phones based stations provides cheap and more accurate time. Some of the GPS applications take this time for display, or other than basic position calculation not use at all.

Anyway four satellites equipped system are needed for normal operation, few number users apply for special cases. Situation like one known variable can help in determining its position using only three satellites by a receiver just like ship and aircraft have known altitude. The additional keys or assumptions may be used by some receivers of GPS resulting past known elevation, dead reckoning, inertial navigation; including data from the vehicle computer in support a position when less than four satellites are in visible position (David, 2009; Air Force GPS, 2010; Anonymous, 2012).

Structure

The present GPS consists of mainly three segments, which are space segment, control segment and user segment. The development, maintenance and operations of space and control segments are basically governed by US Air Force. Fundamentally GPS satellites transmits signals from space, every GPS receiver takes the signals to compute the three-dimensional location (Altitude, longitude and latitude) and current time.

Space Segment

An instance of visualizing 24 satellite GPS constellation in motion having earth rotation is noticed the number of satellites in view from target place on earth under live observation. Space segment composed of 24 to 32 satellites in medium orbit of earth including payload adaptors to the booster need to launch into orbit.

The space segment is comprised of space vehicles (SV) or GPS satellite orbits in parlance of GPS. Originally the design of GPS is called for 24 SVs and every eight in appropriately three circular orbits (GPS programme, 2011), but later it was redesigned orbital planes with every four satellites (Danielle and Britni, 2018). Nearly 55° tilt relative to the earth's equator (inclination) have been equipped with six orbit planes which are separated by 60° right upheaval of ascending node that shows angle along the equator from a referred point to that orbits intersection (Amos and Jonathan, 2019). One half of a sidereal day represents to orbital period which stands for 11 hours with 58 minutes this helps to satellites for passing over the similar locations (Abel and Chaffee, 1991), or in nearly same locations (Fang, 1992) in each day. The orbits are so meticulously arranged for atleast six satellites always align with sight from any places on the earth's surface (Grewal *et al.*, 2007). The main objective of this arrangement can give result that four satellites are not spaced at 90° evenly away within every orbit. Commonly the regular difference between satellites lies at 30°, 105°, 120° and 105° away, which further add as 360° on total (Bosen *et al.*, 2005). Orbiting at the height of nearly 20000 km (12600 mi); orbital radius of almost 26600 km (16500 mi) (NAVASTAR, 2008) is present. In each sidereal day has two complete orbits is made up each SV useful tool representing the same ground surface every day (GPS support Notes, 2007). During development of GPS, it was very useful tool even under only 4 satellites, correctly align collate all four satellites visible from one spot for some hours in a day. Ground track repeat may be used to know good coverage in combat zones for military operations.

The 32 satellites in the GPS constellation and out of 32, 31 are in functional use as per Feb 2016 (Pike, 2009). By providing unnecessary measurement, additional satellites can improve the precision of GPS receiver data calculation. As increased the number of satellites, constellation was turned into non-uniform arrangement and such arrangement prone to increase reliability and also availability of system as in relation to uniform system under multiple satellites fail to perform (GPS Gov, 2010). Approximately nine satellites can be seen from any point on the ground anytime ensuring reasonable necessity over the minimum 4 satellites required for a position.

Satellite steering is not precised by GPS standard to change a satellites orbit, unhealthy mark is adhered with satellite; therefore receivers do not utilize it. Engineers track new orbit from ground surface after the satellite maneuver, and upload new ephemeris, with marking as healthy satellite again. The OCS (Operation Control Segment) presently provides as control segment of stored record. It serves the operational capacity that supports GPS users with keeping GPS operationally perform as per specification.

The operational control segment had replaced the era legacy 1970 as mainframe computer at Schriever Air Force Base in September 2007. The system contributed enabling upgrades with a foundation for new safety architecture which helped military and armed forces. This OCS system continuously be the ground control system of the record till new segment, as next generation GPS operation control system (Real Engineering, 2017) and OCX is a well developed and functionally fit.

Newly developed OCX provided with more capacities as cornerstone for revolutionizing GPS mission enabling their capacities in GPS review from the NAVSTAR joint Programme (Office Archived, 2007). It is greatly enhanced services of GPS operation to united state combat force, civil partners and also myriad domestic and international users. Critical part of GPS modernization is represented by this GPS OCX programme and give significant information surety over current GPS OCS programme.

1. GPS legacy satellites can be controlled and managed through OCX simultaneously next generation of GPS III satellites during arranging full array of military signals.
2. As construction and designed on flexible architecture that may fastly adopts the changing needs of today's and further GPS users to quick access the GPS data and constellation is secured through accurate and reliable data base information.
3. To know the awareness on situations with more accuracy is provided the war fighter highly secure, executable and predictive information to enhance efficiency.

4. Signals like L1C, L2C and L5C have been modernized and M-code capability, which earlier legacy systems do not have such capacity.
5. It also serves as significant information surely as compared to current programme with detection and prevention of cyber crack during containing, isolating and operating.
6. The higher volume near real time command and control capabilities is also supported.

The US Air Force declared the completion of GPS OCX preliminary design review with confirmation of OCX programme is ready to carry new paradigm of development on September 14th, 2011. The GPS based on OCX programme left major milestones and pushed it with GPS IIIA launch beyond April 2016 (USGS Naveen, 2007).

Navigational signals are transmitted by GPS satellites first encode a variety of information with satellite positions, position of internal clocks and health of the working network. The signals are transferred on two different separate carrier frequencies which almost common to the satellites in the network. There are two different encodings are in use: a public encoding with enabling low resolution navigation and US military encrypted encoding.

GPS message format

Sub frames	Description
1	Satellite clock, GPS time relationship
2–3	Ephemeris (precise satellite orbit)
4–5	Almanac component (satellite network synopsis, error correction)

Every GPS satellite regularly broadcasts the messages generated from navigation on L1 (C/A and P/Y) and L2 with P/Y frequencies at a rate 50 bits/second. The 750 seconds ($12^{1/2}$) minutes are required time to complete message. The structure of message consists of basic format of a 1500 bit long frame constituted of five subframes, and one subframe contains 300 bits almost take 6 seconds long. In this sequence, 4 and 5 subframes are subcommutated greater times (25) each, so that whole data message needs 25 full frame transmission. Each unit i.e. subframe consists of 10 words and each word 30 bit longer. Therefore, it consists with 500 bits in a message and the single message has 37500 bit long. This provides 750 seconds to deliver on entire almanac message in GPS. Each 30 second frame begins precisely on the minute or half-minute as displayed by atomic clock on each satellites (Autralian Football, 2016) in table below:

First subframe of each frame encodes week number and time in week (Pacific Northwest Geodetic Array, 2014), even the data about the health of satellite.

The ephemeris precise orbit for the satellite present in second and third sub frames and other 4th and 5th subframes possesses almanac, which keeps coarse orbit and status information for upto 32 satellites in constellation and data related to error correction. As a result, to obtain perfect satellite location from this message and the receiver must demonstrate the message from each satellite including its solution for 18 to 30 seconds. For collecting all transmitted almanacs, the receiver must demodulate the message of 750 seconds to 732, or $12^{1/2}$ minutes (Armed Control Association, 2006).

All satellite discriminate same frequencies, and encoding signals using unique Code Division Multiple Access (CDMA), so receivers may differentiate individual satellites from each. Two distinguish CDMA encoding types is used in the system are coarse or acquisition (C/A) code, and it is accessible to general public, and the precise (P/Y) codes are encrypted so that United State military and NATO nations have properieteries to access to the encryption code may reach it (Sinha, 2003).

GPS frequency overview

Band	Frequency	Description
L1	1575.42 MHz	Coarse-acquisition (C/A) and encrypted precision (P(Y)) codes, plus the L1 civilian (L1C) and military (M) codes on future Block III satellites.
L2	1227.60 MHz	P(Y) code, plus the L2C and military codes on the Block IIR-M and newer satellites.
L3	1381.05 MHz	Used for nuclear detonation (NUDET) detection.
L4	1379.913 MHz	Being studied for additional ionospheric correction.
L5	1176.45 MHz	Proposed for use as a civilian safety-of-life (SoL) signal.

The satellites broadcast L1 signal (1.57542 GHz) and L2 signal (1.2276 GHz) frequencies and satellite network takes a CDMA spread-spectrum (Global Security Org., 2007). Wherein the low-bit rate message data is encoded being a higher PRN (Pseudo-Random) sequence that is different for each satellite. In reconstruct the real message, receiver should be aware of PRN codes in each satellite. Under C/A code for common people, transfer data at the rate of 1.023 million chips/second, whereas for United State Military, P code is used the chips have 10.23 million/second. Real interval reference of satellites have 10.22999999543 MHz to compensate for relativistic effects which provide observers to perceive earth with difference time reference in regard to transmittance in the orbit. Both C/A and P codes modulates L1 carrier while L2 carrier is modulated with P code (Bonsen *et al.*, 2005). Generally P code is encrypted as a P(Y) code which is limitedly available to military equipment having a proper decryption key. Both C/A & P(Y) codes brings precise time of day to users. The L3 signal is utilized to transfer data from satellites to surface stations and the data used by U.S. Nuclear Detonation (NUDETs) detection system (USNDS) to identify place and report NUDETs in atmosphere of earth and near space (National Security Satellite Programmes, 2013) with extending usage enforcement of nuclear ban on treaties. The signal was launched in 2010 is provided by first block IIF satellite (Greenemeir and Larry, 2016). The phase quadrate uses each other with two carrier components of L5. Every carrier component is bi-phase shift key (BASK) regulated by a separate bit train. L5 is also third civil GPS signal, which positively supports the application "Safety of life" for aviation and provide enhanced availability and accuracy (Anonymous, 2019).

Decoding and Demodulation

By using coarse/acquisition gold code GPS satellite signals decode and demodulate in the GPS because whatever satellite signals are subjected to modulate on the L1 carrier frequency and signals should be delineated or separated only after demodulation. Through assigning each satellite has unique binary-sequence called as a Gold Code. The signal is decoded only after demodulation is adding Gold codes responding to the satellites monitored by receiver (Kyle, 2016) and satellite message form (2010).

Geo-metric Explanation

The equation related to GPS may be simplified by numerical and analytical procedures and it can enhance to develop understanding the solution methods:

Spheres: Any measured range is known as pseudo ranges that contain clock errors. For simplifying idealization the range is synchronized, the radii of spheres is represented by true ranges and centralized on transmitting satellites. To solve the position of the receiver does intersection of surfaces in three of the spheres. If higher number of minimum ranges are available then more than three space surfaces might be formed near intersection through least squares.

Hyperboloids

The distance travelled between the receiver and satellite are sequencing *i* and *j* then it is subtracted result is $(t_i\text{-}s_i)c\text{-}(t_j\text{-}s_j)c$ in this equation known or measured quantities. The centre of points having a stable difference in distance with two consecutive points i.e. two satellites are a hyperboloid (Multilateration). From four or more measured reception times, receiver may be kept at the intersection of the surface of these or more hyperboloids (first modernized GPS satellite Buit, 2017).

Spherical Cones

Four dimensional geometric space can be assumed as a solution space like x, y, z and b describing a spherical cone (Borre *et al.*, 2007) alongwith cusp placed in satellite and base has sphere around the satellite. The receiver is located at four or more such cones at intersection in satellites.

Solution Methods

Least squares: The calculation can be based on four or more than four visible satellites simultaneously depending on many receiver channels, capacity of processing, GDOP (Geometric Dilution of Precision). By using more than four satellites include one over-determined pattern of equations without unique solution and the system may be simplified by one least-squares or weighted least squares method (Peter, 2013).

Iterative: Above both equations are used for four satellites whereas least equations for more than four, which are non-linear and need certain solving methods. The very common measure is for linearized way of the equations using by iteration like Gauss-Newton algorithm. Initially the GIS system had been developed assuming a numerical least squares solution method, it means closed-form solution.

Closed Form

S. Bancroft developed above set of equations closed form (Interface Specification IS-GPS-200, 2012, Text Generator Version 2.0, 2011). The properties of closed form is well known sustaining proponents claim it and found superior in low-GDOP situations, compared to iterative least square methods.

Algebraic method is used in Bancroft's equation; it opposes to numerical and can be used for either four or more than four satellites. The key steps are inversion the 4x4 metric under four satellites and solution of one single-variable quadratic equation as well. These methods facilitate one or two solutions for not known quantities. Under availability of two, only one pertains near-earth sensible solution. When receiver utilizes more than four-satellites for solving the issue, and Bancroft takes generalized inverse commonly known as pseudo inverses to find a solution. A case has been made those iterative methods (Gauss-Newton algorithm) for clarifying over-determined non-linear least squares (NLLS) problems generally provides more realistic solution. Bancroft (1985) is so earlier, and not a closed-form solution was first as stated by Leick *et al.* (2015), other hand closed-form solutions had been published later era, even the adoption practices is not so clear.

GPS Working Mechanism

The receivers receive signals from each of the 24 satellites which determine the location or range through computation of difference between sending signals and time taken for receiving. A signal has data which are used by receivers for computing locations of satellites and arranges the adjustment needed for right property. For propagating delays or down signal's speed influenced by ionosphere and the troposphere. GPS atomic clock is carried by GPS satellites that provide highly accurate time. Satellites broadcast the time information that is placed in the codes so that a receiver can regularly determine time of the signal as broadcasted. Regarding information for the ranges to three satellites and the location of the satellite as signals are sent, and receiver may easily compute the own three dimensional positions. GPS is synchronized by an atomic clock, in which order to compute ranges are needed from three signals. By considering a measurement from forth satellite, actually the receiver avoids the need for an atomic clock. So far the matter concerned to four satellites, in receiving signal and receiver uses four satellites to add a computation of latitude, longitude, altitude and time too.

GIS and Remote Sensing

Possibly it can be integrated GPS position into remote sensing, using DGPS or kinematic techniques, depending upon the accuracy needed, Real time or post processing provide for the sensor that can be projected to ground, in place of taking ground control oriented to an image. The GPS gains advantage from using GRS we can capture the location data as in various form of GPS applying. Any appropriate software or computer can be linked with GPS easily, and users may too take all the data on a common base with small distortion. Thus the GPS system can support in many way of construction of GIS data bases timely and accurately.

3

Cartography

Map making involves the application of both scientific and artistic elements, combining graphic experts and specific knowledge of compilation, and frame principles with techniques available for product generation.

History of Cartography

Cartography has much back history than what we seen in portable form by its name or definition. Many prehistoric painting of caves had their own time frame record of maps, artifacts and design have been preserved hoping that they are sufficient to the era of forgotten habit and culture, and treasure explicit ancient world. The ancient wall painting of seventh millenium BC, might have indication of oldest maps in the world and the painting is assumed to be the location of ancient city Antolia as Mellaart, depicted 1967. Onward 600 BC, the modern form of cartography started to develop map. The pioneer contribution in map designing and development, old Greek and Roman were main contributor in this direction. One Greek Philoshopher Ptolemmy, multi-talented genius are recalled in this context, who later credited with first documented map of world during production of Geographica, is a treatise on cartography, very soon one Arabian Scholar Muhammad Al-Idrisi prepared a medieval Atlas involving knowledge of world collected by Arabic merchants in 1154.

India and China east established and set milestone in the area of mapping and designing. Using age old mapping systems of Indian astronomers as well as cartographers had developed some mapping skill on the basis of pole star and other constellations. Qin State of China was associated with production of oldest current map of the world, as dating back for 500 BC (Blegen, 1958).

Invention like telescope, compass and sextant resolutionized the cartography in the world; it was the step forward towards Age of Exploration from 15th century via 17th century. During this period, western world people organized extensive surveys, search of new lands and designed expanding maps whole world in a piece of world. German cartographer Martin Behaim produced oldest recent map of world in 1942. Soon after that so many invention, discovery and explorations surfaced and given window of map-making cartography like science and art of map making (French, 1998).

General Versus Thematic Cartography

The large scope of cartography categorized two broad areas *viz.*, general and thematic cartography with expanding the field.

a) General cartography: These types of cartography include construction of maps that is built for general people and involves wide aspects pertaining to reference and place (location) systems and always given in series. For example, it includes topographic maps of 1:24000 scales in a full series, which created by United State Geographical Survey and Ordnance Survey of 1:50000 maps representing UK by Great Britain Government.

b) Thematic cartography: Specific geographic map based on themes, the themes are designed to deal cartography field and is usually aimed for particular group of audiences. Present heavy inclining about this cartography and also gained popularities among viewers. Faster growth of thematic map in the cartography due to higher volumes of information related to geography in modern time get popular like forest cover map and other features also depicts in this cartography system.

Projection of Map

The projection of map is art of representation of a part or whole earth with meridians and parallels on flat surface. The projection associated with different types of distortions, although globe can exactly represent the areas and shapes along the precision. Even today various types of map distortions have to improve for solving the problems associated to projections.

Projection Classes

Following lists are mainly found the projection classes.

- Cylindrical projection: The global shape is treated like cylinder with horizental parallels and vertical meridians, the Mercator projection is a type of cylindrical projection.
- Pseudo-cylindrical projection: The epitome of this projection is parallel and central meridian which is mapped as straight lines and sometime other meridians are often spaced curved lines.
- Conic projection: This projection map possesses parallels in arcs of circles and meridians in straight lines.

- Pseudo projections: All the meridians except the central meridian (straight line) represent complete arcs in Pseudo-conical projection and parallels are the form of circular arcs.
- Azimuthal projection: If parallels are in form of full and concentric circles, whereas meridians are in straight lines form.
- Pseudo-azimuthal projection: Equators and central meridian intersect each other in straight, perpendicular lines in this kind of map projection and remaining parallels are in complex circles forms that semi-circle bend forms from equator. Other meridians are measured as complex curves bowing towards central meridian.

Topographical and Topological Maps

I. Topography map: Regarding a location, topological maps are simplified map of location or place which represents only those required information to be attributed without scale, and distances, the distance may be varied.

II. Topologic map: This map contains highly detailed information and bulk representation of the relief of an area. The lines that connect places/location of same height/elevation are known as contour lines are always used for this purpose. These types of map generally available in series where two or more map sheets together can represent full topographical details. In this map, drainage pattern, elevation, ground relief, forest area, roads, railways etc. are very common in information.

Cartography Principle in Map

i) **Purpose**: Basically purposeful designed map dictates special purpose of the map that may be integrated only those information which shows the feature based information in the particular map. The first step in the cartographic process, define purpose and meaning, means that you should interpret the requirements of the user when you are thinking about the design of the map. You need to answer two important questions.

ii) **Advance**: It always details the time frame information on map with guiding in advance to understand the quoted information for various level of people who interested in getting information.

iii) **Size & scale**: This contains information according to the purpose of map which size is decided and further throws light on scale for giving perfect information to the target group. The second step in the cartographic process is to choose the scale of the map. Defined, map scale is the ratio of map distance to earth distance. In other words it is the ratio at which the earth has been reduced to fit on the map. Map scale operates along a continuum from large-scale to small-scale. A large scale map is a map that is produced at 1:0 all the way through 1:600,000. A medium scale map is a map that is produced from 1:600,001 through 1:2,000,000. A small scale map is a map that is produced from the scale 1:2,000,001 through 1 to infinity.

iv) **Media (Quality map)**: Use the Media Map template to create apps that display an interactive map including basic tools. This app is a set of options to limit map navigation and is designed to fit into small spaces on a web page or as a stand-alone app.

v) **Focus**: The cartographic process is the abstraction and generalization of data. Once you have determined the purpose, scale, format, and type of map, you then need to determine the data sets and appropriately abstract and generalize.

vi) **Integrity**: Integration of many components in one map is another important aspect in cartographic process, how the integration has to take in consideration for better visibility and understanding.

vii) **Balance**: It mostly looks on different parts of composition in one theme so that the balance of map can be expressed with visibility; sometime tone and shape also place the role in expression of balance.

viii) **Completeness**: Top to bottom and left to right, all the required things are projected in map means the map showing completeness with fine tuning.

Map Elements

Maps are the primary tools by which spatial relationships and geographic data are visualized. Maps therefore become important documents. There are several key elements that should be included each time in a map is created in order to aid the viewer in understanding the communications of that map and to document the source of the geographic information used (Map body, Map title, Map legend, Map scale).

- The data frame is the part of the map displays the layers of data. This part is a important and focal centric of the map document. In the example displayed in figure 12.
- The legend serves as the simplifier for the symbology in the data frame. Therefore, guiding key in identifying objects and their relevancy is used. Detail description of map components indicates about theme for which map is designed with colour schemata. In the legend below, the fire schemata has been categorized with a graduating color scheme. The legend details which colors refer to which years. Legend explains the various features present in map with colour differences.

- The title is important because it instantly gives to the viewer a succinct description of the subject matter of the map (Fig. 5). Bastar division-DEM quickly tells the viewer of the subject matter of map.
- The purpose of the north arrow is for orientation (Fig. 10). This allows the viewers to determine the direction of the map as it related to due north. Always map shows north oriented either side of top of the map, so that due north faces the top of the page. There are exceptions to this, having the north arrow allows the viewer to know direction.
- The map scale depicts, how paper map relates to real world. The description is a ratio (Fig. 4). This can be shown either as a unit to unit or as one measurement to another measurement. So, a scale showing a 1:10,000 scale means that each one paper map unit shows 10,000 real world units. Like 1:10,000 in cm means that a measurement of one cm on the map equals 10,000 cm in existing object on earth. The second method of depicting scale is a comparison with different unit types; other hands, 13:1002 means that each inch measure on the paper map represents 100 feet in the real world because indication symbolization in inch and feet.
- The citation portion of a map is the area where explanatory data about the data sources and currency, projection information and any caveats are placed. In the below example, the citation tells the source and date of the data. Citations help the viewer determination for the use of the map at their own purposes.

Title: A map title is briefly and typically included map purpose as related to the map's topic. The followings are example of map titles. Perhaps a statement about that time period, the map cover would be useful.

Map Body: The map body map element contains the main focus on visually dominant, and also contains the important features to the message of the map. The map body should have larger as it is possible on the medium but not crowded. Map body varieties includes as cropped and floating which are widely used to preference when designing your map.

- **Cropped map:** A map represents area of interest within a geographic location and the surrounding area is separated by a neat line.
- **Floating Map:** This type of map is disconnected from neighboring regions, which can confuse map users.

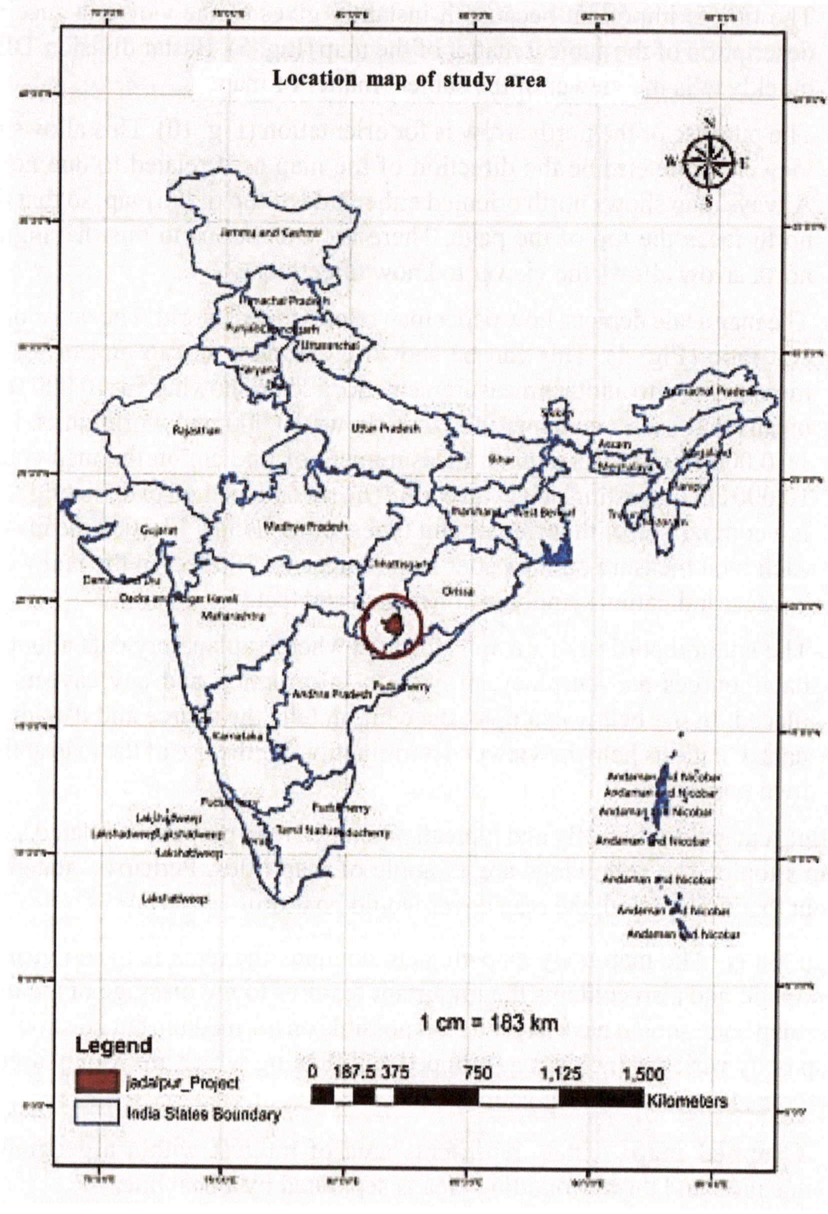

a) Cropped Map

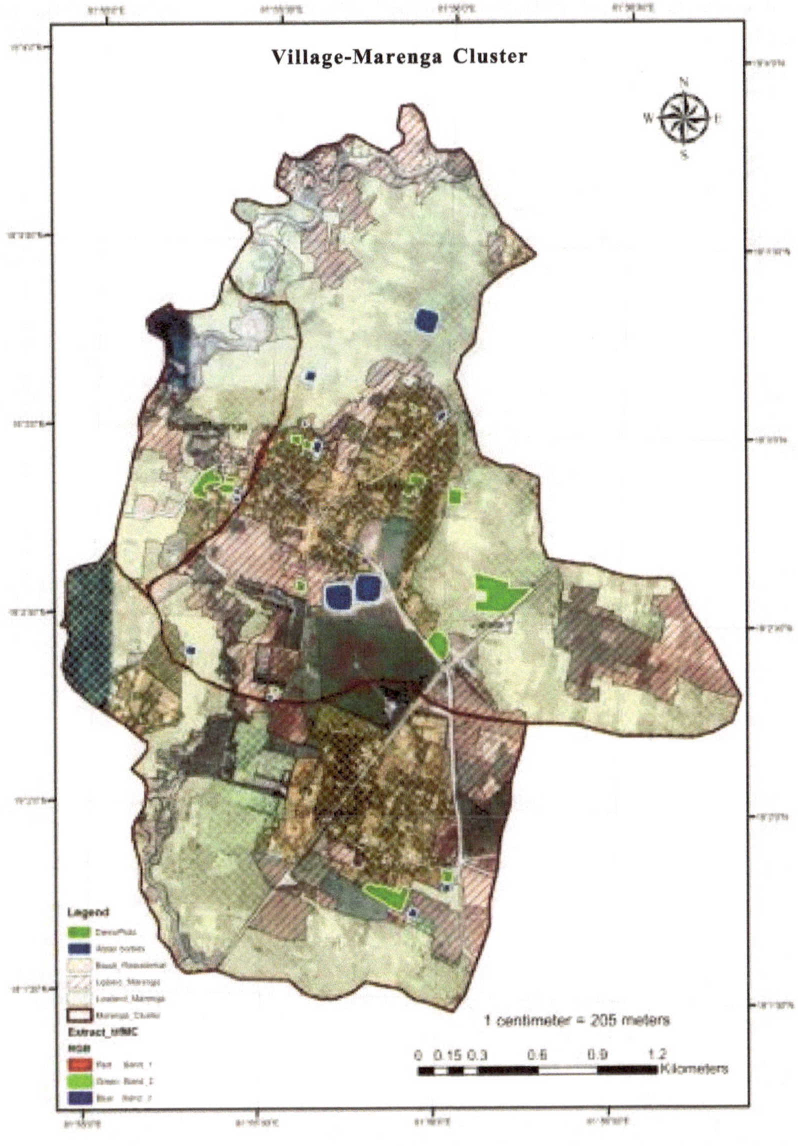

b) Floating Map

Fig. 1: Cropped and floating map

Inset Map: The inset map element is a small ancillary map that is typically larger in scale than the map body; basically the inset map shows more detail in the map body.

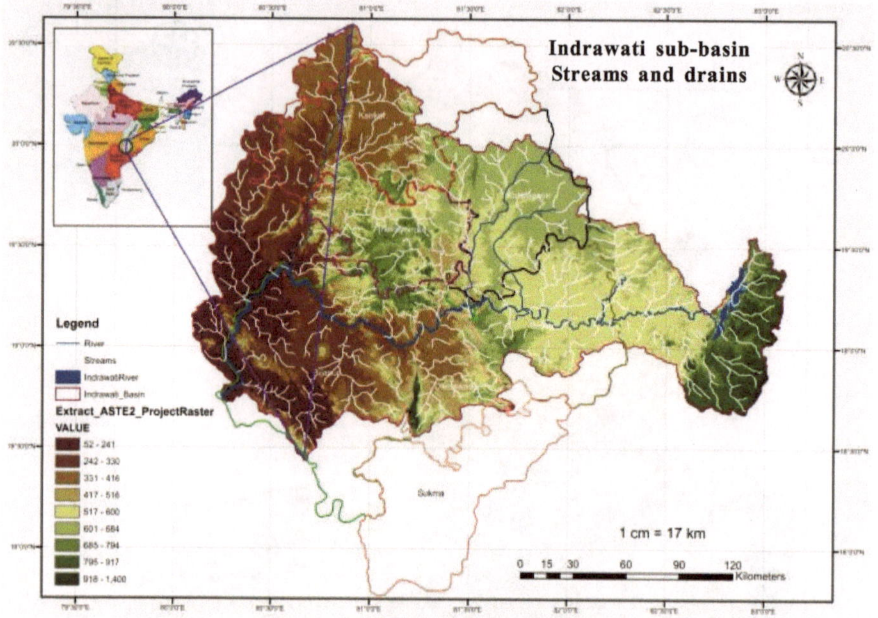

Fig. 2: Inset Map

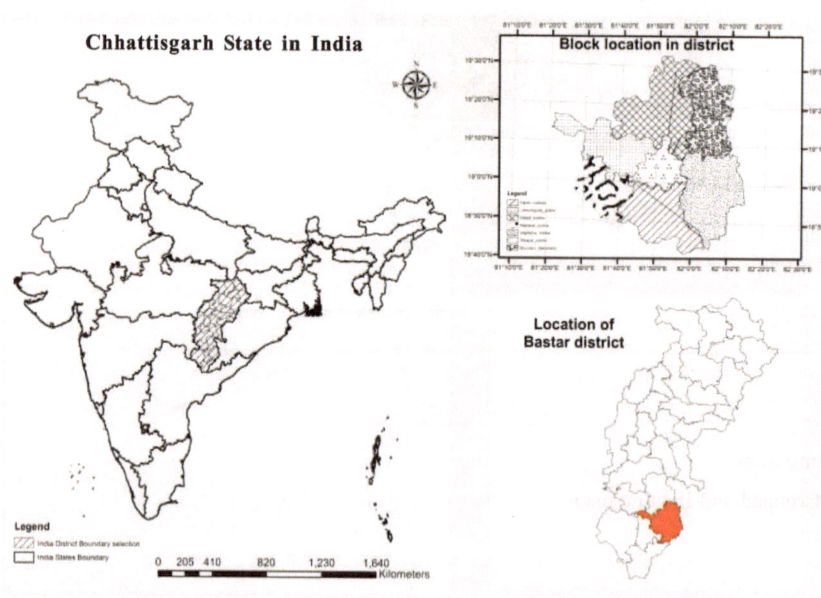

Fig. 3: Location Map

Map Scale: Map scale is used a unit of measurement for the appropriate readers with purpose and the map scale must be subtle and small. The scale should be noticeable but not stand out too much as map readers are expected to search for the map scale when required.

- **Graphic scale:** The graphic scale uses a graphic element, typically a bar or line, to represent a certain distance on the map. The graphic scale bar is often divided at meaningful intervals to assist the map reader. A major advantage of graphic will scale accordingly to be correct.

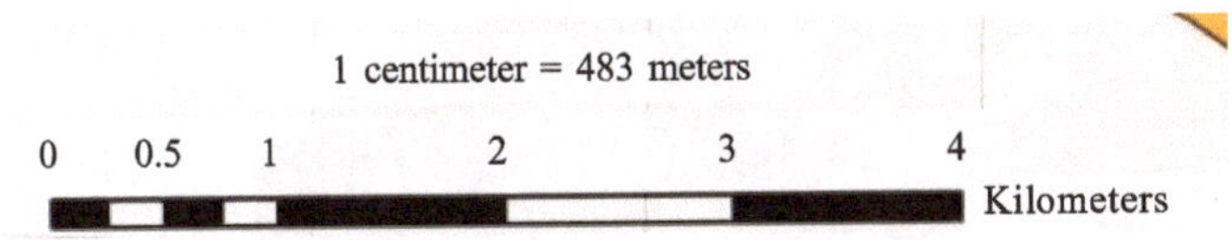

Fig. 4: Graphic Scale

- **Verbal scale:** The verbal scale is a sentence that details the relationship of the distance on the ground to the distance on the map. *One inch on the map equals twenty feet on the ground*
- **Representative Fraction:** In the representative fraction scale, two numbers are written separately by a colon. The number of the left of the colon represents the distance measurement map and a number to the right of the colon represents distance measured on the ground. Representative Scale is always *1:20.*
- **Location Map:** It is also a small ancillary map at a smaller scale, the purpose is to identify the location in the main map in relation to geographic context. It can include a location map on map layout with the area.

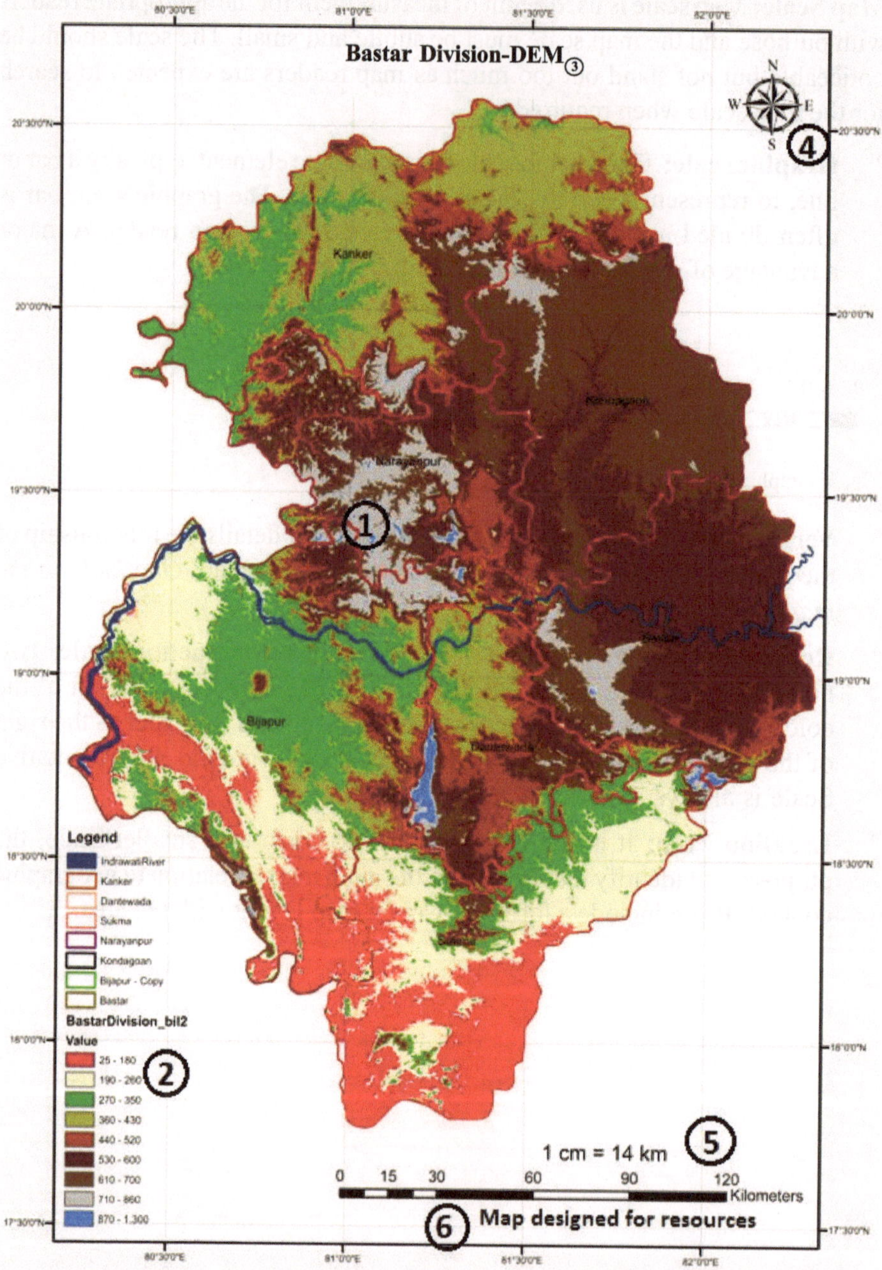

Fig. 5: Scale Bar: The scale bar on the map layout can be made sure that the scale bar is large enough to find, but small enough to be subtle. The top scale bar is quite smaller and it is not so useful for readers when they measure long distance. But the bottom scale is large being visually dominant on the map. So, the map scale in the middle is assumed to be at a reasonable size for this particular map.

Quality Criteria: Basically three criterias viz., scale units that always are in appropriate form to read the map and assess the location with relevant features, a scale unit must be perfect to scale showing a map of a small neighborhood in feet or meters and not miles; the scale interval must be rounded easy-to-use meaningful numbers and last one related to quality is that the number of divisions must divide equally into the scale range.

Legend: The legend is purposely identified unknown or unique map features briefly that map legends do not require to include a representation of all map features that are self-explaining.

General Reference Map Legend: The map legends have two columns of information that are roughly equal in size. Each map feature is identified with a symbol that is similar to the symbol found on the map followed by map name feature to the right of the symbol, where they may not be included on thematic maps.

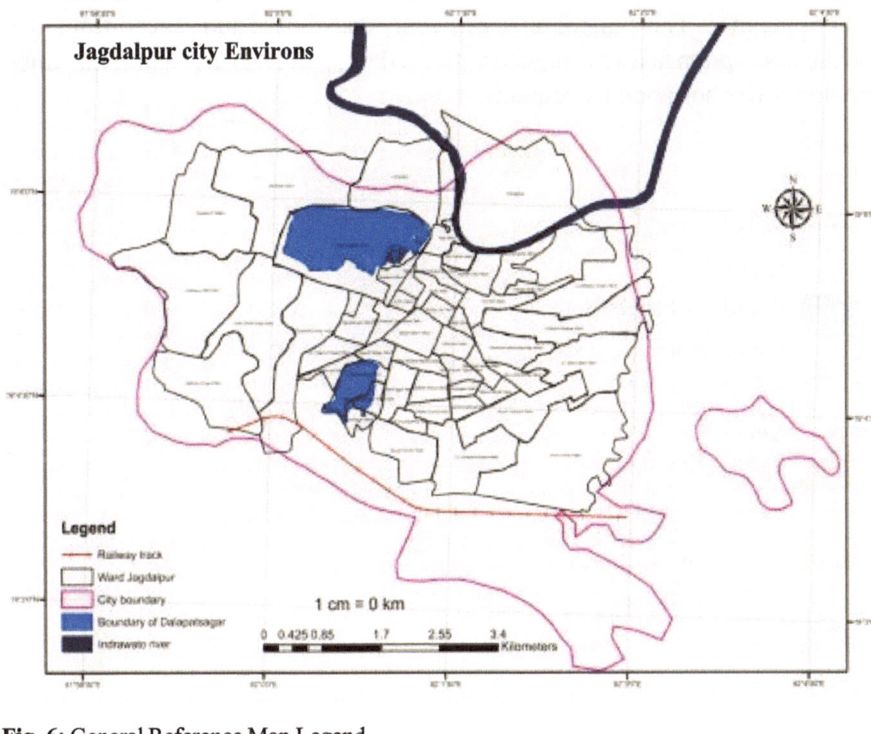

Fig. 6: General Reference Map Legend

Graduated Symbol Map: It represents the graduated symbol varies in size as related to the values. So, it contains important representative size for each value being capable to determine the value at those locations based on the circle size. The Vertical Layout with different size circles, and each circle represents to the right. Another is Nested Layout, the circles are nested inside of each other, and the labels are placed inside the relevent circle.

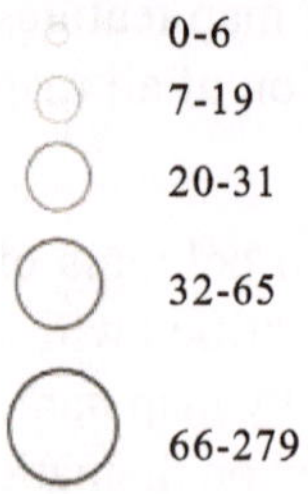

Fig. 7a: Vertical Layout

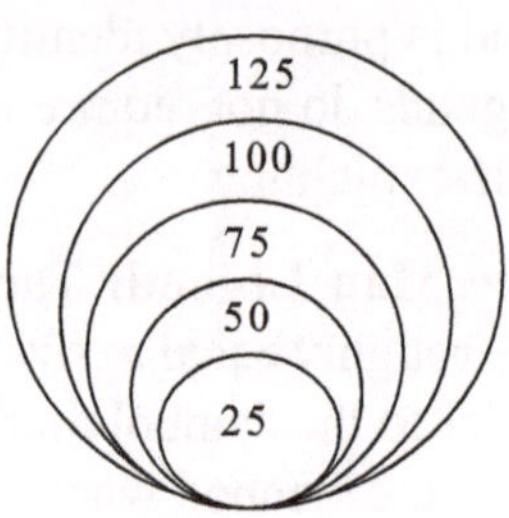

Fig 7b. Nested Layout

Legend Design: First, the symbol must be at the left with the description to the right of the map. The symbol must be evenly distributed and spaced from them and the description and also aligned with the descriptions to the right. The symbol should also be horizontally centered.

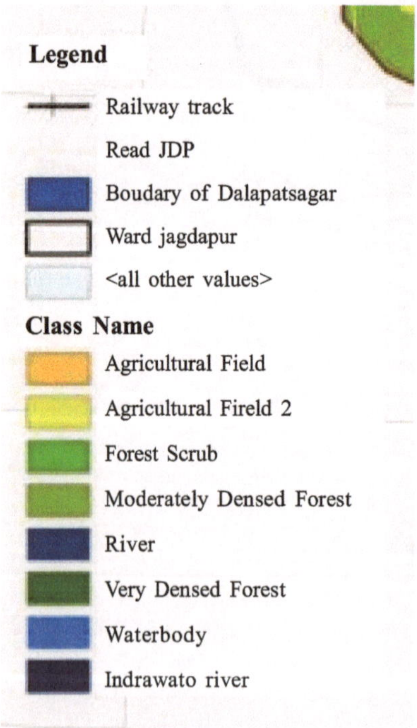

Fig. 8: Legend Design

Columns: Legend can be split in multiple columns so that the map legend is placed properly or the legend entries can be split into comfortable columns.

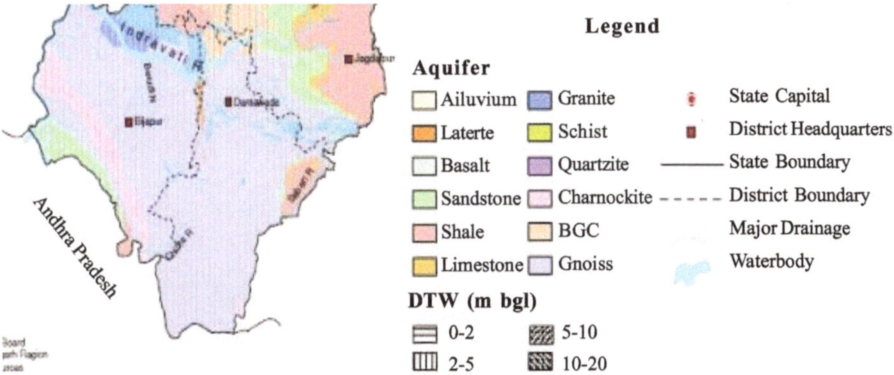

Fig. 9: Columns of Index

Headings: Heading of legend can contain meaningfully separate groups of entries; symbols representing a single feature on the map must have a singular description and multiple features with the plural description.

Directional Indicator: Always North arrow depicts the direction of north upward of map. Map readers are used to most maps showing North as up. So that natural earth information can be matched with map features and readers are familiar with this map.

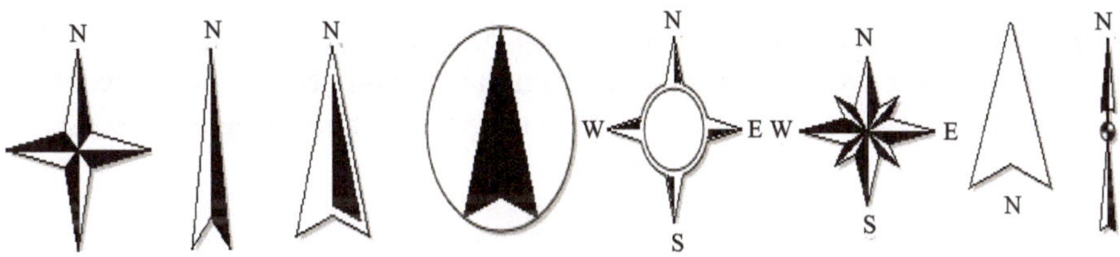

Fig. 10: Directional Arrow

Label: The label is mainly given in map for communicating attributes or ancillary informations to the map readers. It helps in orientation the readers to the map and the features are kept on the map.

Graticule: It is used mainly in reading location coordinate on the map having meaningful divisions and units. The thematic map omits graticule from maps to convey the spatial distribution of a theme, not for determining precise locations.

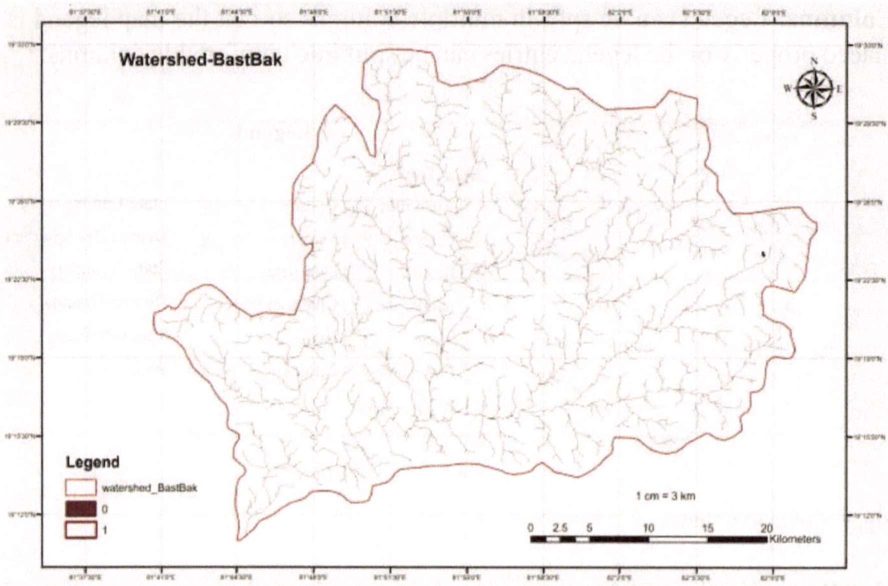

Fig. 11: Graticule

Neat Line: The neat line of map element provides a frame around the whole map or individual map elements, being to be a nice and clean frame of the map.

Ancillary Text and Objects: The term ancillary belongs to a matter that supports another matter, the ancillary information is plus information providing a greater understanding of the topic.

Placement: The map elements and layout is considered, it should carefully accept placement map element. Map elements are positioned and sized according to the importance. You should also strive to reduce white space on the map.

Fig. 12: Map Elements

Use of Map

Base map is a representation of data in pictorial forms, not much detail to come in the conclusion. Some of the important things find in map are picture, representation of landform or features and their relationship in ratio, Scale is very important factor in detailing how the map dealt with real situation involving RF (representation of fraction) i.e. 1:50000; Statement or verbal scale also considered to as a word statement of scale expression, where the response options are presented to the respondent using words, whether spoken or written.

Verbal Scale

A verbal scale that expresses the relationship between distance on the map and distance on the ground in words like one inch equals to 10 miles which is drawn in graphical map scale.

Verbal scale: 1 inch=1 mile

Representative Fraction (R.F.): 1:24000 (1 map unit is equivalent to 24000 land units)

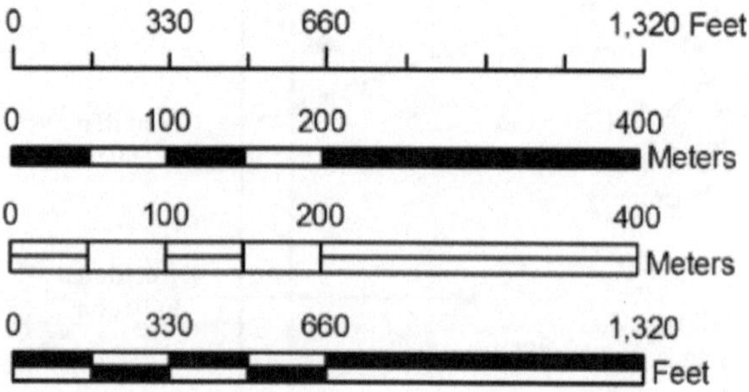

Fractional map Scale

The fractional method involves the scale of a map uses a representative fraction to explain between the map and the real world. This can be seen as 1:50,000 or 1/50,000. Other kinds of scale, survey scales, Guttman scale, largest scale, interval scale, continuous scale, comparative scale, discrete scale, forced choice scale. RF is universal scale but graphical scale change with change in scale extending expression:

Large size: Small area coverage in paper, large scale cadastral map

Small seale: Large area coverage in map, smaller scale According to object, thematic map is developed as soil map, Vegetative map etc.

General purpose map: Map preparation for cities and its locations over the expanded areas.

Scale represents and projects land area in measured paper to assess fastly by normal man without any haphazardness within time frame otherwise wandering and collection of data and their laying with factors might be a link consuming process.

Gratitude map: Geo-referred map (latitude and longitude).

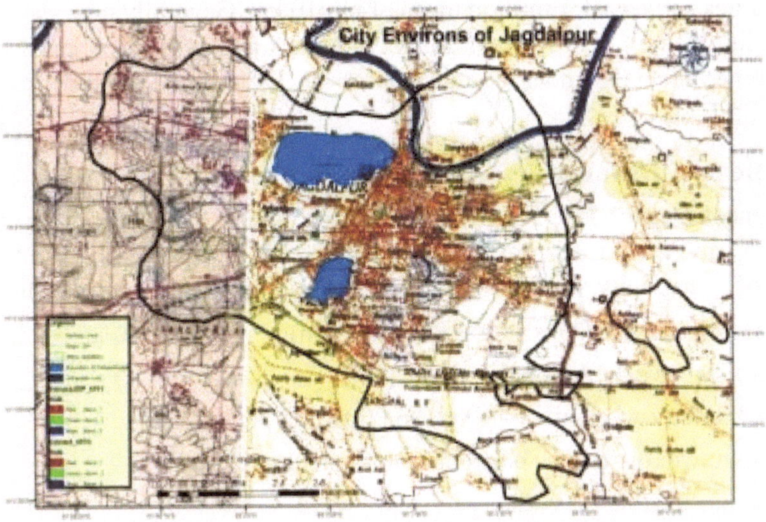

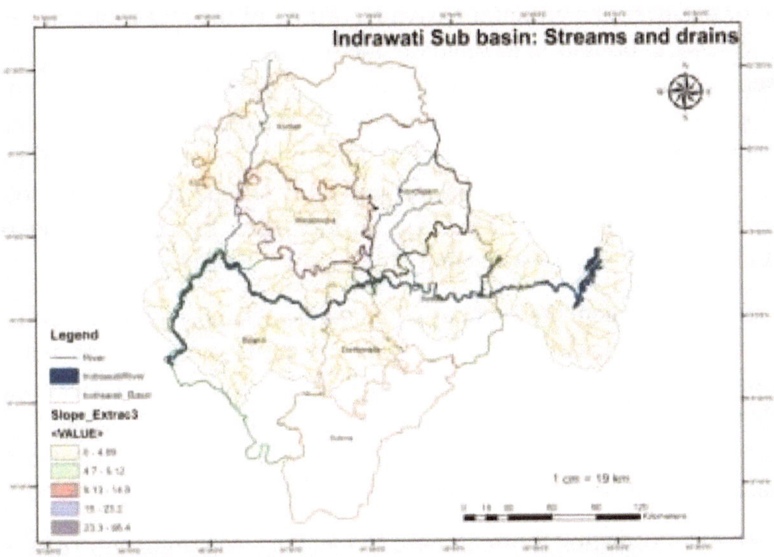

Fig. 13: a) Fractional Sacle Map on Toposheet, b) Drawn Map on Toposheet

Symbolized feature: symbols are used for expressing details about map on paper through vegetation, roads etc., survey of India standardized symbols for map making then 100% match and types of symbol explains in point, linear, and aerial distribution/spatial distribution. Thickness of boundary will be standardized. Original map is drawn on topographical sheet and base map draw from it. Base map is a Skelton of map projection and classification scale for topography as entire India lies between 1:1 million means 1 cm:10 km. Generally map shows vegetation in green, road in red text, railway in black and cultivation lands in yellow. Whole India falls under latitude from 8°4 to 37°7 N and longitude from 68°7 to 97°25 E.

Measurement of Distance

Measurement of distance depends on the below given formula that details distance, light volocity and time. Electromagnetic radiation (EMR) is basically decides the quality of cartography, which is broadcasted the radio signal through satellite:

- Satellites broadcast radio signals (EM radiation)
- Simple distance calculation d = v * t

  Where, Velocity = velocity of light 186,000 miles per seconds

  Time is known (difference between sending and receiving)

  Distance is calculated as "d"

Cadastral Map

A cadastre or cadaster is a comprehensive recording of the real estate or real property's metes-and-bounds of a country (CadastralTemplate.org, 2008). Often it is represented graphically in a cadastral map. In most countries, legal systems have developed around the original administrative systems and use the cadastre to define the dimensions and location of land parcels described in legal documentation. A land parcel or cadastral parcel is defined as "a continuous area, or more appropriately volume, that is identified by a unique set of homogeneous property rights" (Dale and McLaughlin, 2000).

Cadastral surveys document the boundaries of land ownership, by the production of documents, diagrams, sketches, plans (*plats* in the US), charts, and maps. They were originally used to ensure reliable facts for land valuation and taxation. An example from early England was from the Domesday Book in 1086. Napoleon established a comprehensive cadastral system for France that is regarded as the forerunner of most modern versions.

Cadastral survey information is often a base element in Geographic Information Systems (GIS) or Land Information Systems (LIS) used to assess and manage land and built infrastructure. Such systems are also employed on a variety of other tasks, for example, to track long-term changes over time for geological or ecological studies, where land tenure is a significant part of the scenario. Cadastre is technically defined as a set of records having the extent, value and occupancy of lands. A cadastre stored records of areas and land values of owners which purposely compiled for the aim of taxation. So many countries do not impose any land tax, and practically, cadastre serves two more important purposes *viz.*, ready resources of precise description and identification of that specific land pieces, which acts as a continuous record of right in land.

In modern time, normal cadastre map consists of large scale map or plan in series corresponding registers. Both plans and registers can be saved in computers under computerization and registration of maps. This chapter details the essential features of cadastral map with concerned to the state they take when the map is drawn on paper or showing on computer screen. Meanwhile survey of an individual piece of land contains for the plot of land in some country and can have unconnected to side land, the true cadastral map covers all pieces of land within an area than showing in isolated places. This acts as index for other land piece surveys which show higher details of information or may be enough large scale for the dimensions of each piece to receive from the map throughput monograph and termed as cadastral map can include any piece of land that is designated by ownership, value or use provided with land piece having an independent status and also related to the management for land resource. Any cadastral map shows the boundaries of such piece of lands and possibility of additional incorporation of resource it details coupled with them, involving physical structures on geology, soils and vegetation the way land is used.

Scale related with cadastral maps are more important because of objective of map to be provided a precise description and identification of the pieces of land, the scale must be more sufficient for every separate plot which can be subjected of isolated possession (Survey plot or land parcel) to seem as a identifiable unit of a map. Data may be restricted at any scale when map data are stored in computer system and may avail in impression of greater accuracy than quality survey data can warrant. The map and related registers create complementary parts of the system of description and identification, expecting for some system have cross-referencing between things shown on map and recorded in system. Every land piece must be given either name of number and these all references are known as property identification (PID) or unique piece reference number (UPRN). Various reference systems already been created including

- Name of greater or grantee,
- Sequential title number,

- Volume and folio number where plot is registered,
- Name of locality,
- Registration of individual plot,
- Postal address,
- Street index reference and number of land piece,
- Grid coordinate (google).

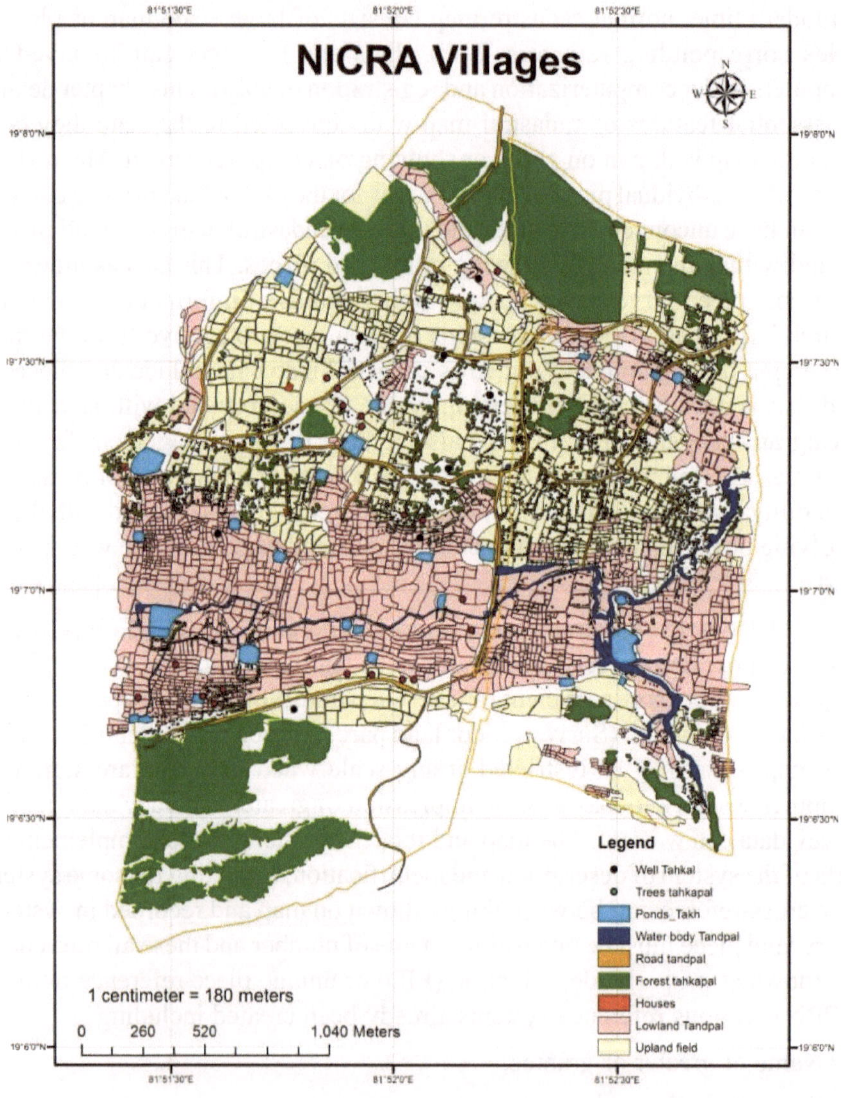

Fig. 14: Cadastral Map of Study Village Cluster (Tandpal and Tahkapal)

4

Principles of Digital Terrain Analysis

Preparation of base map being in mind, the forest, agriculture, water, road and boundary are almost same for all but theme may be different as per requirement. Base information is to survey and need terrain information, the preparation includes land forms by separation of water, kart area, coastal area. Meanwhile preparation of focus might be on DEM (Digital Elevation Model) and water movement helps in demarcation of boundaries on map.

Classification of map depicts different levels of map which denotes various properties to understand easily with simple observations; one million maps explain events in 1:10000 scale hierarchy system which explains. Broad term map (Hill, terrain, hill types) to very detail (high resolution) and more details.

Terrain analysis symbolizes and represents the landscapes; surface of ground is always a matter of interest in delineation surface features for various aspects of human beings. Terrain analysis developed in different years i.e. photo-topography (1946), stereo-photographs (1950), Mars points (1980), automated generated Mars point and in 2000 onward direct generation of DEMs from stores. The data related to source of DEM are photometric data, RADAR (active), radio wave, LIDAR (Light Detection and Ranging), UV, digitalized contours and ground survey. DEM differs on x and y axis with interpolation method, generation method mode (DIM Vs DSM), resolution (scale) and re-sampling and processing. Large scale map detail with map contains scale, resolution, accuracy and contents of maps are related. All layers of spatial database should be stored in a common coordinate and accuracies. The combined data should be considered only as good as the wart input.

GIS Projection

Maps are always visualized flat but they actually represent curved surfaces, changing three dimension space onto a two dimension map is called a projection. Projections are mathematical expressions that convert data from a geographic location (Latitude and Longitude) on a sphere or spheroid to a representative location on a flat surface. Projection always causes distortion in one or more ways: shape, area, distance and direction. That is why projection is set by objective of project for obtaining higher accuracy with right position.

GIS Projections-Datum

Datum defines a coordinate system and a set of control points whose geometric relationships are known. All datums are based on the spheroid and provide a frame of reference for measuring locations on the earth. The earth is not round, on small scale maps, it must be treated as a spheroid. Survey of earth has been done many times. The commonly references spheroid in maps in NAD 27 (North American Datum 1927) which goes back to data collected by Lewis and Clarke in 1966. The origin of these datums is a point on the earth referred more accurate horizontal datum referred to as NAD 83 due to centre of the earth's mass orientated. Under NAD 83, locations of provisions control points shift by as much as 500 feet. Since no one projection is perfect in all respects, choose a projection based upon project needs.

Scale

Resolution is clarity of map visualization to show portion of the surface of earth on map, scale clarity directly belongs to size of a map as increase in scale area reduces vice-versa small area map possesses larger expansion of same area. Map scale is extent of reduction expressed as a ration. 1:24000 is example of representative fraction (RF) because amounts on either side of colon are equivalent. Map scale indicates how much a given area is reduced. On a same size map, features on a small scale map (1:250000) will be small than large scale map (1:1200) small scale can show large amount of area without much detail whereas large scale can only small area but lot of details. Size of scale can represent each horizontal line equals to one unit of distance.

Accuracy

Map accuracy involves resolution, map scale, drafting skills, thickness of lines etc. any number of the factors can cause errors and the errors are accumulative. By knowing error, error can be minimized, the error source may be flattening of earth, accurate location, map interpretation, drafting error (tracing), conversion error, oblong to digital, calibration error, media stability, digitizing error and unexplained errors. National map accuracy standards stands less than 10% of features, more than 1/3rd inch from intended location on scale larger than 120000, less than 10% features, more than 1/50th inch from intended location on scales smaller than 120000. Always map overlay with 0-20 mm per check plot, no gaps should show.

Measurement on a Globe

Spherical geometry consists of lines of latitude (Parallel i.e. equator) and vertical lines of longitude (Meridians). Together, these form a grided network called a graticule (Graticular Networks). Latitude and Longitude are an angle measured from the earth's centre to a point on the earth's surface and define the location of points on the globe. Horizontal axis is equator and vertical axis is the Green which Prime Meridian intersection = 0°0°.

Latitude: Equator equal to 0°, North Pole is 90°, South Pole is -90° represents on globe to give proper projection.

Latitude: East is positive up to 180°, West is negative upto 180° with demarcation locations in coordinating system on earth.

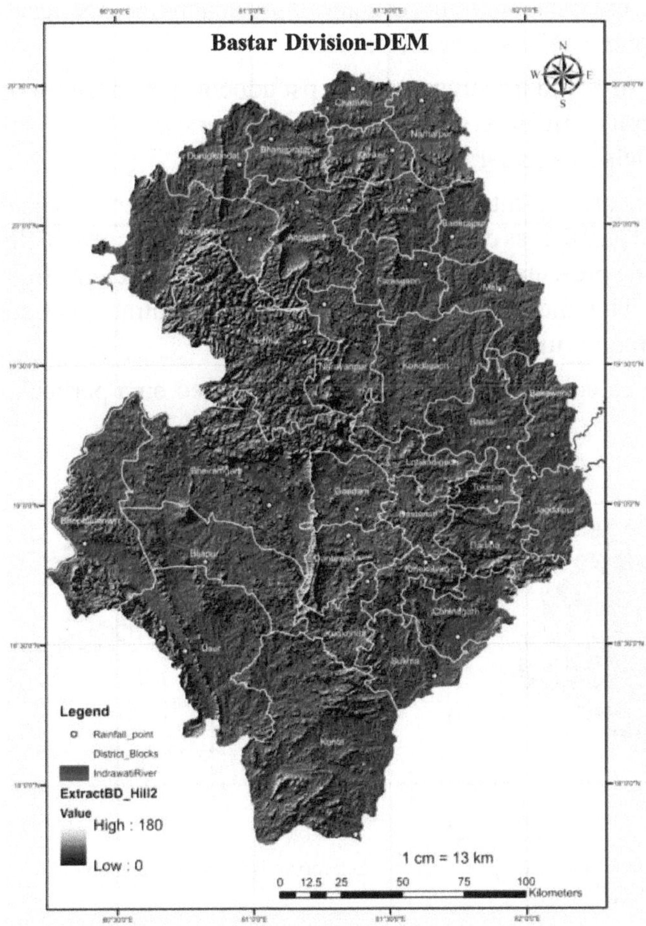

Fig. 1: Digital Elevation Model (DEM)

Type of Projection

- **Cylindrical**: In standard presentation, these map regularly-spaced meridians to equally spaced vertical lines, and parallels to horizontal lines.
- **Pseudo cylindrical**: In standard presentation, these map is the central meridian and parallels as straight lines. Other meridians are curves (or possibly straight from pole to equator), regularly spaced along parallels.
- **Pseudoazimuthal**: In standard presentation, pseudoazimuthal projections map the equator and central meridian to perpendicular, intersecting straight lines. They map parallels to complex curves bowing away from the equator, and meridians to complex curves bowing in toward the central meridian. Listed here after pseudocylindrical as generally similar to them in shape and purpose.
- **Conic**: In standard presentation, conic (or conical) projections map meridians as straight lines, and parallels as arcs of circles.
- **Pseudoconical**: In standard presentation, pseudoconical projections represent the central meridian as a straight line, other meridians as complex curves, and parallels as circular arcs.
- **Azimuthal**: In standard presentation, azimuthal projections is map meridians (straight lines) and parallels as complete concentric circles. They are radially symmetrical. In any presentation (or aspect), they preserve directions from the center point. This means great circles through the central point are represented by straight lines on the map.
- **Other**: Typically calculated from formula, and not based on a particular projection

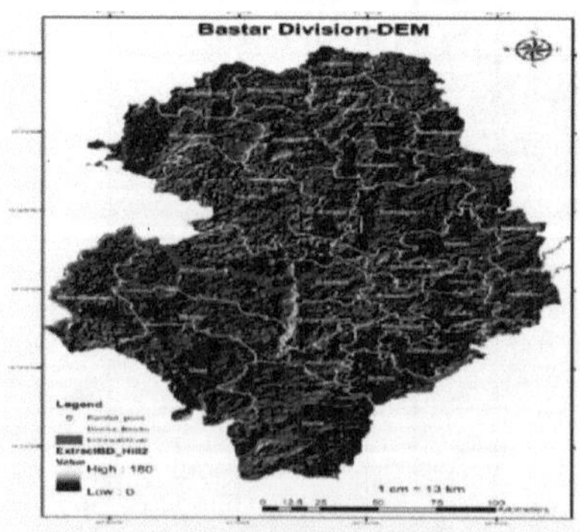

Transverse Mercator-constant Scale along Chosen Central Meridian

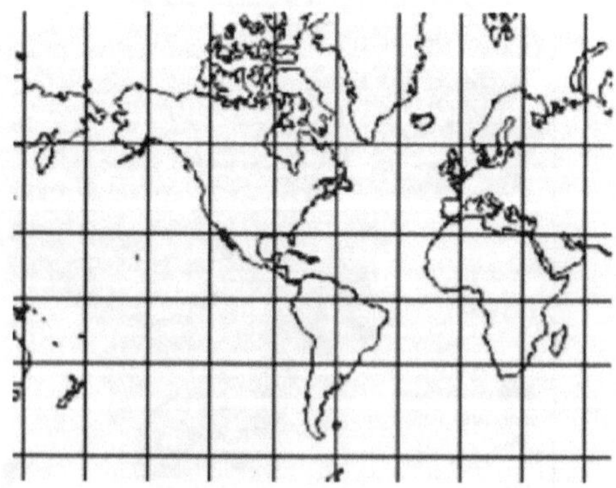

Universal Transverse Mecator

- **Polyhedral maps**: Polyhedral maps can be folded up into a polyhedral approximation to the sphere, using particular projection to map each face with low distortion.
- **Retroazimuthal**: Direction to a fixed location B (by the shortest route) corresponds to the direction on the map from A to B.

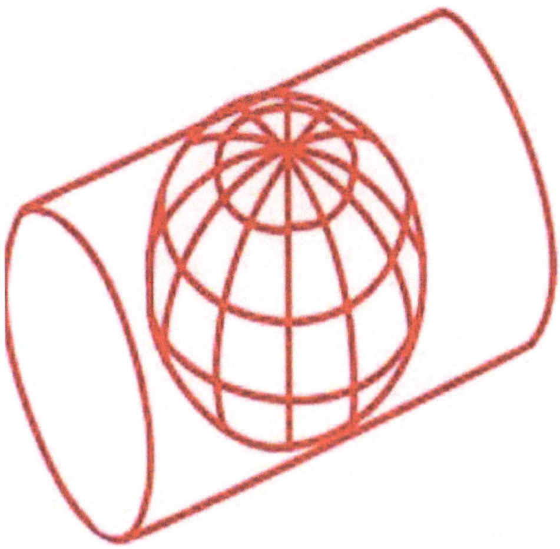

Transverse Cylindrical

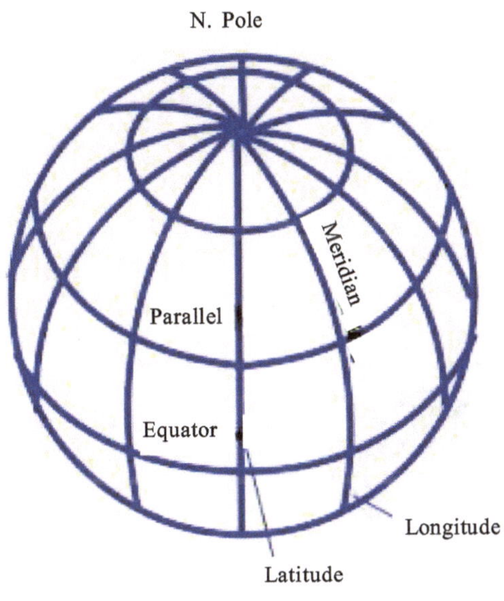

Global Measurement

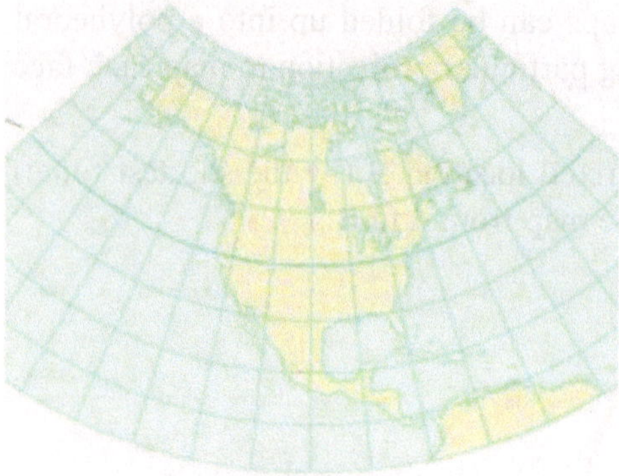

Albers Aqual - Area Conic

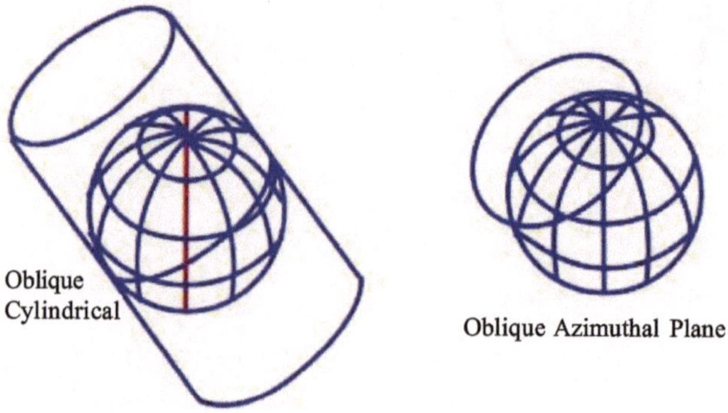

Oblique Projections

Projections

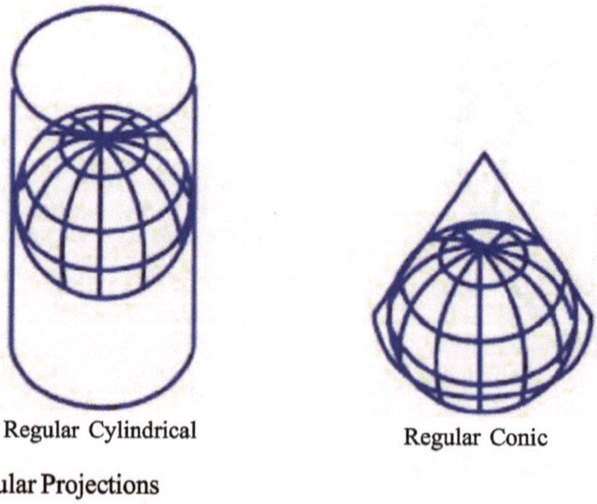

Regular Projections

Polar Azimuthal (Plane)

Fig. 2: Projection of Map

Map Properties

Scale

Scale indicates representing large and small area coverage under scaling along visual for common man. Small map shows 1:250000 measurement in which features of map looks smaller than large scale map (1:10000). The adjustment of feature depends on map theme; it is surveyed for flora definitely many other features which are not targeted would be deleted from map. Reduction of area to show portion of earth's surface on map

Map scale: Extent of reduction expressed as a ratio 1' = 2000; 1' = 24000 inches; 1: 24000 is example of representative fraction (RF) because amounts on either side of action are equivalent, map scale indicates how much a given area is reduced on a same size map (or piece of paper), features on a small scale map (1:250000) will be smaller than on a large map (1:1200). Small scale map can show large amount of area without much details whereas large scale only show small area but lots of details.

Accuracy

Accuracy is a combination of resolution, map scale drafting skills, thickness of lines etc., any number of factor can cause errors and attempting to minimize. The source of error flattening of earth, accurate location, map interpretation, drafting error (tracing), conversion error (analog to digital calibration error), media stability, digitizing cursor error, RMS error (accurate registry of tics), machine rounding errors, unexplained errors. National map has standard accuracy is less than 10% of feature, more than 1/30° inch from intended location on scales smaller than 1:20000, use map overlay with 0.25 mm pen check plot no gap should be shown.

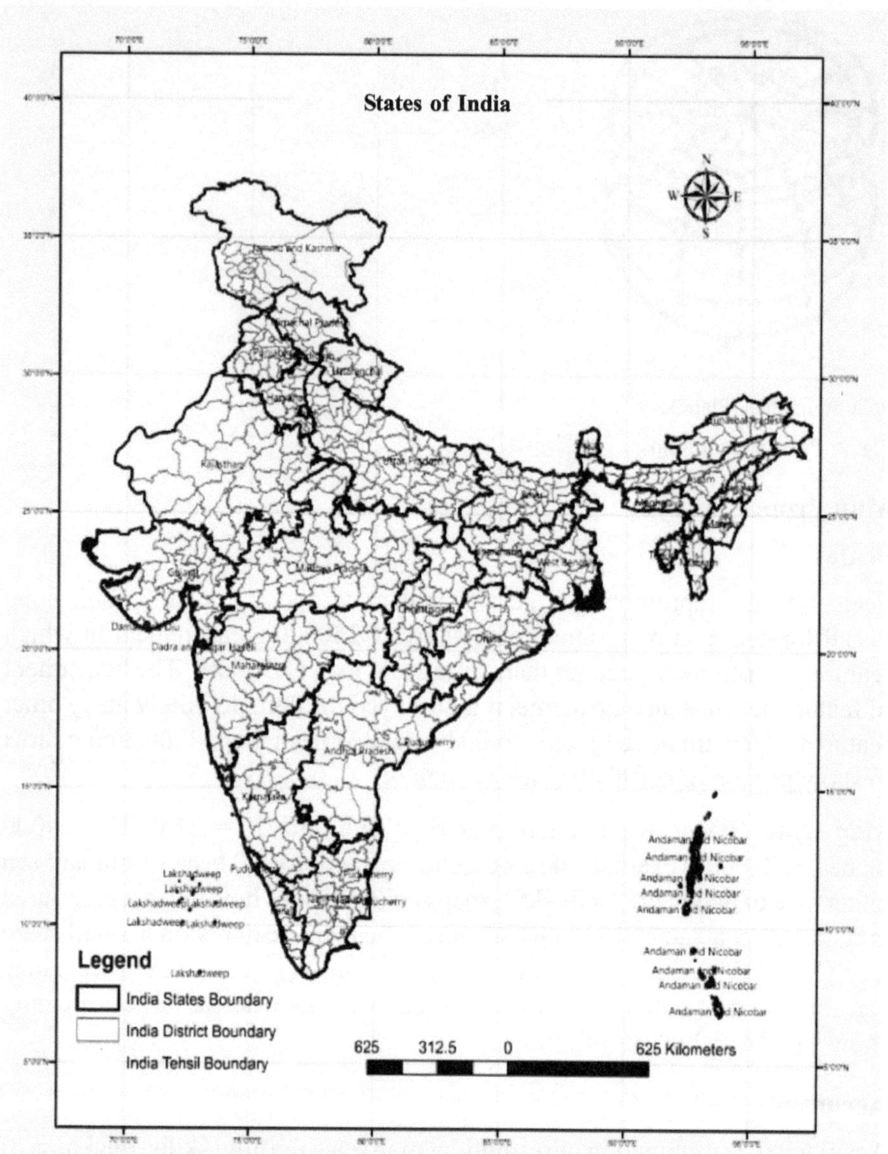

Fig. 3: Latitude and Longitude of Indian Contunent

5

Aerial Photography

Age old practice of photography was taken with still camera in parallel direction, not aerially scan or snapping which really present wider prospective of any object or places in rearranging or planning skilfully in two dimensional working. Earlier aeroplane played a important role in over head condition to capture snaps but again accuracy and angle of camera limited the works because these photographs were diagonally or trigonally not matched the reality of ground.

Aerial photograph is snapshot taken from air which may be any angle to focus. Normally this type of photograph is taken vertically using low altitude aircraft, drone, unmanned aircraft or any object is used for snapping scene overhead. There are many things to determine that makes one photographs different from another to same area considering film type, scale and overlap. Aerial photography needs same conceptual components are used like stereoscopic coverage, fiducially marks, focal length, roll and frame number and flight lines and atleast index maps. The below given details may assist to develop understanding fundamental information of aerial photography with basic technics.

Historical Events in Photography

French photographer and balloonist, Gaspar Felix Tournachon was the first known aerial photographer who took photographs in 1858 as "Nadar". The idea had been patented in 1855 using aerial photographs in map making and surveying, but three years long time was spent in experimenting before the remarkable success, which produced the very first aerial photograph at a view of French village of Petit-Becetre taken from a tethered hot-air balloon above 80 meters from ground. Although the photograph was of no mean feat, due to exposure of light as collodion photographic process, to be carried in the basket of the balloon. Unfortunately, Nadar's earliest photographs no longer survive, and the oldest aerial photograph known to be still in existence is James Wallace Black's image of Boston from a hot-air balloon in 1860. Later the development of the dry-plate process, aerial photography was no need to carry so much equipment, and the first free flight balloon photo mission was carried out in 1879 by Triboulet over Paris.

The devastation of San Francisco after the 1906 earthquake in California and fire was captured by George R. Lawrence, using a camera attached to a string of kites high above the city. He specially designed large-format camera had a curved film plate to provide panoramic images, which remain some of the largest aerial exposures ever seen. The camera was larger and heavier, took as many as 17 kites to lift it 2,000 feet into the air. Lawrence also used ladders and high towers to capture lower level "aerial" photographs.

The Bavarian Pigeon Corps use their pigeons in carrying messages and for aerial reconnaisance. In 1903, Julius Neubranner designed a tiny breast-mounted camera for carrier pigeons. The camera could be set to take automatic exposures at 30-second intervals as the pigeon flew along. The flight path was not always reliable, and mostly it was used for military purposes, the birds were introduced at the 1909 Dresden International Photographic Exhibition, where postcards of aerial photographs taken above the exhibition were very popular with the public.

Later rocket mounted camera was used for obtaining aerial photographs by the Swedish inventor, Alfred Nobel in 1897 and Alfred is best known nowadays for the Nobel prize. In 1906, Albert Maul produced a more reliable method in Germany using a rocket propelled by compressed air, which was taken an aerial photograph at a height of 2,600 feet, before being ejected and parachuted back to earth. He had patented the idea of using power rockets in 1903, and by 1904 it was testing gyroscopically-stabilised cameras launched by rockets and recovered by parachute. In 1912 he demonstrated his perfect rocket to the Austrian Army, but by then airplanes were found to be more effective.

Aerial Photography from Airplanes

The airplane was used first time in 1909 for aerial photography by Italian Wilbur Wright, engaged in marketing planes to the Italian government, when he carried a passenger who took motion pictures of the military field at Centocelli, near Rome.

During World War I, aerial photography soon replaced sketching and drawing by the aerial observers. The battle maps used by both sides were produced from aerial photographs, and by the end of the war, both sides were recording the entire front at least twice a day. Cameras especially designed for use in airplanes were being produced including thermal infra-red detectors. Stability and shutter speed remained a problem, and towards the end of the war Sherman M. Fairchild developed a camera with the shutter located inside the lens. This design significantly improved the quality of the images, and became the standard for aerial camera systems over the next 50 years.

Fundamental Concepts

Film: Commonly aerial photography is taken using film; however colour, infrared, and false-colour infrared film are also used for special purpose.

Focal length: The distance from the middle of the lens to the focal plane. As focal length increases and image distortion decreases. The focal length is perfectly measured when the camera is calibrated.

Scale: It is ratio of the distance between photo distance and ground distance which represents real ground on paper map. If one km stretch of highway covers 4 cm on an air photo, the scale is calculated as follows.

$$\frac{\text{PHOTO DISTANCE}}{\text{GROUND DISTANCE}} = \frac{4\text{cm}}{1\text{km}} = \frac{4\text{cm}}{100000\text{cm}} = \frac{1}{25000} \text{SCALE :1/25000}$$

Another method utilized to determine the scale of a photo is to get the ratio between the focal length of camera and the altitude of plane above the ground being taken photograph.

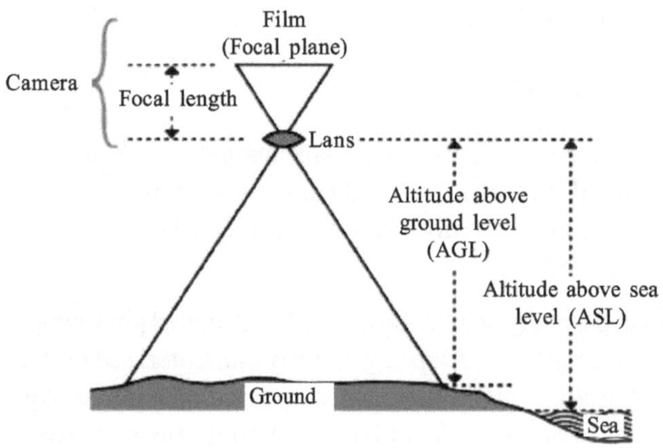

If a camera's focal length is 152 mm, and the plane's altitude Above Ground Level (AGL) is 7 600 m, using the same equation as above, the scale would be:

$$\frac{\text{FOCAL LENGTH}}{\text{ALTITUDE (AGL)}} = \frac{152\text{mm}}{7600\text{m}} = \frac{152\text{mm}}{7600000\text{mm}} = \frac{1}{50000} \text{SCALE :1/50000}$$

Scale may be expressed three ways

1. Unit Equivalent
2. Representative Fraction
3. Ratio

A photographic scale of 1 millimetre on the photograph represents 25 metres on the ground would be expressed as follows:

- Unit Equivalent expresses as 1 mm = 25 m
- Representative Fraction means 1/25 000
- Ratio details 1:25 000

Types of scales

Two types of scale generally mentioned when scale is discussed

1. **Large Scale:** Larger-scale photos (1:25 000) cover shorter area with more detail. A bigger scale photograph explains that ground features are larger with more detailed size and vice-versa actual ground coverage seems smaller in aerial photograph at smaller scales.
2. **Small Scale:** Smaller-scale photos (1:50 000) include more areas with smaller detail. A small scale photo simplifies the earth features are at a smaller, less information. The area of earth coverage that is seemed on the photo in greater than at larger scales.

Basic Components of Photography

Fiducial marks: Little registration marks exposed on the margin of a photograph. The distances between fiducial marks are perfectly assessed when a camera is calibrated, and this information is mainly preferred for cartographer when compiling a topographic map.

Overlap: Frequency of click basically decides how much overlapped photographs each other while aerial photography, overlap is generally charcaterized by area covered two or more photographs each other, and expressed as a percentage. The photo survey is framed to acquire 60% forward overlap means between photos along the same flight line and 30% lateral overlap shows between photos on adjacent flight lines.

Stereoscopic Coverage: 3-D image which produces two overlapping photos is called a stereo pair, are seen as stereoscope. Every photograph of the stereo pair gives a slight different view of the same area, is the brain combined and interpreted as a three dimensional image.

Roll and Photo Numbers: Each aerial photo has a unique index number as per the photo's frame and frame. For instance, photo A23819-32 is the 32th annotated photo on roll A23819. This unique number permits you to find the photo in NAPL's archive, along with metadata information including date of day, the plane's altitude (above sea level), the focal length of the camera, and the weather conditions.

Flight Lines and Index Maps: The aerial survey contractor arrays the location of the first, last, and every fifth photo, along with its roll and frame number in centre, on a National Topographic System (NTS) map. Photo centres are represented by small circles, and straight lines are drawn connecting the circles to show photos on the same flight line. Small-scale photographs are indexed on 1:250 000 scale NTS map sheets, whereas larger-scale photographs are indexed on 1:50 000 scale NTS maps.

6

Topographical Maps

Toposheet

Fundamentally toposheet represents a kind of map in which topographic features of particular area is given details on the map features in two dimensional land surfaces. It shows both horizontal and vertical portion of the terrain with a combination of contour lines, contours, symbols, labels and related representation together in one piece of paper. Toposheet portray the shapes, location of mountains, many natural and manmade features, and the toposheet combinedly uses for extracting accurate information about particular area containing land surface features.

Scale Based Classification

1. Large scale map represents a scale of 1 in 1000 or less than 1000
2. Medium scale map ranges in between 1 in 1000 to 1 in 10000 representation of real ground
3. Small scale map covers either 1 in 10000 or greater than 10000 scale for toposheet.

Topographic survey was very much needed for assisting in reparation of plan in battle field and defensive emplacement under military action initially, that period of time elevation based information was so crucial. Now, topographic map series become national resources in planning infrastructure and resource utilization. By the moderating for common uses, it needs in print forms with arbitrary contents, area coverage and scale under google platform.

The topographic map is characterized by large-scale detail representation of relief using contour lines. Traditional definitions require a topographic map to show both manmade and natural features. This map has published typical map series of two or more map sheets that combine to create the whole map.

Topographic Map Conventions

The different features are represented through conventional signs or symbols usually explained in the margin of map or given in separate sheet. Tradition of showing topography or land contours are common features, this is not limited upto contour, even significant streams or other water bodies, forest cover, built up areas or building as per scale and other features may also be depicted on points of interest. Presently, topographic maps are prepared by photogrammetric interpretation of aerial photography, LIDAR and remote sensing techniques, whereas older map were prepared by traditional surveys.

Left side Toposheet Header

Top left side of toposheet has district name, surveyed year, state name, region, latitude and longitude degree with further fraction. Minutes are expressed in 15 horizontal and 30 vertical then 35 in the same corner.

Right Side Toposheet Header

It gives the details of toposheet number as 43 p/12 means 12th sheet of series 43, also depicts magnetic variation of true north (geodetic north) is the direction along the earth's surface towards geographic north pole. Actually, magnetic variation is angle between magnetic north (the direction shows the north end of a compass needle) and true north.

Forest and Contours

Generally green colour denotes forest in toposheets based on geo-references in topographic map. Contour lines are drawn as brown lines with line number of four digits in irregular manner, it means representing earth's hill features. A contour line is combination of two line segments that connect but do not intersect, which represents elevation on a topographic map. Technically it is defined as a line of function of two variables or curve which the function has a constant value. In cartography, contour line joins points of equal elevation (height) above at given level like mean sea level.

Contours: Imaginary lines which joins all the points of equal altitude above mean sea level. They are also called as level lines.

Contour Interval: It is interval between two successive contour lines. It is also called as vertical interval, usually denoted as V.I. Often, contour interval is constant for map.

Cross-section: A side view of the earth cut vertically along a straight line. It is defined as a section or profile.

Hachures: Short straight lines drawn on the map along the way of maximum slope, connecting across the contours. They detail about slope of the earth.

Topographic Map: A map of a small area is drawn on a large scale explaining details of surface features both natural and is manmade. Contours represent relief in map, in survey of India for the topographical maps. The new series kept the numbering system and the layout plan of the left over India and Adjacent Countries Series.

The topographical maps are prepared on 1:10,00,000, 1:250,000, 1:1,25,000, 1:50,000 and 1: 25,000 scale serving a latitudinal and longitudinal coverage of 4° x 4°, 1° x 1°, 30' x 30', 15' x 15' and 5' x 7' 30", respectively. The system of number of each one is a topographical maps.

International Map Series of the World: Topographical Maps under this map series of the World are designed to make standard maps for the whole World on a scale of 1:10, 00,000 and 1:250,000.

Reading of Topographical Maps: The study of topographical maps is simple. Map reading includes a trick for reading being familiar with the legends, traditional sign and the colours shown on the sheets. The traditional sign and symbols depicts on the topographical sheets.

Survey of India

The SoI (Survey of India) is pioneer institute having responsibility of mapping and surveying, which was set in 1767 to help consolidate the territories of British India. It is a oldest engineering departments of government of India, its distinguished history includes handling of Mammonth Great Trigonometric Survey under William Lambton and George Everest.

The Great Trigonometric Survey was a project of surveying of India throughout 19th century, and was led by William Lambton and later by George Everest. Many surveyors were demarcated the British territories in India and measurement Himalaya height like Everest, K2 and Kanchanjunga. The Great Trigonometrical Survey was near Madras. In beginning, East India Company thought that this project would complete in five years but eventually it was the work of 60 years or more incurring financial onus on the company and brought under the crown after 1957.

National Map Policy

National Topographic Data Base (NTDB) of survey of India confirm on national standards to provide, maintain and access; making available in convenient form.

The policy further ultimate with promoting the use of geo-spatial knowledge and intelligence via partnerships and other mechanisms by all section of society with aim of knowledge based society.

Map Series

Generally a map series is published on several sheets, and a map series is a group of topographic maps usually having same scale and specification of topographic. Each sheet can appropriately identified by publisher which belongs to same series. Map series is prepared to cover an area in map due to its scale and spread over several sheets.

One individual sheets of a map series can be used quite independently, which is generally have complete map details of surrounding along legends. The toposheets are series of maps, index explains what the neighbors of current sheet are, and current sheet will be highlighted. Bird's eye views of administrative regions are covered in administrative index.

Number of map is technically difficult and impractical to print, only Switerzerland national map is capable to print in single sheet at a scale of 1:25000 that particular map approximately covers print area of 9x14 metres in sheet that is the problem behind the map series is issued and preserved loose leaflet form. In extreme cases map series may include thousands of sheets. The greatest map series ever created in 1:25000 topography map of Soviet Union, about 300000 sheets were completed in 1987.

There are Two Series of Maps

i) **OSM (Open Series Map):** It supports for developmental activities in the country. OSM contains different map sheet number and projected in WGS-84 datum, each of the OSM becomes unrestricted after clearance of Ministry of Defence-Survey of India ensure about avoiding civil and Military Vulnerable Areas (VAs) and Vulnerable Ponits (VPs) to print on OSM.

ii) **DSM (Defense Series Map):** These are the topographical maps on everest/WGS-84 datum and polyconic/UTM projection with various scales (Height, contour and full content without dilution of accuracy). This map is mainly used in defense and national security requirements. Both DSM and OSM are derived from NTDB. National Topographical Data Base (NTDB) is analogue and digital forms consisting of the data given below.

- National Spatial Reference Frame
- National Digital Elevation Model

- National Topographical Template
- Administrative Boundaries
- Toponomy (Place names)

Methods of Relief Representation

Basically physical or relief features of ground surface represents different elevation and depressions containing mountains, hills, plateau and plain as varies with location and landforms, these all features of map is known as a relief map. Over the years, so many attempts have already been taken to express the relief features of ground surface on maps, which include hachure, hill shading, unit layers, benchmarks, height and contours. Although all topographical maps, contours and spot height are mainly used to express relief of an areas.

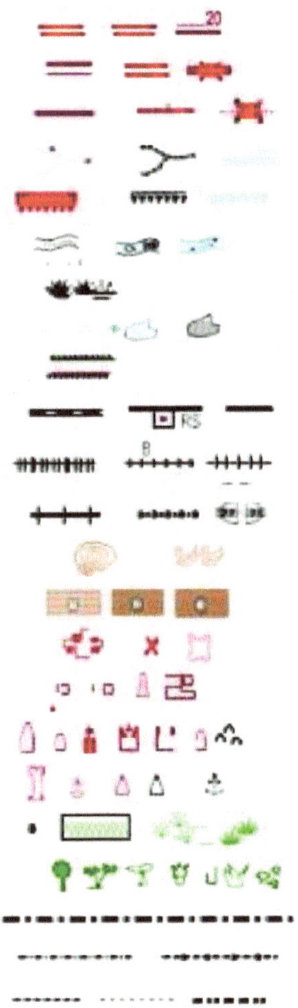

Roads, metalled: according to importance distance stone
Roads, unmetalled: according to importance bridge
Cart-track, Pack track and pass, Foot path with bridge
Streams: with track in bed undefined, cabal
Dams: masanory or rock-filled, earthwork, Weir
River dry with water channel, with islands and rocks, tidal river
Swamp reeds
Wells: Lined, undefined, Spring, Tanks: Perenniel dry
Embarkments: road or rail
Railway: broad gauge, double, single with station, under construction
Railway other gauges: double, single with distance stone, under construction
Light Railway or trainway, Telegraph line, Cutting with tunnel
Contour Cliffs
Sand features (1), Flate (2) sand hills (permanenet) (3) dunes (Shifting)
Towns or Villages: Inhibited, desserted Fort
Huts: permanent, temporary, Tower, Antiquets
Temple, Chhatri, Church, Mosque, Idgah, Tomb, Graves
Lighthouse, Lightship, Buoys: Lighted, Unlighted, Anchorage
Mine, Vine or Trellis, Grass, Scrub
Palms: palmyra, other, Plaintain, Conifer, Bamboo, other trees
Boundary, International
Boundary, state: Demarcated, undemarcated
Boundary, district: subdivision, tehsil or taluk forest

■ ⅄	Boudary, pillars: surveyed, unlocated, village injunction
△200 •200 •200	Hieghts, triangulated: station, point, appropriate
BM 63.3, DM 63.3,	Bench-mark: geodetic, tertiary, canal
PO, PS	Post office: Police station
DB, IB (Canal), RH (Forest)	Bunglows: dark or travelers, inspection, Rest-house
CH, CG	Circuit house, Camping ground
RF, PF	Forest: reserved, protected

Conventional Sign & Symbol

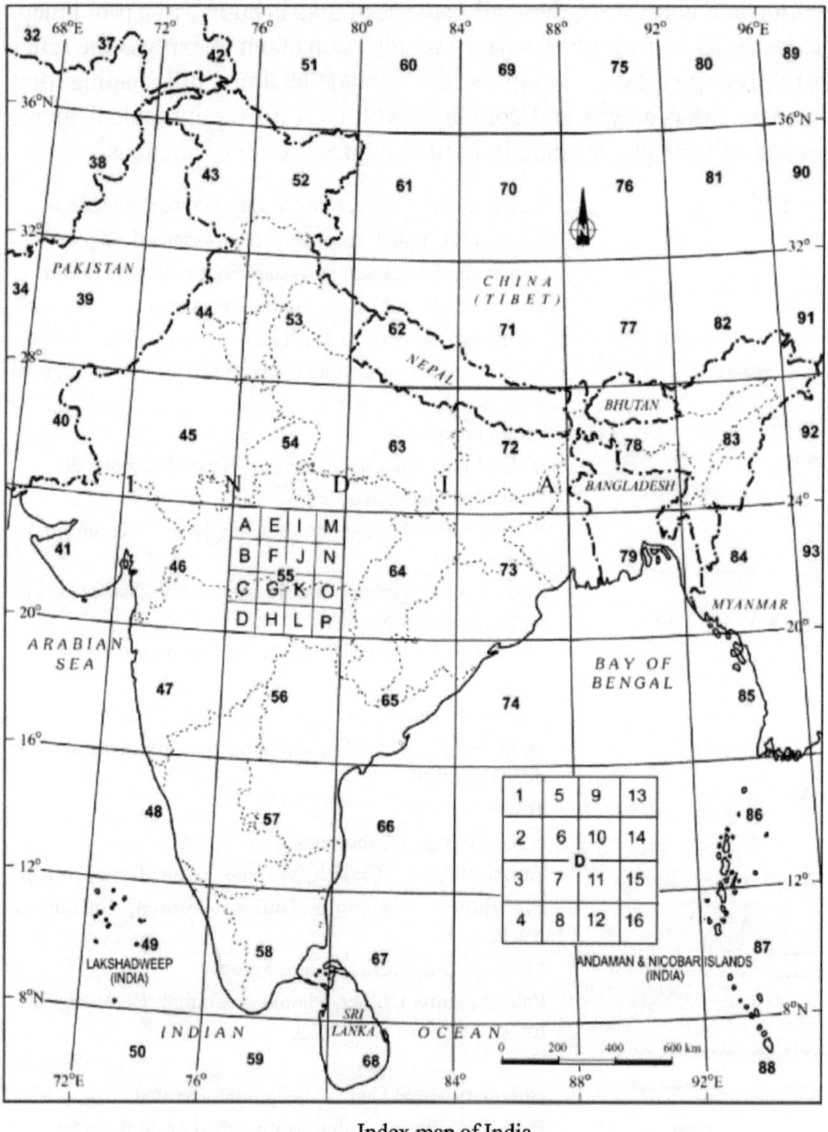

Index map of India

Contour of Map

Overall earth's surface is not uniformly similar and varies according their geo-morphological variations which contain mountains to hill to plateaus and pain relief feature of the earth depict elevational and drought depressions, when map shows these features are known a relief map.

Many procedures have been used to showing the relief features of surface on map in last a few years. These all methods involve hachures, hill shade, layer tints, spot height, contour and benchmarks. Nut moreover contours and spot height on topographical maps.

Contours

It is imagery lines joining spot with same elevation above mean sea level, (MSL). Any map shows the land form by contours is said to be contour map and the methods used for showing relief features by contour line is very useful and versatile along with providing useful insight into topography of particular area. In the beginning, surveys of ground and levelling methods were widely used in drawing contours on topography maps. Earlier method of surveying, leveling and mapping has been replaced by aerial photography. Now these photographs are in prime use of topography mapping contour may have different vertical interval (VI)viz, 20,50,100 meter above mean sea level, which is known as contour interval and always constant in the map. vertical interval between the two successive contour lines stays constant, while horizontal distance varies from place depending on slope nature, the horizontal distance also knows as horizontal equivalent with increasing slope gradient.

Basic Feature of Contour

- Always, contour line is drawn to show equal height places, which means any structure is constructed follows contour lines.
- The shape and lines represent the hight and slope/gradient of land surface on earth.
- Closely found contours express steep slopes, while wider line space represents gentle slope.
- Two as more contours do not show crossing each other mean contours are different elevation.

Contours Drawing and Cross Sections

The varying degree of slopes are presented in any topographical map, like a flat plain show gently slops, diffs, gorges are associated with steep slopes in same way, valley and mountain ranges are represented varying degree of slops (steep to slops). Space between contours is important because it indicates the slopes.

Types of Slope

The slopes are generally categorized into gentle, steep, concave, convex and irregular or undulating. Various types of contours exhibit different slopes which follows distinct pattern and slopes express a distinct spacing pattern.

Gentle Slope: The degree of slope is very less in a feature, the slope called gentle. The distantly placed contours represent gentle slope.

Steep Slope: When the degree of a feature is more and the contours are closely spaced is known as steep slope.

Concave Slope: A slope with slope gentle gradient different in the lower portion of a relief feature and steep in its upper portion is called the *concave slope.* Contours in this type slope are commonly spaced in the lower portions and are closely spaced in the upper portions.

Convex Slope: Other hands, the *convex slope* is little gentle in the upper portion and steep in the lower portion. As a result, the contours are often spaced in the upper portion and are closely spaced in the lower portions.

Types of Landform

Conical Hill: It creates almost uniform from the surrounding land as conical flask of laboratory. A conical hill with uniform slope and narrow top by concentric contours spaced with at regular intervals.

Plateau: Wide flat-tapped highland having comparatively steeper slope, rising above the adjoining plain is known as *plateau.* The contour lines representing a plateau are commonly close spaced at the margins with the innerest contour exhibits wide gap between its two sides.

Valley: It is a geomorphic feature presents between two hills/ridge which forms gully like structural output of erosion by water stream:

'V'-shaped Valley: It looks likes the letter V, V-shaped valley is mostly found in hilly areas. The inside of the V-shaped valley is displayed by the inside contour line having smaller gap between its two sides and the lowest value of the contour is commonly associated. The outward side, the contour value increases in uniform interval.

'U'-shaped Valley: This valley is formed in glacier region caused by high lateral erosion at higher altitudes. The broad bottom with steep sides forms valley in V-shape. The lowermost portion of the U-shaped valley is displayed by innerest contour line with a large gap between its two sides. The contour value rises with uniform intervals for all other contour lines outward.

Gorge: In high altitude areas, the gorge is formed and characterized by vertical erosion of river flow than lateral erosion. This may be deep and narrow river valleys having side steepness. Always, the gorge is exhibited with so close wider contour lines on map, inside contour exhibit small gap between both sides.

Spur: A tongue like structure of any hill or land projecting from highland into lower side. It seems like V-shaped contour but in reverse in manner. The arms of V tend towards higher ground and pointed position of V to lower sides.

Cliff: Cliff is perpendicular face of landform with very steep feature. It may be identified by contour runs very close to another and further merges in one.

Waterfall and Rapids: A sudden perpendicular descent of water from a considerable height in the river bed is broken as water fall. Cascading stream with succeeding or preceding is formed rapid downstream and upstream of any waterfall. Contour always represents a merge of waterfall into another when crossing a river stream and rapids by relatively distant contour lines.

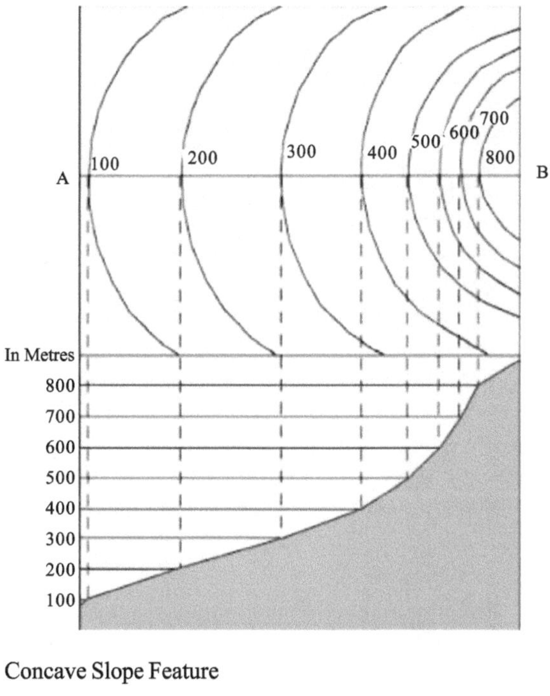

Concave Slope Feature

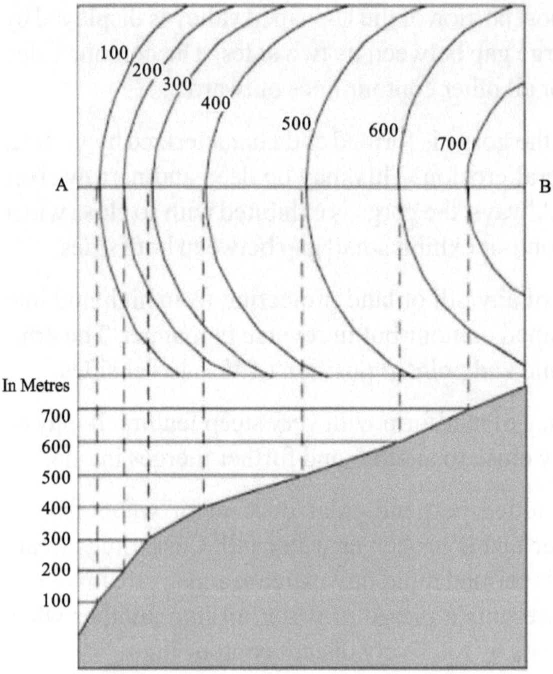

Convex Slope Feature

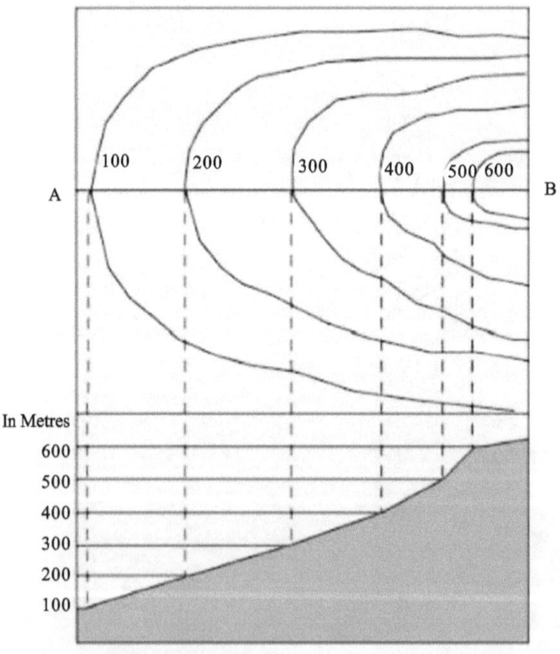

Gentle Slope Feature

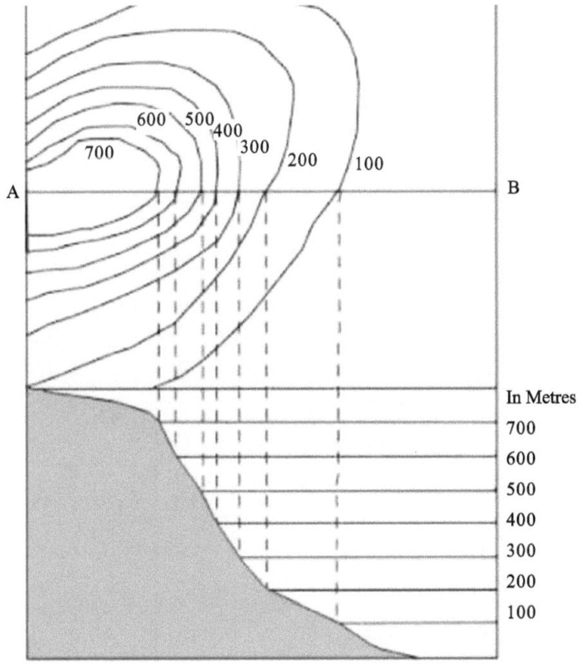

Steep Slope Feature

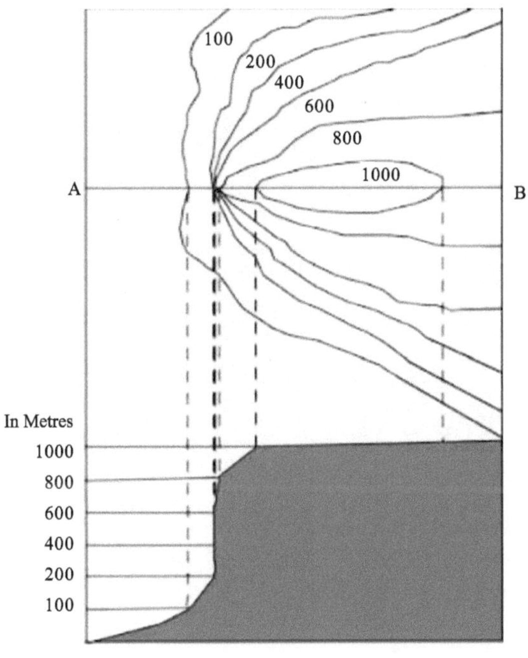

Cliff Faeture

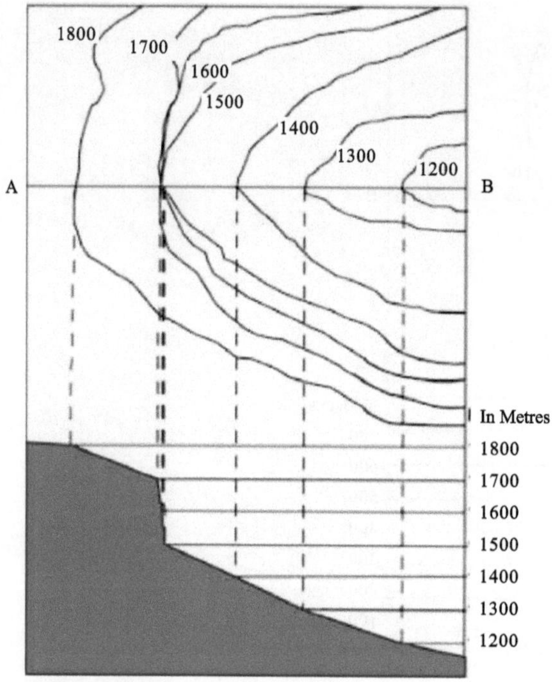

Water Fall Feature

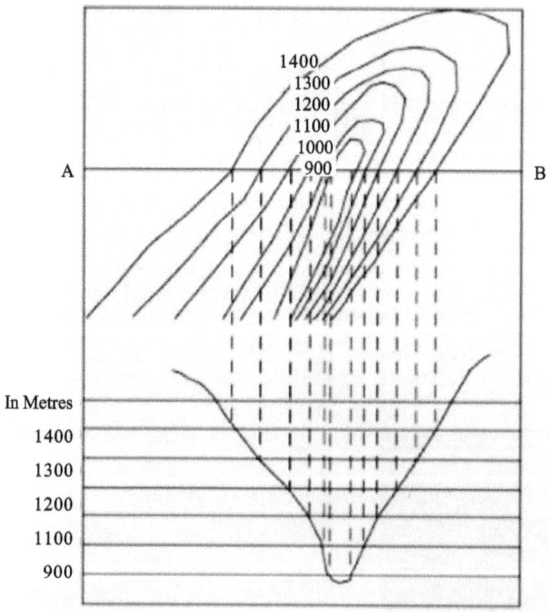

V-Shaped Valley

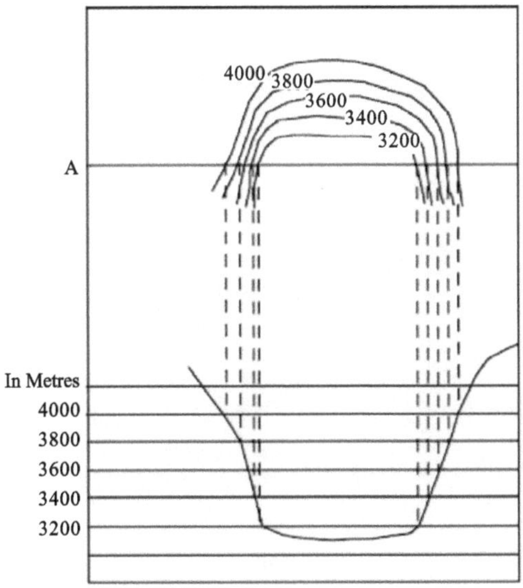

U-Shaped Valley

Steps for Drawing a Cross-section

The below given steps should be followed for drawing cross-sections of different relief features based on the contour.

1. Draw a straight line across the contours on the map and give them as AB.
2. Take a strip of white paper or graph and place its edge along the AB line.
3. Mark the position and value of every contour that cuts the line AB.
4. Choose a suitable vertical scale, like ½ cm =100 metres, to draw horizontal lines parallel to each other and equal to the length of AB. The number of such lines should be equal or more than the total contour lines.
5. Mark the feasible values connecting to the contour values along the vertical cross-section. The numbering may be started with the lowest value exhibited by the contours.
6. Now put the edge of the marked paper alongwith the horizontal line at the bottom line of the cross-section in such a way that AB of the paper corresponds to the AB of the map and mark the contour points.
7. Draw perpendiculars from AB line, intersecting contour lines, to the corresponding line at the cross-section base.
8. Smoothly join all the points marked on different lines at the cross section base.

Toposheet Study

4x4 = 4 latitude x 4 longitude

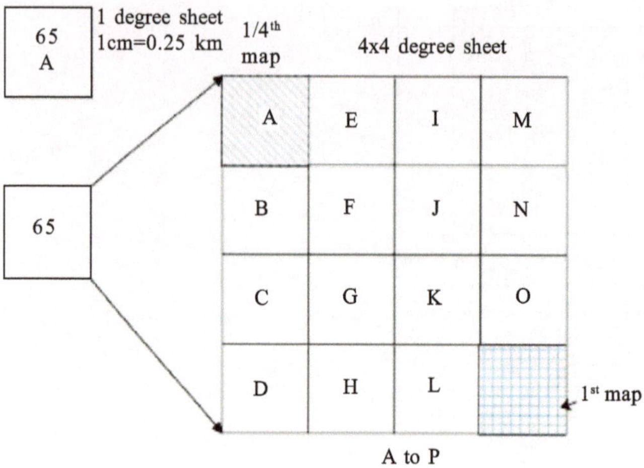

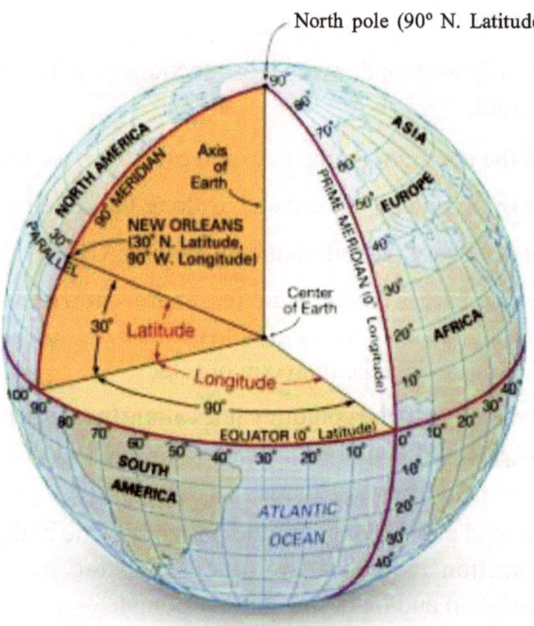

Toposheet Indexing

Actually toposheet represent ground surface detailing in measured scales index in division of degree box and toposheet which explains all information concerned to area with mentioned scale below in symbol box & map. There may be degree sheet comprising of due degree onwards. Four x Four degree Contour interval: Sheet divides into A to P of one degree. Each degree comprises of 4x4 bones.

0 to 1 Degree

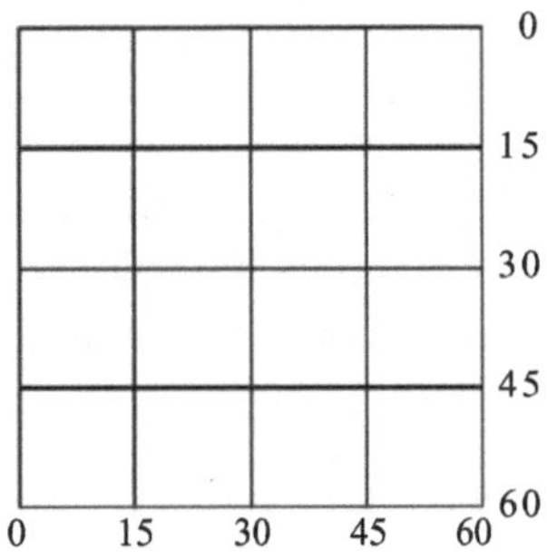

1 Degree sheet

Contour interval: Contour interval represent the level of interval of landform moving in same line of height alongwith their measured spots plus specific interval. Million sheet means 1:1000000 scale further which divided into finer scale for study of all scale map.

- 1:1000000 of 55 degree
- 1:250,000 of 55 G (G is degree sheet)
- 1:50,000 4 55 G/5
- 1:25,000 of 55 G/5/2

Contour interval

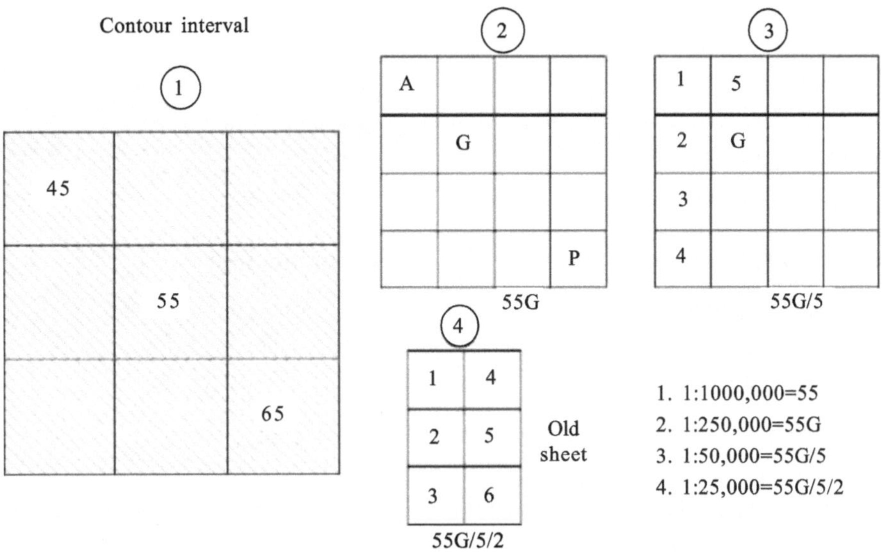

1. 1:1000,000=55
2. 1:250,000=55G
3. 1:50,000=55G/5
4. 1:25,000=55G/5/2

Elevation of area shows landforms denoting contour pattern, closed contour line that explains steep contour and conical slope contour, the place mentions spot height with black colour. Contour line is often drawn in brown colour with thick line value then it calculates. Down side of each map may be two box, one is administrative map another is toposheet index.

Identification of Cultural Features

The major cultural features include settlements, buildings, roads and railways displayed on topographical sheets through specific signs, symbols and colours. The location and pattern of distribution of various features guide to understand area for map reader.

Distribution of Settlements

Map may be shown through its site, location pattern, alignment and density. The nature and causes of different settlement style can be easily identified by comparing the differences in settlement with the contour map. Basically 4 types of rural settlements may be focused on the map:

a) Compact
b) Scattered
c) Linear and
d) Circular

Similarly, urban centres may also be differentiated as

a) Cross-road town
b) Nodal point
c) Market centre
d) Hill station
e) Coastal resort centre
f) Port
g) Manufacturing centre with suburban villages or satellite towns
h) Capital town and
i) Religious centre

Different factors determine the *site* of settlements like

a) Source of water
b) Provision of food
c) Nature of relief
d) Nature and character of occupation and
e) Defence

Settlement should be precisely assessed in relation to the contour and drainage map. Density of settlement is directly correlated with food supply. Most of the time, village settlements along a river valley, road, embankment, coastline, are pronounced *linear settlements*. On other hand, urban settlement has a cross-road town assumes a fan-shaped pattern, the houses being settled along the roadside and the crossing being at the centre of the town and the main market. In a nodal town, the roads radiate in all directions.

Transportation and Communication Pattern

Relief, population, size and resource development pattern of an area directly affect the sources of transport and communication with density. These are detailed through conventional signs and symbols. Sources of transport and communication provide useful information about the area shown on the map.

Interpretation of Topographic Maps

Map reading may be easier by knowing map language and directional sense in interpretation of toposheets. Always we must be taken north lines and map scale guides us effortlessly. We should know thoroughly legends or keys depicted in map to assess the features. All toposheets possess a table having conventional signs and symbols found in map, which are intentionally accepted so that anybody may read the map without knowing the languages.

A topographic sheet is usually depicted under the following points

a) Marginal Information
b) Relief and Drainage
c) Land Use
d) Sources of Transport and Communication and
e) Human Settlement

Marginal Information: Actually marginal information includes sheet, location grid references, degree, lower side with scale and districts cover etc.

Relief of the Area: Basically topography of the area is considered to identify the plains, plateaus, hills or mountains along with peaks, ridges, *spur* and the common direction of the slope studies to recognize under common topography. The features are below different heads:

- *Hill*: With concave, convex, steep or gentle slope and shape.
- *Plateau*: Whether it is broad , narrow, flat, undulating or dissected.
- *Plain:* Its types, i.e. alluvial, glacial, karst, coastal, marshy, etc.
- *Mountain*: Elevation, peak, passes, etc.

Drainage of the Area: The prominent rivers and its tributaries with extending of valleys formed by them, the types of drainage pattern, like dendritic, radial, ring, trellis, internal, etc.

Land Use: LULC involves various categories of natural vegetation and forest which shows dense or thin forest and also categorizes like Reserved, Protected, Classified/Unclassified.

- Agriculture, orchard, wasteland, industries etc.
- Facilities and Services like schools, colleges, hospitals, parks, airports, electric substations, etc.

***Transport and Communication*:** All transportation related information given in this section of information. The transportation involves the means as national or state highways, district roads, cart tracks, camel tracks, footpaths, railways, waterways, major communication lines, post offices, etc.

Settlement: It basically includes as rural settlements- exhibit types and patterns of rural settlements (compact, semi-compact, dispersed, linear, etc.).

Urban Settlements: Type of urban settlements and their functions like capital cities, administrative towns, religious towns, port towns, hill stations, etc.

***Occupation*:** The two information like land use and types of settlement details about occupation of the people belong to area, rural area means major group of people do agriculture; in tribal areas, lumbering and primitive agriculture. In rural areas, the main occupation of majority of the people is agriculture; in tribal regions, lumbering and primitive agriculture are prominent. Similarly in coastal areas, fishing is practiced. Cities and towns exhibit services and business appear to be the major occupations of the people.

Map Interpretation Methods

Generally map interpretation is the study of factors present in map and that detain the casual relationship among many features, for instance. Natural vegetation and farming land can be assessed easily following drainage and landform, whereas settlement and its distribution may be judged by transport network system are highly associated alongwith nature of topography. The following steps can be taken care in map expression:

- First get out the index number of the topographical sheet, location place of India. This gives detailed idea of general features of major and minor physiographic block of area. Note both scale and contour interval of map gives recent and common landform of area.

- Trace out the features using tracing sheets.
  a) Major landforms by contours and other graphical features
  b) Drainage and water features (Main river and its important tributaries),
  c) Land use (Forest, agricultural land, wastes, sanctuary, park, school, etc.) and
  d) Settlement and Transport pattern.
- Describe the distributional pattern of each of the features separately drawing attention to the most important aspect.
- Just superimpose the pairs of maps with note down the relationship, if any, between the two patterns.
- Aerial photographs and satellite imageries of the same area and of the same scale can also be compared with the topographical map to update the information.

Topography and cartography: Improving digital elevation models; it improves DEM (Digital Elevation Model).

Agriculture: It monitors the biomass of land vegetation.

Forest: Monitoring the health of crops, mapping soil moisture.

Botany: forecasting of crop yields.

Hydrology: Quantify water resources from snow, rainfall and underground aquifers.

Disaster warning and assessment: Help in monitoring of floods and landslides, monitoring volcanic activity, assessing damage zones from natural disasters.

Planning applications: It maps ecological zones, monitoring deforestation, monitoring urban land use.

Oil and mineral exploration: Location of natural oil seeps and slicks, mapping geological structures, monitoring oil field subsidence.

Military: Development of a precise maps for planning, monitoring military infrastructure, monitoring ship and troop movements

Urban: Determining the status of a growing crop

Climate: It affects climate change on glaciers, and Arctic and Antarctic regions

Sea: Extent of flood monitoring

Rock: Recognizing rock types

Space program: Backbone of the space program

Seismology: As per permissible level

7

Drone Technology

Aerial photography is objective of getting panoramic view of earth surface to analyze the features of earth and their interrelation at particular time period which may be changed in further events. In this concerned, the observation may play a vital role in achieving the goals of photography. Undoubtedly it is widely used in social function and so on, but still awaited for scientific or research use. Drone can measure the geometry of ground surface at lower altitude with more accuracy in the form of visual feature in natural colour. flight height of drone mainly limits the large area coverage due to lower flying and drone can work perfectly at low altitude planning with good quality feature/photography.

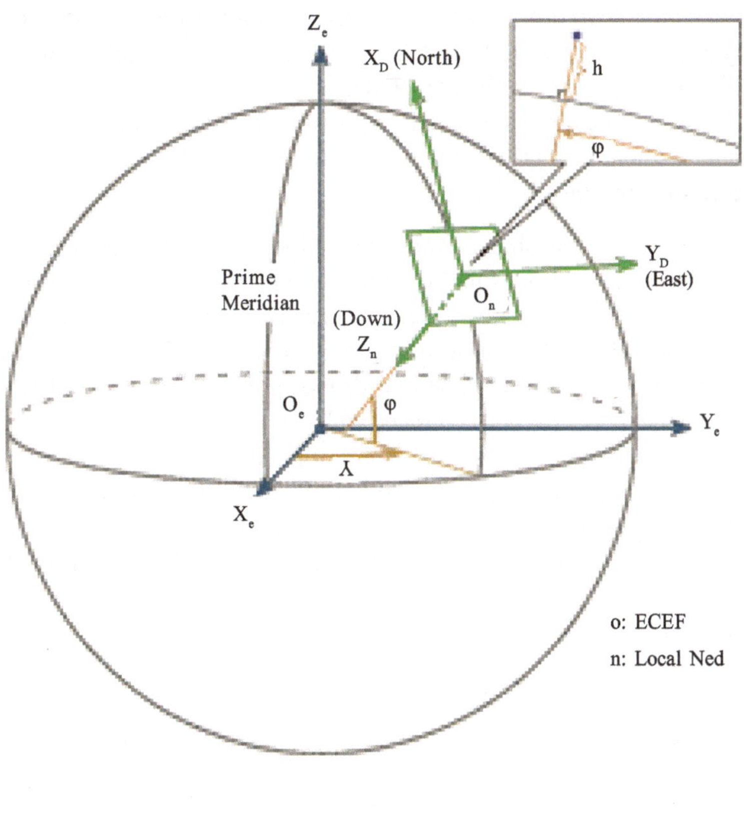

History of UAVs

Fig. 1: Aerial view of village landscape by drone

The concept of drone was initiated not longer than 1849, when Venice was attacked by Austria with an unmanned balloons loaded with explosives. The Venice were besieging by Austrian force at the time and launched nearly 200 of incendiary balloons over the Venice, in which each balloon could have the capacity to carry 10 to 14 kg of bombs. Once they dropped bombs and created havoc on the city. But fortunate things for Ventians were only one bomb found the target remainings were blown away with sudden change in wind direction. It was a effort in innovation of military technology. Although the balloons were used for the purpose of current meet and not really defined the drones but opened new pathway for drone concept. If you find the basic concept of drone is quiet interesting which was being considered by military technologies for more than 170 years ago, it is type of one vision that boosted up the technology development in further coming decades and even centuries. Recent drone has one common feature is quadcopter configuration. Beginning of this technologies appeared in 1907, when two brother viz., Jac Ques and Louis Bregnet with help of French Physiologist Charles Richet developed on early development with their gyroplane, a fare runner of helicopter, and design of copter was visionized. Even this progressed to achieve the first ascent of vertical flying aircraft with one pilot, reached a height of 60 m. it was not a free flight because four men were required to the structure.

Last one decades, so great explosion in drone innovation and commercial interest took place. But before this, drones had limited use with military operation or others like hobbyist. From 2010 onwards a new uses were exhibited for drones like delivery vehicles. By middle of decade, a massive growth in demand, for permission of drones with 1000 commercial drones got the permits in 2015, which was tripled in next one year and continued with exponentially. In commercial photography and videography, the drones are equipped with high resolution cameras. This is a combination of radio-controlled (RC) aircraft and smart phone technology. High Degree of cell phone used among the people reduced prices of microcontrollers, and camera sensors, which are so feasible for use in fixed wing hobbyist is aircraft. Further advancement in drones has been visualized and allowed a drone with four or more rotors to be controlled by setting the adjustment of individual rotors.

Drone Evolution

Unmanned Aerial Vehicles (UAVs): Generally UAV is known as drone, is an aircraft without pilot, crew or passengers on board. Monitoring of earth surface with small areas is expanded to capture interested area by controlling from ground conveniently.

Types of UAVs

1. **Single rotor:** Similar to helicopter with a large rotor along with a smaller one in height and it is more efficient to multi rotor.
2. **Bicopters:** It has 2 motor and propellers helps in flying comfortable and are cheaper with provides a longer endurance but flight control is difficult and complicated and present result are in experimental mode.
3. **Tricoptors:** It is cheaper alternative to a quadrotor adding mechanical complexity, provide better option than quadrotor or hexa rotor in consideration of endurance. The stability is reduced due to tricoptors and jittery flight is commonly associated with tricoptors.
4. **Quadcopter:** The four-wing drone is very commonly used in society due to cheaper and easy in manufacturing, good camera control by reducing endurance.
5. **Hexacoptors:** Being six wing of rotor it offers a more stable flight with backup inner motor failure in arms/wings.
6. **Octacoptor:** It provides very good flight control and impenetrable to turbulent winds and even rains. it may be good choice for high altitude aerial photography but cost is very expensive.
7. **Fixed wing**: It seems to be conventional airplanes having wing structure to lift the body in air and characterized by high speed and endurance with no hovering capacity and low mobility.
8. **Flying wing:** Flying wing type drone is tailless aircraft without a definite fuselage, faster and efficient aerodynamics than conventional fixed wings.
9. **Hybrid VTOLs:** It is combined form of multirotor and fixed wings with interchangeable configurations can take off and land vertically and hover with multirotor, good endurance in fixed wing mode.

Applications of UAVs

Unmanned aerial vehicles as drone mainly offer easier observation of surface from aerial distance in primary and simple consideration. Real time photography is taken by flying drone can compare with easier photograph to assess change or development of given task. Drone can be used in family function to scientific research easily with wide area data and coverage. Presently every field become a digital, in which these data and feature are captured and stored in soft form. In such case all data can be stored digitally without much space capturing. Application of drone itself opens the window of wider area having its capacity to easier use and hover with sensor.

Following Fields are Very Important in Applying Drone for Smooth Works

1. **Traffic monitoring:** Now-a-day every small to big city or urban area facing problem of traffic jam, which unnecessarily enhance sound as well as air pollution through emission gases from motor vehicles and exposure of human being loner time with this situation, sometimes VIP movement can cause thronging people in same route or market area, mob clearance can be managed by shifting traffic in nearby route though drone monitoring.
2. **Disaster management:** Unfortunately, disaster area accrues suddenly and rampages assets, properties and people life, just after disaster no one can observe the real situation immediately in such condition, drone plays a role to view the pathetic situation offers to mange by plans. Flood situation may be a serious if it stays longer, it can be cleared the blockage of water movement through drone monitoring. During natural calamity, small scale management may be managed by monitoring the existing situation.
3. **Wildlife monitoring:** Obviously animals are moveable creature of earth and monitoring by humans is a difficult and confusing because real time intervening with count is a problematic issue can instantly be observed by available resources in around their habitat. Anti-poaching, Anti-trafficking, geo-mapping, Tracking feet step.
4. **Defense system:** Manual collection of information is difficult task in defense monitoring, exact number and location even may not be assessed during war or peace period activities. Another risk is fatal for man with unmanned vehicle, avoids this risk. Surface morphology is a issue in moment of troops can be monitored by drone instantly.
5. **Infrastructure inspection:** General erection of building is easier than further regular monitoring for either supervision or maintenance of infrastructures. Hence drone can inspect building, valuable assets, parking and so on being stable in a place by single man repair estimates and damage control can also be an idea in this direction.
6. **Agriculture:** Agriculture is actually vast area possess wide scope of regular monitoring the natural and cultural change over the season or cropping season, land form planning may be performed under drone mapping using

aerial photography, which may be a part of watershed planning in execution of drain line delineation and construction of conservation structures, crop monitoring, even insect-pest and disease occurrence, moisture stress-based drying of crop. Crop damage by animals; water logged condition, climatic effect on crop and loss percentage with land measurement.

Guidelines and Regulations

Since drone aviates in open sky which can be a route or path of regular mounting of defense and government organization, it is obviously imposed guidance to be followed by users without violation rules set by government organization. Therefore, some regulation is set to strictly obey by users. The following norms were presently incorporated into the DGCA (Directorate general of civil aviation), RPA (Remote piloted aircraft) directory:

- It includes the norm NPNT (No Permission, No Takeoff) into autopilot firmware.
- Drone is to be registered when drone weight is greater than 250 gms. due to heavy size can be used in different purpose.
- Drone larger than the nano class requires mandatory flying license, otherwise they can not pose the information in legal platform.
- Unmanned aerial vehicles are classified according to their weight.
    1. Nano (less than 250g)
    2. Micro (250 to 2.00 kg)
    3. Small (2.00 to 25 kg)
    4. Medium (25 to 150 kg)
    5. Large (More than 150 kg)

Obstacle and Path Planning

By using artificial potential field algorithm, the depth camera based static and dynamic obstacle is avoided. Depth camera with range of 70m and 60 degrees of FOV (field of view) is sufficient to avoid close obstacle. Combination of Dijkstra and bendy ruler algorithms is used in dynamic obstacle avoidance base on radar.

Global navigation satellite system (GNSS): Autonomous takeoff pay points navigation and landing in GNSS denied regions. It is almost 96% accuracy in waypoint navigation cost makes it comfortable and affordable the frame rate up to 20 frames per second at a resolution of 640 ×480 for the effective feature with maintaining speed limit of 5 meter per second. Maximum flying altitude is 70 m above ground level.

Multispectral Sensors (MS)

Modified MS: Modified sensors are designed by placing a filter on a standard visual sensor, which collect tree bands of light at once through the same lens. For capturing different combinations of spectral bands, various filters are used in MS. R-G-NIR filter sacrifices blue for near infrared energy under the view observation.

Multiband MS: A multiband multispectral sensor simultaneously collects several individual bands instead of a single combination of three bands.

UAV Sensor: Basically object from ground surface are sensed by camera mounted on drone that decides how much clarity of feature will be obtained completely based on the sensors' ability and decides quality photography. There are so many sensors; some of them are given below.

- Consumer grade camera
- Multi spectral camera
- IR Sensor
- Thermal camera
- LIDAR sensor
- Hyperspectral sensors
- Temperature and pressure sensors
- Ambient temperature
- Barometric pressure sensors
- Panasonic cameras
- Video camera
- Oblique camera
- UAV - based sensor
    - Sony nex 5n RGB camera
    - Canon power short IR camera
    - MCAG multispectral camera
    - Spectrometer (UAVSTS)

Mission Planning

Most of the commercial UAVs available with flight planning software like AIPRDFLIGHT, Pix 4 Capture, Map made easy, Aerial imaging, Geoplanid, Emotion etc. these software providers the flexibility to modify the flight parameters and enables both topographical map and imagery view, so that the target area can be easily delineated.

Mission planning or field preparation: Field planning is the limit step and important for suitable data acquisition over the desired study, which includes identifying/ defining the area/ terrain in the form of polygon layer with number of height required covering the desired area. Single flight depend on a life of battery where multiple height also depend a battery plus marking the waypoint. Meanwhile, working in flying flight it needs identification and specification of take off and distance of ground sampling, overlapping images whether that side and lateral overlap, flight height, direction and speed, number of flight lines. Apart from these parameters estimating flight duration, camera condition and setting GCPS (Ground Control Points) are the main guiding tools in achieving goal of study under drone flying.

8

Image Processing

The information of image is perfectly accepted by eyes when the image will be in convenient form. Always pictures accurately detail about information related to their position, sizes and inter-related with each other is objects. Actually images portray positional information which can be recognized as objects. Human eyes are exact example for differentiating that information from images to innate visual and mental ability.

Digital and Analog Images

In real sense we can confirm that 2-dimensional representation of any objects with either in digital or analog form. From space, satellite based image extraction of earth surface is roughly called remote sensing image, may be analog or digital as it seems from space. Aerial photographs are specific characterized red by electronic sensors because of digital images. The digital image is arranged in a a two-dimensional array of pixels. Every pixel is characterized by its intensity value through a digital number and address of location or represented by row and column numbers.

Pixels

A pixel is defined as comprised of two dimensional array of individual picture elements which are arranged in rows and column, and every pixel contains a particular area of earth's surface. Pixel has two special features *viz.*, intensity value and a location address in 2-D image. Basically the intensity value assesses physical quantity like solar radiance at given wavelength band that reflects from ground, backscattered radar intensity or emitted infrared radiation, which is a normal value of average for whole ground covered area of the pixel.

For recording and digitalization, the digital number stores the intensity of a pixel. Because of defined storage capacity, the digital number can store with that defined number of bits called a binary digits. The radiometric resolution of the image is determined by bit numbers. For instance, 8 bit digital number has 0 to 255 range details measuring 2^8-1, whereas 11-bits digital number has 0 to 2047 ranges. The identified intensity value requires to scale and quantity fitting within the value ranges. Actual intensity value can be called from digital number of pixel in a radiometrically calibrated images.

Multilayer Image

Many types of measurement can be performed by one single pixel covering ground surface with a single pixel. Each type of measurement creates a image carrying specific information of the areas. Through arrangement by stacking these images from the same area together, multilayer image is formed. In multilayer image, every component image is layer. These multilayer images may also be created by comprising images obtained from various sensors and other attributing data.

Multispectral Images

Data having different bands is utilized for multispectral images for displaying visual image; single band can display one band at a time in a grey scale image or three band combinations as colour composite image. The knowledge of the spectral reflectance signature of the object is required for interpreting these composite images with spectral information content of image. Multispectral image extracted from SPOT multispectral scene at 20 m ground resolution. The same area coverage is shown variation. The vegetation area appears bright in NIR band because of high reflectance of leaves in wavelength region of NIR. Many shades of grey can be identified for greenery areas differing vegetation types, water mass looks darker in NIR band.

Superspectral Images

Recent advances turned the images quantity high with help of satellite sensors, which are well equipped or designed to capture images at several wavelength bands. Several satellites are composed of 36 spectral bands in wavelength regions of visible, NIR, short wave infrared and thermal IR. Any band contains narrower bandwidths, always make enable finer spectral features of targets going to capture by sensor. The super spectral expresses such sensors have finer spectral.

Hyperspectral Image

This spectral image comprises of hundred or more continuous spectral bands creating a 3-dimension images form cube. The targeted pixel has characteristic spectrum is built in a hyperspectral image for exact identification and characterization of this image has great potential of applications in thus fields as precision agriculture and different fields.

Image Resolution

Fundamentally the quality of image depends on remote sensing data which consists of their spectral, radiometric, spatial and temporal resolutions.

1. Spatial Resolution

Imgeries-KOMPSAT-3A (Korea Multi-Purpose Satellite-3A)of Kosarteda dam, Bastar

Images Resolutions

The quality of remote sensing data consists of its spectral, radiometric, spatial and temporal resolutions.

i) **Spatial Resolution:** The pixel size limits the resolution in a digital image, and smallest object with resolvable can not be smaller as compared to the pixel size. Internal resolution of any system does imaging is decided primarily via IFOV (International Field of View) of sensor which shows a measurement of the surface area seen by a detector element in a real time. However, other factors blur the image such as imperfect focusing, atmospheric scattering and goal of motion. Sampling distance decides pixel size.

A small resolution size always is referred to a high resolution images with expressing fine details of objects, and in other hand, a low resolution image has large size in which surely visualizes coarse features in image. Any small pixel size does not show necessarily high resolution. Three images are quoted for example, first one is a SPOT image of 10 m pixel size, is derived by merging a SPOT panchromatic image of 10 m resolution with a SPOT multispectral image of 20 m resolution. Colour panchromatic image using colour derived is merged procedure from the multispectral image. In this way, effective resolution of a 10 m. The image is further processed to degrade. Other two images are to be blurred forms of image with larger resolution size, although still digitalized at same size of 10 m, even they have the same pixel size as the first image, but not the same resolution.

ii) **Radiometric resolution:** Radiometric resolution governs sensing system which details the minute change in intensity level. The internal radiometric resolution of sensing system depends on signal to noise ratio of the detector. Number of discrete quantization levels limits the radiometric resolution in the digital image used to digitize the continuous intensity value. The SPOT panchromatic image quantizes at 8 bits (256 levels) per pixels. Succeeding images exhibit the effect of lowering radiometric resolution by using lesser quantization levels.

iii) **Spectral resolution:** Wavelength width with different frequency bands stored normally is related to the frequency bands, involving several in infra-red spectrum, special resolution of 0.07 to 2.10 um. On earth observing-1, Hyperion sensor resolves 220 bands from 0.4 to 2.5 um having spectral resolution of 0.10 to 0.10 um/band.

iv) **Temporal resolution:** Flyover frequency of an plane or satellite, is only related in time based studies or required average or mosaic image as monitoring degrading forest. It was the first use by skilled community when repeated coverage showed the changes of infrastructure, development unit or modification of equipment. Repeat collection is subjected under cloud cover over certain area for accuracy in same location.

Visual Interpretation

Discussion and information extraction is done by recognizing object, observation of targeted object and their surrounding involves variation that variation is required for interpretation on the basis of visual elements like tone, shape, pattern, texture, shadow and their association with object in remote sensing-based target visual element allows us to interpret and analysis; interpretation of these elements is described as:

1. **Tone:** It represents relative brightness of things in an image for comparison. Often, tone is main basic elements for distinguishing among targets and their features. The variation of tone also helps in distinguishing the element of shape, texture and pattern of object, color pattern itself describes variation which makes interpretation easier.
2. **Shape:** It explains general form, structure and their relative proportion of appearance as sometimes outline of individual object. Shape always poses distract key for interpretation of any object under particular study. Urban and agriculture feature are typically represented by straight edge shape, whereas natural images are commonly more irregular shape showing undisturbed shape.
3. **Size:** Size of any object is directly related to scale, is main factor to determine the size of target in comparison to other objects in same image, about size to the interpretation of object, as approximation of object size can quickly interpret to proper result. Orderly repeating similar tones and textures will have distinction and recognizable pattern.
4. **Shadow:** Shadow of any image provides an idea of profile and relative height of a target makes identification smoothly. The shadow may also eliminate interpretation in their space of effect, since object within shadow are hardly demonstrable from arounds.
5. **Association:** It focuses a related between other recognizable objects in approximating to the target of interest. Always identification associates with features available in around target objects that one expects to provide information in identification.

Table. Aerial and satellite imagery of various scale for appropriate grassland management

Image scale	Usage
1:100 to 1:500	Species identification, including grasseses and seedlings, identification and measurement of erosion features, forage production estimates, rodent activities in the surface soil, assessment of amount of other surface features such as litter, and wildlife habitat assessment
1:600 to 1:2000	Species measurement, erosion estimates over larger land areas, condition and trend assessment, production and utilization estimates, and wild life habitat assessment
1:5000 to 1:10000	Detailed vegetation mapping, ccondition and trend assessment, production and utilization estimates, and wild life habitat assessment.
1:15000 to 1:30000	Vegetation mapping at the habitat-type or ecological site level, allotment management planning, and planning for multiple use, including wildlife habitat assessment.
1:30000 to 1:80000	Planning for range management, vegetation and soil unitmapping on a grassland or allotment basis, and multiple-use planning, including wildlife habitat mapping.
1:100000 to 1:250000	Synoptic views for planning grassland use and mapping large vegetation zones covering large areas such as entire mountain grassland.

(*Source:* Trueller, 1996)

Image Correction

Radiometric correction (Radiance value)

Gives a scale to the pixel values, means the monochromatic scale of 0 to 255 will be changed to actual radiance values.

Atmospheric Correction (Rescaling)

It ends atmospheric barrier by rescaling each frequency band so that its minimum value (usually realized in water bodies) corresponds to a pixel value of 0. The digitizing of data also creates possible to improve the data by changing gray-scale values.

Concept of Signature

Signature is a unique identity of each particular wavelength and also identified by their unique features as find in radiation due to length and frequency. Various types of specific signature separate spectrum with unique colour ID becoming part of remote Sensing by showing different reflectance. These all specificity creates interest on sensible data, the variation 'includes shape, size, texture, Wavelength, time etc. in which whole concept of signature variations detail as Spatial, temporal and spectral variation. Spatial variation includes shape, Size and texture based information on ground surface shows variation on mentioned specificity and distance between two or more objects are differentiated on their emission. This Signature can easily be identified. Wavelength based variation is Spectral, either high, medium or low intensity and their emission or absorption by particular object at particular time scale. Another variation is studied under time interval expresses time frame variation with time slots changes over the period of time.

NDVI is calculated from the visible and near-infrared light reflected by vegetation. Healthy greenery absorbs most of the visible light that hits it, and reflects a large portion of the near-infrared light. Unhealthy or sparse vegetation (right) reflects more visible light and less near-infrared light. The representatived actual value may vary with real when it is closely observed. Nearly all satellites, vegetation Indices employ this difference formula to quantify the density of plant growth on the Earth-near-infrared radiation minus visible radiation divided by near-infrared radiation plus visible radiation. The outcome of this formula is known as NDVI (Normalized Difference Vegetation Index).

NDVI = (NIR-VIS)/ (NIR+VIS)

NDVI = - 1 to+1, calculations of NDVI for a counted pixel always represents a number that consider from minus one (-1) to plus one (+1); however, no greenery gives a value close to zero. A zero expresses no vegetation and +1 (0.8-0.9 μm) indicates the highest density of greenery.

Spectral Behavior

Spectral behavior changes with change in electromagnetic radiation (EMR) as incidents on earth surface and according to surface features reflection is achieved due to component of the target. Since each component exhibits typical spectral signature as influenced by several parameters of own inbuilt properties. Hence, it is assumed to understand the nature of EMR interaction with every component. Nature of spectral signature along with earth surface is discussed as:

- Soil: Flux incident on soil surface is started the process of reflection, absorption and transmission, the reflection properties of the soils is almost similar with positive relationship between reflection and wavelength present in spectral behavior. The factors influence the spectral signature are mineral composition, moisture, organic matter, soil texture, structure different size and shape of aggregate that also affect the reflectance in the images.
- Mineral composition: This affects the reflectance spectral, reflectance of soil poses increasing from the visible to shortwave infrared (IR) absorbing band around 1.4μm and 1.9μm reposed to the level of soil moisture.

- Effect of texture, structure and moisture: Relationship among these three can be best describer to rough texture of soil, and more soil moisture results a fairly low diffuse reflectance, on the reverse, sandy soil has a weak structure gives to smooth surface, where low soil moisture condition shows fairly high and always estimate reflectance properties. The soil moisture remarkably decreases the surface reflectance of soil unless the soil is saturated under visible wavelength, unlikely near and middle IR wavelength is negatively related to the soil moisture. Any change in soil moisture results fast reduction of reflectance in water and hydroxyl absorbs wavelength. It is very noticeable in soil day time because of high bound water and absorption of hydroxyl properties.
    - Organic matter is not directly influence the spectral influence as belongs to soil moisture and water holding capacity. OM (Organic Matter) exhibits dark colour that properties matter but further it is increased beyond this level hardly affects.
    - Iron oxide has the properties of rusty red color which selectively reflect especially red light, due to the soil property the reflectance shows variation in distinct feature.
    - Soil aggregate includes shape and size which directly affects to reflectance properties. The larger size of aggregate decreases the reflection of incident solar energy.

Signature of Vegetation

Classification of vegetation from remote sensing images include chemical and physical properties collected for the vegetation like texture, roughness and local slope. Factors influence the vegetation quality on satellite and remote sensing image, which includes brightness, greenery and moisture, the brightness is analyzed as weighted sum of all bands and defines in the way of major variation in reflection of soil. Greenness shows orthogonal to brightness and contrast in between near infrared and visible bands, which related to quantity of green vegetation in image. Reflectance is more in moist vegetation than dry vegetation, leaf characters that influence optical properties of leaf, are basically depend on internal or external structure, age, moisture stress and overall health of leaf. The important point is to be noted that optical properties and their reflectance of leaf are same over the species. But the peculiarity of leaf spectral signature feature for three main optical spectral domains may be related leaf pigments, cell structure and water content.

Leaves, stems, flowers and stalks of a plant are responded to electromagnetic wavelengths differently, the wavelengths length is important in the total of reflection that prevails. Tree leaves and canopies reflect higher in the shorter wavelengths, whereas the longer wavelengths reflect more with trunk and branches. The density of the tree canopy will affect the back scattering of the wavelengths.

The bands produce different status of refrectance rates within electromagnetic spectrum. The visible bands (400-700 nm) exhibit various reflectance, in which lower reflectance shows more light is observed by pigments of leaves comparatively more reflectance. The leaf pigment absorbs mainly blue (450 nm) and red (670 nm) wavelength bands.

Remote sensing images are influenced by these factors which are considered as quality, scale, season, film type as well as background. Apart from these factors, some factors directly affects. Vegetation classes are depend on time of day, sun angle, atmospheric barrier, clouds, errors in processing of transparencies/ prints alongwith interpretating the images. Smoothness and coarseness of images (Photographic texture), colour contrast, relative sizes of crown images in photo scale and topographic location supports to determine the vegetation. Various types of images display different characteristics of greenery. Sometimes images of satellite may be hybrid with topographic data (ancillary data) for interpretation properly.

Spectral Reflectance and Signature of Water

In visible range of wavelengths, little light is taken, generally below 5% is reflected and remaining is transmitted. The blue-green wavelength of the spectrum has a high transmittance rate. The most specific characteristic of water in reference to spectral reflectance, is the energy absorption at the near-infrared wavelengths. Generally water takes Infrared high. By leaving small quantity radiation either to be reflected or transmitted resulting in string contrast in water and land boundaries. The factors, responses the differences in reflectance of a water body are in depth, suspended material alongwith surface material of the water.

Water absorbs energy at various wavelengths, which will interact in a simple form with the water and available matter. The function of the water and the inert matters whatever radiation is not reflected by waterbody but contribution in refraction is due to bottom (organic and/or inorganic material) governs reflectance properties. In shallow water, therefore, in such stream, always the bottom materials confirm the water body's reflectance properties and colour in FCC. The water body contains a large amount of suspended sediment visible reflectance will result. Turbulent water will also affect the amount of energy absorbed and transmitted. The chlorophyll presents in plants which also affect the amount of water reflectance. An increase in chlorophyll decreases blue wavelengths with increase in green wavelengths. Water bodies have very high amount of greenery via similar reflectance properties, at least in part, those of vegetation with increased green, decreased blue and decreased red reflectance. Thermal variations also affect the reflectance of water whole day.

The smooth surface refrects light giving very high or very low reflectance, depends on the location of the sensor. On other hands, in case of rough surface it will be increased scattering at the surface, resulting increase trend of the reflectance.

Image and Photograph

Large accounts for pictorial data in the form of pixels in definite dimension is image whereas photograph depends on photography film (0.3 to 0.9) with reaction of time and camera.

Colour and Channel

Human eye is perfect colour identifier but in case of Satellite is techno Guilt machineries works according programmed process and limits if condition varies but human eyes sudden change with changing objects. Channel comprised of narrow wavelength range generally described as band and their composition. Change appearance simultaneously needs perfect analysis using proper software otherwise never draw the preferably outcomes. Mostly primary colour is widely used to slow useful information from imageries which are BGR (Blue, Green and Red) on general term and can be assigned anywhere in world.

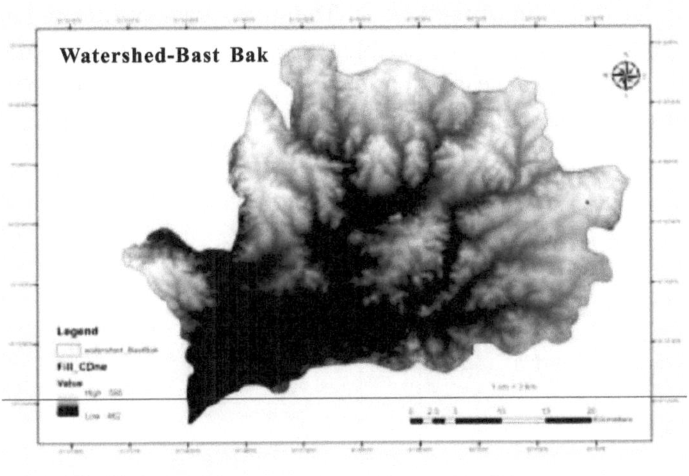

Fig. Black and White and colour images

Spectral Reflectance Signature

The commonly occurrence of transmittance, absorption or reflectance when solar radiation hits the surface of target. Various materials reflect and absorb at different wavelengths. Some radiation reflects far away due to depending on ground roughness and also the angle of the sun directs rays relative to ground inclination; and some part is being directed back on line with the observing sensor. The reflectance spectrum of a material is a part of the fraction of radiation reflected as a function of the incident wavelength and serves as a unique signature for the material. Any material may be identified from its signature of spectral reflectance having sensing system contains sufficient spectral resolution to differentiate the spectrum from other materials, and this condition previlages the platform for multispectral remote sensing.

The clean water exhibits low reflectance whereas maximum is experienced at the blue end of the spectrum and decreases with increasing wavelength. Due to this process, the clean water looks dark-bluish. Turbid water presents sediment suspension that increases the reflectance in the red end of the spectrum, and its brownish appearance with presence of sediment suspension. Commonly bare soil reflects according its composition and reflectance enhances monotonically with increasing wavelength which is looked yellowish-red to our eyes. Greenery has a special spectral signature which enables for readily distinguishing from other types of land cover in an optical/near-infrared image. The blue and red regions have low reflectance in the spectrum, due to absorption by chlorophyll. It has a peak at the green region which gives rise to the green colour. In near infrared (NIR) region, the reflectance is much higher than that in the visible band due to the cellular make up of the leaves. Therefore, vegetation can be distinguished by the high NIR but often low visible reflectance. This characteristic has been used in early reconnaissance missions during war times for camouflage detection. The shape of the reflectance spectrum can be used for identification of vegetation type.

9

Remote Sensing

In beginning of aerial photography, the photos were taken to evaluate existing topography, plan observation and sampling incursion. After World War II, the assessments of aerial photographic data were much more difficult, and real geological data started to be extracted. The use of stereoscopic pairs enabled geologist to explain height structural features. But, the basic use of remote sensing data were collected was in explanation. These trends of comparative photography until development took place into the satellite age when satellite imagery began popular and commercially available. The availability of various imageries in several combinations opened a option to analyze regions in much more detail. Apart from this, the multiple flying allowed a prospect to be viewed in various light during differnt seasons. The development drastically decreased the cost of regional exploration by minimizing repeated trips to a place for reassessing. This permitted data to be gathered from the tropics and arid regions that was previously difficult task in wide regional field exploration. As computer age progressed being developed and enhanced the value of data that allows imagery as digitally highlighted specific features. Ground features like differential cropping, drainage patterns, and folds/faults may be identified.

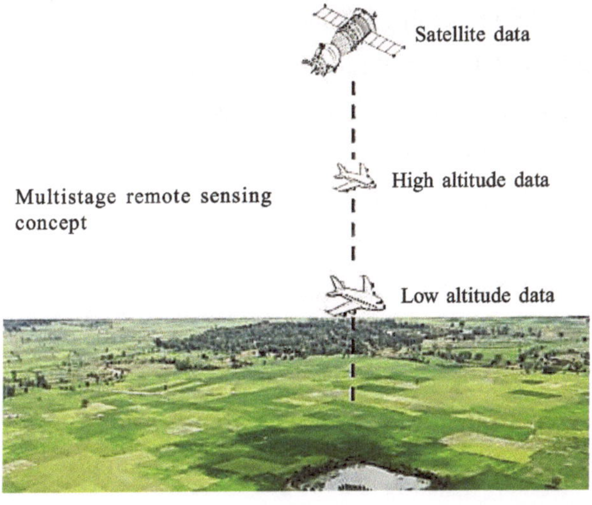

Multistage remote sensing concept

With first satellite images in earthquake research through remote sensing was used in structural geographical and geomorphological aspects. Functional fault and structure were mapped on satellite images. Active tectonic analysis with applying alignment analysis, even before and after earth quake, the time series of alignment distributions on earth surface were explored. These were initial milestones in remote sensing and following milestonied foot mark is being given below:

Milestones in the History of Remote Sensing

1800 Discovery of Infrared by Sir W. Herschel

1839 Beginning of practice of Photography

1847 Infrared Spectrum Shown by J.B.I. Foucault

1859 Photography from Balloons

1873 Theory of Electromagnetic Spectrum by J.C. Maxwell

1909 Photography from Aeroplanes

1916 World War I: Aerial Reconnaissance

1935 Development of Radar in Germany

1940 World War II: Applications of Non-Visible Part of EMS

1950 Military Research and Development

1959 First Space Photograph of the Earth (Explorer-6)

1960 First TIROS Meteorological Satellite Launched

1970 Skylab Remote Sensing Observations from Space

1972 Launch Landsat-1 (ERTS-1): MSS Sensor

1972 Rapid Advances in Digital Image Processing

1982 Launch Commercial Earth Observation Satellite SPOT

1986 French Landsat-4: New Generation of Landsat Sensors: TM

1986 Development of Hyperspectral Sensors

1990 Development High Resolution Space borne Systems
First Commercial Development in Remote Sensing

1998 Towards Cheap One-Goal Satellite Missions

1999 Launch EOS: NASA Earth Observing Mission

1999 Launch of IKONOS, very high spectral resolution sensor system

Remote sensing deals the art and science of obtaining information on area, object or phenomenon via the analysis of data collected by sensor which is not directly contacted with object (Schultz and Engman, 2000; Ritchie and Range, 1996). The use of recording or real time sensing device fitted on aircraft, spacecraft, satellite, ship or any buoy. In last 40 years, travelling in space have opened new pathway for not only absorving cosmos deeply but we can see the dimension of our world. Phenomenons, object and ground surface are epicentre of remote sensing which enables in acquiring information. Further, 1960 onwards inception of space flight evergrowing information is regularly gathered by space based remote sensing. All the technically involvement in obtaining information to act as complete system is for providing perfect data. In coming decades, remote sensing will be used in decision making process on the factors affect more to earth and its resource. Remote sensing does perform many number of work as links minimizing time and enhancing efficiency.

- EMR: Emission of electromagnetic radiation.
- Transmission of energy from source to surface of the earth, interaction with the atmosphere as well as absorption and scattering.
- Interaction of EMR with the earth's surface: absorption, reflection and emission.
- Transmission of energy from surface to remote sensor.
- Data transmission, processing and analysis.

RS gathers information or data through sensor without direct contact to objects/ substances, while gathering information sensor uses EMR or acoustical waves that are major issue on interested target. Aerial photography is the best example of remote sensing result.

Principles and Process of RS

In remote sensing, instruments mounted sensor to view spectral, spatial and radiometric connection of targeted objects and substances from distance photons based corresponding frequency spectrum in EMR.

The process generates an interaction between incoming radiation and the targets of interest. This is done using image systems where **seven elements** are included. The remote sensing uses emitted energy and non-emitted sensors.

1. **Energy Source:** The requirement for remote sensing is to be an energy source which illuminates electromagnetic energy to the target.
2. **Radiation and Atmosphere:** During movement of travelling energy from its source to the target, it contacts with and interacts through atmosphere passing through. This interaction can occur as the energy travels from the target to the sensor.

3. **Interaction with the Target:** Through atmosphere, once energy passing and interact with object, it completely depends on properties of both (target and radiation).
4. **Recording Energy by Sensor:** Object emits or scatters energy from target require a sensor to trap and record electromagnetic radiation.
5. **Transmission, Reception, and Processing:** The process of data acquiring is finished and then it is transmitted in electronic forms to receive and process.
6. **Interpretation and Analysis:** The illuminated information is interpreted visually, digitally and electronically to get information.
7. **Application:** The collected information is used finally for various field to reduce labour, time and haphazardness.

Types of Remote Sensing System

1. Visual Remote Sensing System

Human eyes are sensitive to two types of photosensitive cells, known as cones and rods in retina of eyes. There is basically 3 types of them are sensitive to the region of visible spectrum viz., red, green and blue. Cones become sensitive under low light condition with job performing by rods, ultimately sensitive to total light intensity. So, the things look in grey shades are in insufficient light. If the object are observed and situated for away from the eyes, this time information requires carrier for travelling from the object to our eyes. Under this situation the carrier is visible light as a part of electromagnetic spectrum and objects, sufficient light falling on them. Some portion of scattered light is intercepted by the eyes creating image in retina after being through eye's optical system. Retina generates signals are carried through the nerve fibres leading to brain. On the basis of previous experiences, it is helped to process and interpret signal at brain. The visual system is true representation of passive remote sensing system which completely relies on external source of energy to regulate.

Optical Remote Sensing

The optical sensors can detect the reflected and scattered solar radiation from ground surface, creating images in space, in which the region of wavelength are commonly extended from the range of visible and near infrared (VNIIR) to short-wave infrared (SWIIR). Materials like water, soil, buildings, roads and vegetation easily reflect the visible and infrared light in different manners. These have various colour and intensity with available sun light. Knowledge of spectral reflectance signatures of different composition in earth surface helps in interpretations of optical images.

Infrared Remote Sensing

The emitted or reflected infrared radiation from earth features can be detected by infrared sensors. In thermal infrared region, middle wave infrared (MWIR) and long-wave infrared (LWIR) are in this limit. The energized earth (Warmed earth) release the radiation, they are utilized in remote sensing satellite to measure the earth's surface and temperature of sea. It is also used in detection of forest fire, volcano eruption, oil fire etc.

Microwave Remote Sensing

Some of the satellites contain passive or active micro-wave sensors, in case of active sensors, which emit pulses of radiation from microwave to light object proceeding to take images. Earth surface images are measured by microwave energy scattered from ground surface or sea sensors because these types of satellites possess own flashlight emitting microwaves to lighting the objects. Thus images can be obtained in day as well as night. The special microwaves have ability to penetrate to clouds, it means cloudy day is even not hurdle in taking image due to this specific character. Synthetic aperture radar (SAR) supports to microwave imaging system in producing high resolution images of earth. To providing useful information of ocean, land and atmosphere, EMR in microwave wavelength range is used in remote sensing. Many factors influence the image when microwaves strike on surface and part of back scattering energy to sensors.

- Dielectric constant of surface materials depend on moisture content is a physical factors.
- Roughness, slope, orientation of objects referring the radar beam direction are main surface feature affects remote sensors.
- Land cover features like soil, vegetation or object creation.
- Other factors *i.e.* polarization, microwave frequency and incident angle.

Radar Sensing

Radar follows the phenomenon of sending radio signal out and then waiting for bounce back from object. The time required to return the signal is calculated in featuring perfect topography. Radar has capability to penetrate thick clouds and moisture, and the feature of radar enable us to map area like rainforest accurately sensed images by providing day light even under bed weather condition. This radar images are used to draw a map related to landforms and geographical formations, different soils, crop, greenery, ice area, oil licks from ocean etc.

Synthetic Aperture Radar (SAR)

The transmission of microwave pulses to earth via antenna and microwave energy is measured while scattering back to space aircraft. SAR works similar principle of radar to create an image through utilizing the time delay during back scattering signals. Ground resolution is a limiting factor by microwave beam size transmitted from the antenna.

Satellite Remote Sensing

Orbits are the platform for satellites monitoring of earth imaging and well equipped sensors look to earth surface. From different part of EMR, the orbital platforms gather and transfer data, which are conjunction with larger scale ground sensing and analysis gives enough data/information to monitor trends. Many other use of satellite remote sensing involves various areas of earth sciences like natural resource management, agriculture as land use and planning conservation, security and overhead observation and standoff collection on border areas.

Basically sensors or satellite record sunlight intensity is technically called electromagnetic radiation are reflected different wavelength from the earth and some of the energy is absorbed. Energy features have their own unique spectrum value.

Due to structural features of any object has specific look that specefic features of the surface like shrub, crop and moisture all are reflected light variation in different wavelengths. Mostly actual colour of object back to environment and absorbs other visible wavelengths. This may be observed as a peak in the green band in the reflectance spectrum. The grass reflectance shows even more strongly in the infrared portion of the spectrum, which can't be detected by our eyes and only detected by an infrared sensor. The detectors are having sensitive to specific ranges of wavelengths, called as 'bands'. The satellite systems are specialized by the bands at which that measure the reflected energy. The Landsat TM satellite, specialized provides the data bands at the blue, green and red wavelengths in the visible portion of the spectrum and at three bands in the near and mid infrared portion of the spectrum and other band in the thermal infrared portion of the spectrum. The satellite based detectors measures the intensity of the reflected energy and store it.

7. Airborne Remote Sensing

For accuracy, many time airborne remote sensing images are highly predictable in small area measurement using downward or sideward facing sensors and fitted on aircraft to get earth images. It provides high spatial resolution images

(20 cm or less) can be obtained comparing the satellite images, whereas less area coverage is disadvantage. It is expensive to map a large area by an airborne remote sensing system. Airborne remote sensing projects are always dealt as one-time operations, while earth observation satellites provide the possibility of continuous monitoring of the earth.

8. Acoustic and Near-acoustic Remote Sensing

Acoustic remote sensing is sound based remote sensing with two distinct passive and active sonar, are used in acoustic system of remote sensing in passive, listening for the sound made by another object and active sonar, emitting pulses of sounds and listening for echoes, used for detecting, ranging and measurements of underwater objects and terrain. Seismograms of different locations can locate and measure earthquakes by comparing the relative intensity and accurate timing.

Electromagnetic Waves

Electromagnetic waves transport energy through space in the form of certain periodic disturbances of electric and magnetic fields. All electromagnetic waves pass through space at the similar speed, c = 2.99792458 x 10^8 m/s, (Light speed). An electromagnetic wave is identified by a frequency and a wavelength.

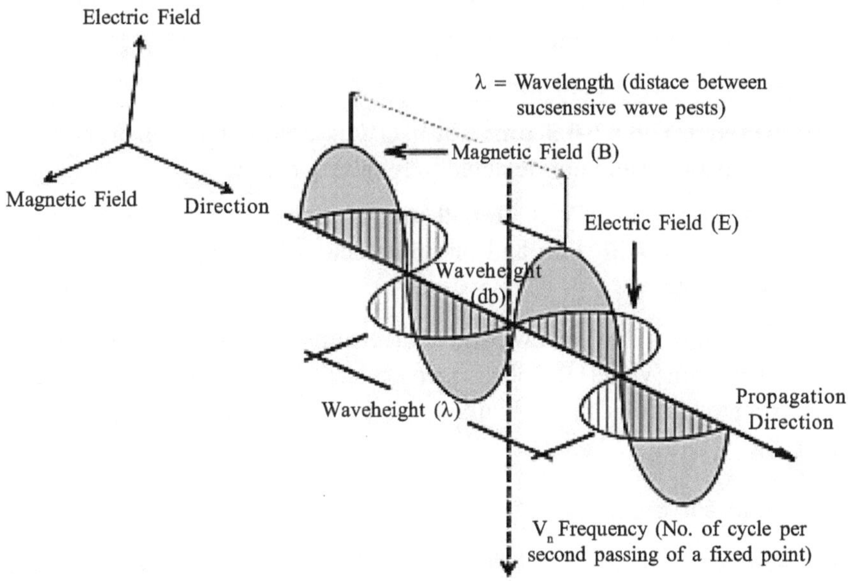

Fig. 1: Electromagnetic wave, components include a sinusoidal electric wave (*E*) and similar magnetic wave (*M*) at right angles, both being perpendicular to the direction of propogation

Photons

As per quantum physics, the energy of an electromagnetic wave is quantified, it means exist in discrete amount. Basic energy unit for an electromagnetic wave is known a photon. The energy E of a photon is proportional to the wave frequency γ, the constant h is the Planck's Constant, h = 6.626 x 10^{-34} J s.

$$E = h\gamma = \frac{hc}{\lambda}$$

The frequency (wavelength) of an electromagnetic wave decides on its source. The wide range of frequency consolidated in our physical world, ranging from the low frequency electric waves obtained by the power transmission lines to the very high frequency of the gamma rays generating from the atomic nuclei. These wide frequency ranges of electromagnetic waves make Electromagnetic Spectrum. The electromagnetic spectrum in a narrow band from about 400 to 700 nm is visible and no sharp boundary can be seen between these regions. The boundaries are approximate and there are overlaps between two adjacent regions (Wavelength units: 1mm = 1000 µm; 1 µm = 1000 nm).

1. **Gamma Rays <0.30 nm:** This range is completely absorbed by the upper atmosphere and not available for remote sensing.
2. **X-Rays 0.03-30.0 nm:** This range is totally absorbed by the atmosphere and not deputed in remote sensing.
3. **Ultraviolet**: **0.03-0.40 µm**
   - **Hard UV 0.03-0.3 µm:** Hard UV is completely absorbed by the atmosphere and not depicted in remote sensing.
   - **Photographic UV 0.30-0.40 µm**: Not absorbed by atmosphere and detectable with film and photo detectors but with high atmospheric scattering.
4. **Visible Light:** This narrow band of electromagnetic radiation lies between about 400 nm (violet) to 700 nm (red). It is widely used available for remote sensing the Earth, can be obtained with photographic film.

Violet: 400-430 nm

Indigo: 430-450 nm

Blue: 450-500 nm - Since water absorbs electromagnetic (EM) radiation at longer wavelengths, band first gives the best data in mapping detail and water depth covered areas. It is also used for soil-vegetation discrimination, forest, and distinguishing cultural features

Green: 500-570 nm - The blue-green region corresponds to the chlorophyll absorption of healthy greenery and better for mapping detail the depth or sediment in water bodies. Manmade feature (Cultural features) roads and buildings also exercise up well in this band.

Yellow: 570-590 nm

Orange: 590-610 nm

Red: 610-700 nm - Chlorophyll absorbs these wavelengths from healthy vegetation. Thus, this band can be used for distinguishing plant species, as well as soil and geologic boundaries.

5. **Infrared (0.7 to 300 µm wavelength):** Infrared region is sensitive to plant water content, which may be tool in studies of vegetation health and also used for distinguishing clouds, snow, ice, mapping geologic formations and soil boundaries. Apart from this, it responses to plant and soil moisture content. This region is further divided into the following bands.

   A. Near Infrared (NIR): 0.7 to 1.5 µm.

   B. Short Wavelength Infrared (SWIR): 1.5 to 3 µm.

   C. Mid Wavelength Infrared (MWIR): 3 to 8 µm.

   D. Long Wavelength Infrared (LWIR): 8 to 15 µm.

   E. Far Infrared (FIR): longer than 15 µm.

The NIR and SWIR are also called a Reflected Infrared, corresponding to the main infrared component of the solar radiation reflected from the earth's surface. The MWIR and LWIR comes under thermal Infrared.

6. **Microwaves (Radar) 1 mm to 1 m wavelength:** It can penetrate clouds, fog, and rain. Images can be acquired in the active or passive mode. Radar is the active form of microwave remote sensing. Radar images are obtained at various wavelength bands.

7. **Radio and TV Waves:** It is characterized as10 cm to 10 km wavelength. The longest-wavelength part of the electromagnetic spectrum is radio and TV waves.

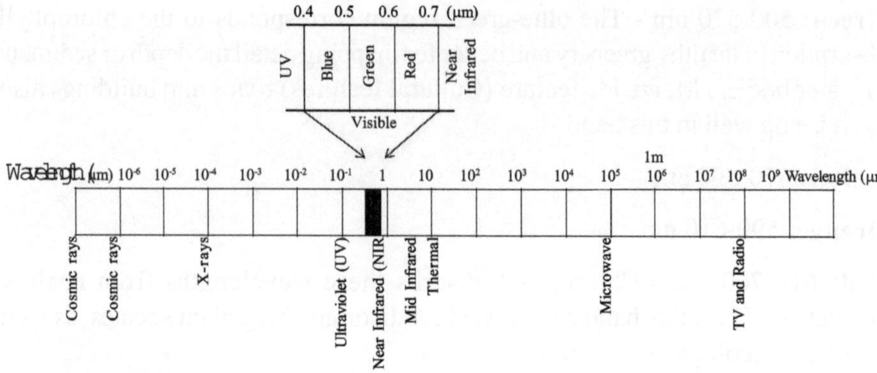

Fig. 2: Electromegnetic spectrum scale division

Kinds of Remote Sensing

Sun is a universal source of energy for remote sensing. The energy of sun is either reflected (visible wavelengths) or absorbed or re-emitted (thermal infrared wavelengths), which ultimately creates two kinds of remote sensing *i.e.* passive and active remote sensing.

1. Passive sensors object naturally radiated or reflected energy in surrounding area is being observed in presence of sun light and sun is obvious source of radiation in passive remote sensors include film photography, infrared, and radiometers.
2. Active remote sensing emits energy to scan objects and areas where a sensor can then detect and measure the radiation which is reflected or backscattered from the object. RADAR is type of active remote sensing where the time delay between emission and return is assessed by fixing the location, height, speeds and direction of an object.

Applications of Remote Sensing

Now-a-day remote sensing is gaining popularity due to its wider expansion of realistic parameters to measure present and past situation of object, make vulnerable the situation, same time it opens vast scope of application.

Meteorology: Atmospheric temperature, pressure, water vapour, and wind velocity.

Oceanography: Sea surface temperature, mapping ocean currents, and wave energy spectra and depth sounding of coastal and ocean depths.

Glaciology: Ice cap volumes, ice stream velocity, and sea ice distribution.

Geology: Identification of rock type, mapping faults and structure.

Geodesy: Figure of the Earth and its gravity field.

Interactions Between Matter and Electro-magnetic Radiation

The matters always behave the process of observation, reflection, penetration and emission with electromagnetic radiation in specific way. The specific appearance and composition directly response to spectrum, like chrolophyll presents in leaf, which absorbs blue and red spectra and same time reflects green spectrum, this is a unique character of matter.

The inner state of an atom relies on their inherent and discrete energy level, the orbit of electron is decided by level of energy. As electromagnetic radiation is incident on an atom of H with lower level of energy (E1), a part of energy is absorbed and electron is included by excitation to rise the energy level (E2) resulting in upper orbit. The electro-magnetic energy E is given as follows:

$E = hc/\lambda$

Where, h = Plank's constant; c = velocity of light, λ = wavelength

The difference of energy level

$E = E2\text{-}E1 = hc/\ \lambda$ h is absorbed

The change of the inner state is an H-atom is realized when electro-magnetic radiation at the particular wavelength λh is absorbed in an H-atom. Conversely electro-magnetic radiation at wavelength λh is radiated from an H-atom when the energy level changes from E2 to E1.

At a particular wavelength, the matter emits or absorbs electromagnetic radiation due to all matter is comprised of atom and molecule regarding to inner state. The types of inner state are categorized into various classes, such as ionization, excitation, molecular vibration, molecular rotation etc., which radiate the associated electro-magnetic radiation, visible light is radiated by excitation of valence electrons, while infrared is radiated by molecular vibration or lattice vibration.

Characteristic state	**Energy (eV)**	**Associated EM wave**
Nuclear transmission and disintegrations	$10^7\sim10^5$	y- ray
Ionization by inner electron removal	$10^4\sim10^2$	X-ray
Ionization by outer electron removal	$10^2\sim 4$	Ultra-violet
Excitation of valence electrons	$4\sim1$	Visible
Molecular vibration, Lattice vibration	$10\sim10^{-5}$	Infrared
Molecular radiations, electron spin resonance	$10^{-4}\sim10^{-5}$	Microwave
Nuclear spin resonance	10^7	Meter wave

Unit, energy of 1eV=1.60219x 1010_{-19} joule, wavelength of 1eV light =1.23985 μm

Schematics of characteristic states associated with electromaguetic radiation

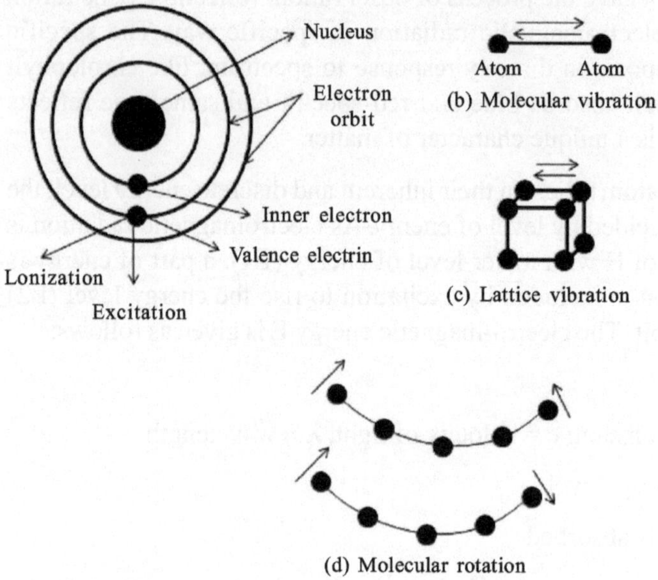

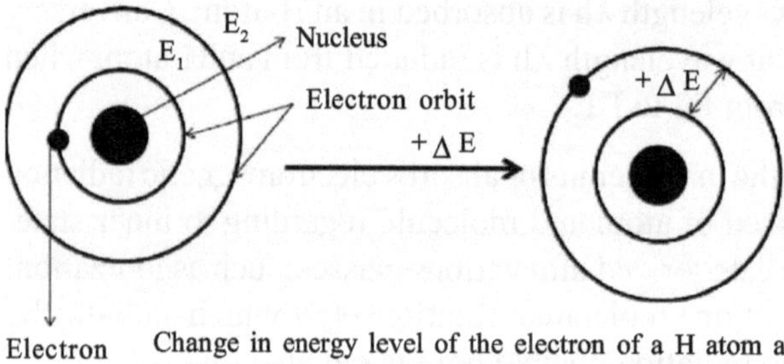

Change in energy level of the electron of a H atom according to absorption of electromagnetic wavelength λ H

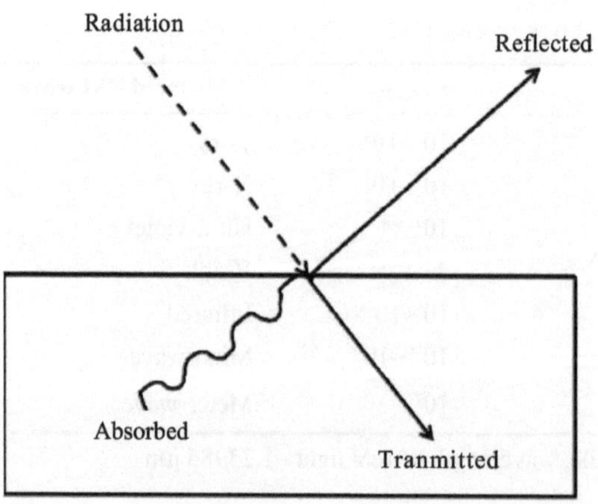

Energy Interaction with Targets

The radiation comes to earth is absorbed by O_3, CO_2 and water molecules then different Wavelength can reach to ground surface through atmospheric window, the Wavelength is further classified as ultra violet rays (0.30 to 0.75 μm), near Infrared and mid infrared commonly ranges from 0.77 to 0.90 μm and 1.75 to 1.99 μm, respectively. Scattering is another kind of obstacle in receiving proper Wavelength an ground surface, which always defined as Rayleigh ($a < \lambda$), Mie scattering ($a < = > \lambda$) and third one is non-selective ($a > \lambda$ i.e. all BGR equal). Interaction equation expresses wavelength variation may be through.

$$E_I(\lambda) = E_R(\lambda) + E_A(\lambda) + E_T(\lambda)$$

Where, λ = wavelength.

$E_R(\lambda)$ = Energy of wavelength reflected from object.

$E_I(\lambda)$ = Energy of wavelength incident upon the object.

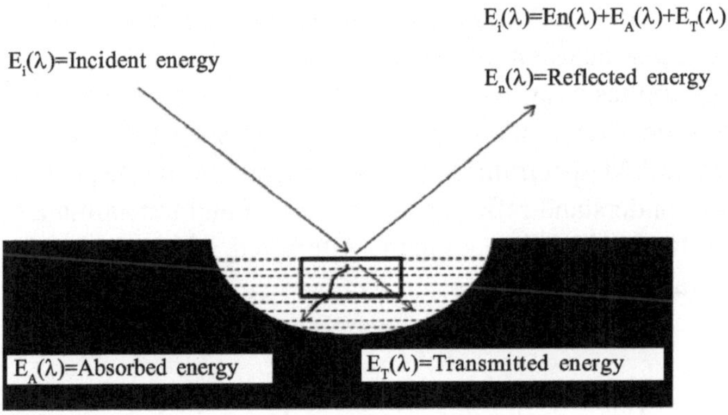

Fig. 3: Basic interactions between electromagnetic energy and earth surface

Any object receives incoming energy that objects behave three fundamental interactions are in response, different fraction of incident energy are reflected, absorbed and transmitted singly or in combination.

Interaction of Electromagnetic Energy with a Target

Interrelationship between these interactions as

$$\mathbf{E_I = E_R + E_A + ET}$$

Where $\mathbf{E_I}$ stands for the incoming energy, $\mathbf{E_R}$ stands for the reflected energy, $\mathbf{E_A}$ denotes the absorbed energy and $\mathbf{E_T}$ denotes the transmitted energy, and with all energy components become a function of wavelength. Three possible relationship may be seen.

The parts of energy reflected, absorbed and transmitted may offer varying for different objects depend on their material type and condition. These distructions are basically used to differentiate between objects in an image; bright objects, such as sand, have higher reflectance than blur objects.

The parts of reflected, absorbed and transmitted energy for a object differs with wavelength; an high absorption object at green and red wavelengths and high reflectance at 'blue' wavelengths can be appeared with a blue' colour to the our eyes.

Green objects such as grass has higher reflectance at green wavelengths than at blue or red wavelengths. Yellow is the product of EM energy at red and green wavelengths. Here a yellow target may have high reflectance at these wavelengths and relatively high absorption at blue wavelengths. The principle of **multispectral reflectance** demonstrates combinations of primary (visible) wavelengths. On the basis of specific illumination and view angles, remote sensing calculates the fraction of reflected energy. At certain geometry, the word used for measurement is bidirectional reflectance; such set of measurement explains the bidirectional reflectance distribution function (**BRDF**). The principle of conservation of energy applies at all wavelengths, however by building tools that record the level of reflected radiation we are able to extract the information content across the whole EM spectrum. For easier interaction multispectral images, first it needs to understand reflectance, absorption and transmittance characters of earth surface, which is commonly interacted with soil, water, vegetation etc. at the wavelength.

Solar Irradiation

Sun as source of light is used by optical remote sensing, solar irradiation spectrum can be modeled by a black body radiation spectrum being temperature source of 5900 K at peak irradiation located about 500nm wavelength. Physical scale of solar irradiance has been performed using grouped and space borne sensors. When they pass through atmosphere, solar irradiation spectrum at surface is modulated by atmospheric transmission windows. Remarkable energy rest within the wavelength of 0.25 to 3.00 um.

The Earth's Atmosphere

Surrounding of earth is consisted with different layers of atmosphere which is mix form of gases and others (solid and liquid particles). From earth to 80 km atmosphere contains 99% or more total mass of the earth's atmosphere, this vertical expansion of atmosphere is in four layers, namely troposphere, stratosphere, mesosphere, thermosphere. Top of the every layer is called pause.

- **Troposphere:** Troposphere has phenomenon of decreasing thermal value with regard to height, at a rate of 6.5°C per kilometer, up to a height of 10 km. Whole weather phenomenon: water vapour, clouds, precipitation are found in this layer. A layer of aerosol particles normally present near to the gound surface. The aerosol concentration lowers nearly exponentially with height, with a characteristic height of about 2 km. The upper atmosphere commonly assures to the region of the atmosphere above the troposphere.
- **Stratosphere:** In this layer, temperature is constant at lower 20 km further which enhances with height upto 50 km. Ozone exists mainly at the stratopause. The troposphere and stratosphere both account for more than 99% of the total atmospheric mass.
- **Mesosphere:** Mesosphere expresses decreasing temperature trend from an alttitude of 50 km to 85 km.
- **Thermosphere:** Extending from 85 km upward to many km is basic character of this layer and temperature from 500 K to 2000 K, in this layer gases mainly exist in the form of thin plasma, because of ionization and energetic cosmic rays. Most of the satellites are set near polar sun-synchronous orbits at a height around 800 km always being above the thermopause.

Atmospheric Constituents

As EMR passes through atmosphere, can be taken or scattered by basic particles presents in atmosphere. Conversion of radiation energy into excited energy of moleculars scattering helps in redistribution of the energy of incident beam to every direction. The various effects of absorption and scattering are lined up in the following sections. The atmosphere consists of the following components.

- **Permanent Gases:** Some gases present nearly stable concentration having small spatial variation. About 78% of the atmosphere nitrogen by volume while the life-essential oxygen occupies 21%. The remaining one percent consists of the inert gases, carbon dioxide and other gases.
- **Gases with Variable Concentration:** The concentration of gases can vary much over space and time. They make up of water vapour, ozone, nitrogenous and sulphurous compounds.
- **Solid and liquid particulates:** Apart from the gases, the atmosphere also possesses solid and liquid particles such as aerosols, water droplets and ice crystals. These particles can congregate to create clouds and haze.
- **Ozone layers:** Ozone presents in stratosphere absorb almost 99% of ultra violet radiation shorter than 320 nm. The ozone is formed of three body collisions atomic oxygen (O) with oxygen molecule in presence of third

atom/molecule. Photochemical dissociation also takes place in ozone molecules to atomic and molecular oxygen. Both the processes (Formation and dissociation) are in balance, ozone remains constant in concentration level. Presence of some specific atoms (Atomic chlorine) catalyzes the dissociation of O_3 to O_2 and ozone which reduces ozone concentration. From the space platforms, it has regularly been noticed that ozone layers are decreasing over the time owing to little increase in solar radiation and part of it reaching the earth. In recent past, higher use of CFCs compounds in aerosol sprays and refrigerant releases the atomic chlorine into top atmosphere because of photo-chemical dissociation, which contributes to ozone layer ultimately.

Absorption by Gas Molecule

Basically energy presents in gaseous molecules are in different forms, which briefly details below.

- Translational energy: Centre of mass in molecule is source of energy due to translational motion. The mean translational kinetic energy of molecule is nearly equal to KT/2, where K stands for Boltzmaan's constant and T for absolute temperature of gas.
- Rotational energy: Molecule rotation creates energy due to rotational movement about an axis via centre of mass and energy is released.
- Vibrational energy: Vibrational energy movement of component atoms also generates energy against their balance position.
- Electric energy: Energy states of electrons of any molecule release energy.

Rotational, vibrational and electric energy are the forms to be quantized, it means energy can change in discrete quantity which is called translational energy. A photon of EMR may be observed by a molecule when the frequency synchronizes with one of the present translational energies.

Solar Radiation in the Atmosphere

When sensors penetrate via atmosphere layer, it obstacles to receiving signal under atmosphereic composition presents in the path. Wavelength based absorption and scattering of radiation are caused due to atmosphere constituents, subsequently the effect reduces the quality of images. Perfect analysis and interpretation of images effect can be reduced for better image. Ultimately atmospheric absorption is in a certain wavelength bands in EM spectrum are highly observed and effectively blocked by the atmosphere. Wavelength regions are usable for remote sensing and determined by capacity to penetrate in atmosphere, which is called windows of atmospheric transmission. The design of remote sensing system always gets privilege to operate within one or more atmosphere windows, the windows present in the microwave zones, infrared wavelength bands, the whole visible region and portion of NIR regions.

Atmospheric Effects

As we understand that atmosphere is transparent to light and tend to believe same situation presents for all EMR, the gases also exist in atmosphere are separately scattered the light of different wavelengths. These gases absorb EM energy at certain interval of wavelength known as absorption bands. The intervening zones of high energy transmittance are known atmospheric transmission bands/windows. Gases and particles are important in affecting the incident light and radiation, which is attributed by mechanisms of transmittance, scattering and absorption.

1. **Transmittance portion of radiation:** The radiation penetrates via atmospheric water or other materials having special characters. Every molecule contains own observation set and their bands in various portion of EM spectrum. A part of their wavelength region from absorption bands of gases can be used in remote sensing. The portion is called ATW (Atmospheric transmission Windows). For reducing atmospheric absorption effects, the wavelength bands are utilized in remote sensing systems and framed to receive within ATW. The windows are occurred in visible, NIR, specific bands in thermal IR and microwave regions.
2. **Scattering:** Large gas molecules and particles present in atmosphere affect electromagnetic radiation from their basic path. Many features like wavelength, abundance particles or gases and travelling distance of radiation via atmosphere. Mostly three types of scattering are considered which are: i. Rayleigh, ii. Mie and iii. Non-selective scattering, these behave without changing wavelength by absorption and re-emittance of electro-magnetic energy with particles.
    - **Rayleigh scattering:** When particles are minute as coupled to wavelength of radiation, which may be nitrogen and oxygen molecules and small specks of dust. This scattering mostly affects shorter wavelengths of energy compared to long wavelengths and is prominent mechanism of scattering in upper atmosphere. Due to this phenomenon actually creates appearance of sky "Blue" in day time. As radiation passes via atmosphere, shorter wavelength (Blue) of visible spectrum starts scattering more as compared to other longer visible wavelengths. During sunset and sunrise the radiation is to pass through atmosphere than midday, scattering of short wavelengths is more, this gives up a

greater part of longer wavelengths to penetrate the atmosphere and sky looks red.

- **Mie scattering:** The particles and wavelength are just about some size in scattering, which have tendency to influence longer wavelengths. Mie scattering presents in lower parts of atmosphere where more abundant of large particles, and it becomes dominant when cloud conditions show overcast in sky.

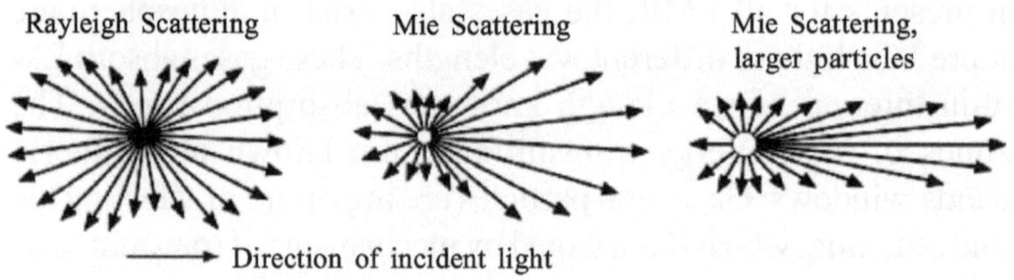

Non-selective scattering: The particles are much larger than wavelength; non-selective scattering is occurred in presence of water droplets and large dust particles. By name of this scattering, fact follows that wavelengths are scattered uniformly. Due to equally scattering from three light (Blue, green and red) causes showing fog and clouds white to our eyes in totality of similar scattering.

3. **Absorption:** The sun light is absorbed via electron or molecular reactions within media consorted, a part of energy involved it can be re-emitted more with longer wavelengths, so that part of radiant energy of sun uses in heating target for rising to thermal response. In opposite to scattering, this mechanism causes molecules in the atmosphere to absorb energy at different wavelengths. O_3, CO_2 and water vapour are major atmospheric constituent which absorbs radiation energy. The measurement of spectral properties of material through planetary atmosphere should know the atmospheric absorption.

   a) **X-Ray and Gama Ray Absorption:** This whole range of X-Ray and Gama Ray is absorbed by the atmosphere and even not receive on the earth.

   b) **Ultraviolet Absorption:** Due to electromagnetic transmission of atomic and molecular O and N causes the absorption of UV (Ultra Violet) in atmospheric phenomenon. Some part of O and N molecules process under photo-chemical degradation to form atomic O and N in upper atmosphere. These atoms are important in the absorption of solar UV radiation in the thermosphere. The photochemical dissociation of oxygen is also poses positive impact for the formation of the ozone layer in the stratosphere.

c) **Visible Region Absorption:** There is small absorption of the EMR in the visible part of the spectrum.

d) **Infrared Absorption:** The absorption is mostly cause of rotational and vibrational transitions of the molecules in infrared region. The major atmospheric elements like water vapour (H_2O) and carbon dioxide (CO_2) molecules are responded for IR absorption. The H_2O and CO_2 molecules have absorption bands at centre of the wavelengths from near to long wave infrared (0.7 to 15 μm). In the far infrared region, maximum radiation is absorbed by the atmosphere.

e) **Microwave Region Absorption:** The atmosphere is realistically transparent to the microwave radiation, which is why it is used for receiving image during cloudy weather.

Basic Components of Remote Sensing

Solar energy is the major source of energy which radiate and illuminate. All time, sun bombards various wavelength of electro-magnetic radiation on earth as visible light, infrared, radio and microwaves; detection and discrimination of surface features is reflected as emitted by surface (Joseph, 2004; Lillesand and Kiefer, 1987; 2000). This special property depends on the property of material (structural, chemical and physical), surface roughness, angle of incidence, intensity and wavelength of radiant energy (Elachi, 1987). Various features of earth returns different amount and types of energy in different band of EMR. Naturally everything on this earth has its own distribution. The spectral characteristics, may be utilized for differentiate one thing from another or even data also be useful in shape, size with other physical and chemical properties. but detection of electromagnetic radiation can be identified by instruments for knowing the emission and reflection under remote sensing, even year wise data, a construction of conservation structures in certain area can be grouped according their size, place, frequency etc. within minute either a desktop and google earth platform model-based execution may be a recant demand in consisting whole work, in which we can easily execute the prospect of the structures. Thus, to know remote sensing, it is necesary to first understand the fundamental of EMR.

Electromagnetic Radiation

EMR (electromagnetic radiation) is a basic form of solar energy in the world, which is dynamic form of energy that generates wave movement at the light velocity ($C=3\times10^{10}$ m/s), electromagnetic energy follows main wave principle; describe the energy as moving in a harmonic sinusoidal manner at the light velocity.

Here, **c = vλ** 3.1

Where, v, λ and c stand for frequency, wavelength and velocity, respectively Although several characteristics of electromagnetic energy are easily described by wave theory, another theory popularly called as particle theory offers insight into how EM energy interacts with matter. It considers that EMR is composed of several discrete units known as photons/quanta. The energy of quantum is.

Q = h c/λ 3.2

Where Q and h stand for energy of quantum and plank's constant, respectively. Here, from equation 3.1

Q = h cv 3.3

Electromagnetic Spectrum

EM energy is source of generating energy required to transfer from object to the sensor, is a important media which is detailed as an EM spectrum. Various fundamental types of energy in the universe are related as portion of this spectrum, several forms existing, the energy mentioned in specified region of electromagnetic spectrum, may be visible light, radio waves microwaves, infra-red, UV rays, X-rays and gamma rays. The spectrum shows continue electromagnetic energy from higher short wavelength (cosmic ray) to extreme long wavelength (radio and television waves), and mind that wavelength of energy declines, the frequency increases. The separation can not be pure and well definite and occur overlapping.

Table: Major regions of the electromagnetic spectrum

Region Name	Wavelength	Comments
Gamma Ray	< 0.03 nanometers	Entirely absorbed by the atmosphere of earth and not available for remote sensing.
X-ray	0.03 to 30 nanometers	Entirely absorbed by the atmosphere of earth and not available for remote sensing.
Ultraviolet	0.03 to 0.4 micrometers	Wavelengths from 0.03 to 0.3 micrometers absorbed by ozone in the atmosphere of earth.
Photographic Ultraviolet	0.3 to 0.4 micrometers	Available for remote sensing the Earth. Can be imaged with photographic film.
Visible	0.4 to 0.7 micrometers	Available for remote sensing the Earth. Can be imaged with photographic film.
Reflected Infrared	0.7 to 3.0 micrometers	Available for remote sensing the Earth. Near Infrared 0.7 to 0.9 micrometers. Can be imaged with photographic film.

Thermal Infrared	3.0 to 14 micrometers	Available for remote sensing the Earth. This wavelength cannot be captured with photographic film. Instead, sensors are used to image this wavelength band.
Microwave or Radar	0.1 to 100 centimeters	Longer wavelengths of this band can pass through clouds, fog, and rain. Images using this band can be made with sensors that actively emit microwaves.
Radio	> 100 centimeters	Not normally used for remote sensing the Earth.

(*Source: http://www.physicalgeography.net/fundamentals/2e.html*)

Electromagnetic Radiation Quantities

Radiant Energy (Q)

Actually this type of energy is completed by EMR, radiant energy exists for detecting the element of sensor to respond the electromagnetic energy in proper manner, which is measured in Joule (Q) as unit.

Radiant Flux (ϕ) (Phi): Means the time rate for flowing radiant energy. Basically measuring unit is Joule per second per Watt (W).

Irradiance (E): It means the Radiant flux intercepted by a plain surface per unit area of any surface. This reaches at the surface from all sides within a hemisphere on the surface. The measurement unit is W per m^2 (Watt per square meter).

Radiance (L): The radiant flux per unit solid angle except extended source in a direction for projection in per unit area in the same direction. The concept of radiance is targeted to respond with brightness concept. The projected area in a direction which makes an' angle θ (Theta) with the normal to the surface of area A is A cosθ. Unit for Radiance is $Wm^{-2}sr^{-1}$.

Spectral Reflectance ($p(\lambda)$) : This is defined as the ratio of reflected energy to incoming energy as a function of wavelength.

Spectral Signature: This represents values of the spectral reflectance of any objects meaned over variation proper defining wavelength intervals composed the spectral signature of features by which they may be distinguished.

c) Interaction of EMR with atmosphere and earth surface

Unlimited source of radiation and EMR an earth reflects and sensor detected by satellite or aircraft go through the atmosphere twice i.e. once its journey to earth surface and once when radiation is being reflected back to the sensor, atmosphere effect is known when interactions between direct solar and reflected radiation from object with interference of atmospheric comonents by remote sensing process.

The atmosphere constituents always process scattering and absorption of the radiation, change the reflected radiation from objects by dwindling, spectrum variation affects both the divertions (scattering and absorption) in their effect. Even existing solar energy is matter of modification by many physical process when the energy passes the atmospherie scattering, absorption and reflection.

1. **Scattering:** Suspended particles present in atmosphere are responsible for radiation of electromagnetic radiation through scattering, or by larger molecules of atmospherie gases or water vapor, the scattering basically depends on size and frequency of particles, the wave length and atmospheric depth by which the energy is travelled, it varies in time and season their scatting difference time to time, scattering decreases image contrastness and change in spectral signature of earth object by the sensor.
2. **Absorption:** When EMR passing through the atmosphere, specific bands is absorbed by the gas molecules present in the atmosphere strongly. Mainly three gases viz., O_3, CO_2 and water vapour absorb the most of solar radiation. The absorption makes darkar the image/scene looking to our eyes due to radiation of the light amount.
3. **Atmosphere window:** The atmosphere is related to the spectral bands are called atmosphere window. Ozone absorption and molecular scattering mainly affect visible part transmission.
4. **Refraction:** Refraction concept is that light band at the contact between two media is followed by atmosphere as light passes through the atmosphere layers characterized with varied clarity humidity and temperature.

Solar radiation incidents on earth's surface are reflected by the ground transmitted into the surface, similarly absorbed and emitted energy on the same ground plays important role in development of satellite image. Meanwhile EMR, interaction experiences a several changes in magnitude, direction, wave length, phase and polarization. This level of change is detected by remotely placed sensor and enables the persons to get useful data about object available on earth. The collected information contains two types of information, one is spatial information (size, shape and orientation) and spectral information (tone color and spectral signature). Spectral band of 0.3 μm to 3 μm is called as reflection signature in the band, radiation sensed by the sensor owing to the sun, reflected by earth's ground.

5. **Reflection:** Ground reflections are the most valuable and reveling in RS application through interactions in the reflected region. The ray of light is radiation when it strikes on non-transparent surface then the reflection occurs. The intensity of reflection mainly decides on the ground refractive index, absorption coefficient and the angles of both incidence and reflection.
6. **Transmission:** The radiation goes through a substance without many losses, the transmission of radiation occurs in any thickness, or depth of a matter, the ability of a medium to transmit energy is accounted as transmission (T).

T = Transmission radiation/ incident radiation

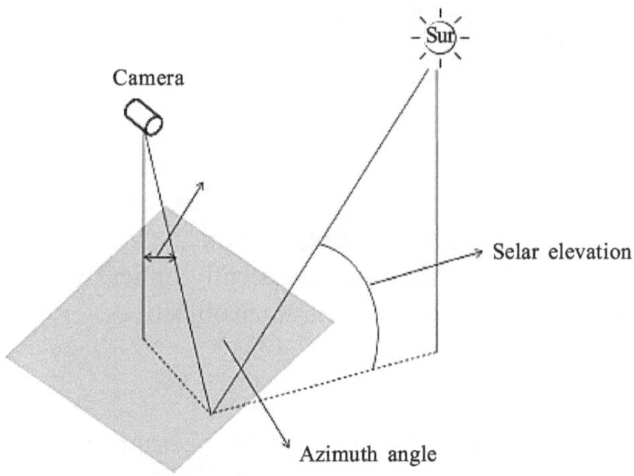

Fig. 4: Sun-object-angular relationship

Data detection and output: The detector is a most important factor of remote sensing which collect the variation of surface material, specific sensors sensible response to several parts of EMR spectrum, works of recording system to be converted the energy detected by sensors in particular form may be perceived the process and assessed by dividing the incoming energy in each wave length band into electrical signal. The electrical signal is further gone for processing to get radiometer data in every band which is always recorded in digital format.

Remote Sensing Systems

Remote sensing system: Normally RS systems are two types as imaging which includes image forming and non-imaging means no image forming. Large image forming system have two categories of system *i.e.*, forming and scanning types. In scanning type, the information is obtained sequentially from earth in pieces of picture or pixels, point by point and line these can be arranged after obtaining in a frame format.

Remote sensing may be either passive or active. In the active systems, own source of energy is used such as RADAR; on other hand, the passive systems depend upon external source of energy is required for illumination like sun for remote sensing.

Active sensors: These types of sensors are used own source of energy to lightening earth and a portion of it is reflected and received to get information.

Passive sensors: The sensors do not have own generated energy source; it receives solar EM energy reflected from surface or energy emitted from surface. Therefore, the satellite cannot be utilized at night time, exceptional is in thermal sensors. Energy is naturally released like thermal energy may be detected both day and night, and also the amount of energy is enough to be recorded (Sabins, 1997).

Types of Remote Sensing

Remote sensing can broadly categorized into three kinds in consideration to wavelength region and types of sensor to obtain data, are optical (Visible and Reflective Infrared); thermal Infrared and Microwave. Recently, optical remote sensing technique is being used in achieving the pre-framed objectives.

Optical Remote Sensing

Optical remote sensing (ORS) uses the visible part of EM spectrum. Energy released from sun is utilized visible and reflective infrared RS. The International Commission on Illumination (ICI) has defined the visible spectrum (0.38 to 0.79 μm). The peak sensivity of human eyes (0.55 microns) is appropriately highest curve of sun (Jensen, 1996; Sabins, 1987; Gupta, 1999; 2003). The data belong to visible and reflective infrared regions primary decides on reflectance of features on earth ground. So, information related objects may be received from the spectral reflectance (Elachi, 1987).

Thermal Infrared Remote Sensing

Source of radiant energy is primarily utilized in thermal infrared remote sensing, is itself object, due to features of a common temperature emits EMR with a peak about 10 μm (Sabins, 1987; Gupta, 2003).

Microwave Remote Sensing

In microwave region, there are two types of microwave RS are used as passive and active. The microwave radiation released from a feature/object is detected under passive microwave RS, whereas in active microwave remote sensing, source of electromagnetic radiations and detector is fitted on the sensor (Elachi, 1988).

Platforms and Sensors

The data take from a feature to a sensor in radiation transmitted through the atmosphere. To gather and record energy reflected or emitted by sensor from object or surface, it should be stable platform away from the object or surface being observed. On the basis of elevation above earth surface, platforms are categorized as ground-borne, air-borne and space-borne.

Space-borne platforms are in space, moving in orbits around the earth through these space-borne platforms getting huge amount of RS data. Based on their elevation and orbit movement the platforms can be two categories.

i) **Geostationary satellites:** An equatorial west to east based satellite orbiting the earth on elevation at which the satellite runs one revolution in 24 hours synchronizing with the earth's rotation. Therefore, it avails regular coverage over the same place. Communication and weather applications are a major works (INSAT satellites).

ii) **Polar orbiting or Sun-synchronous satellites:** The satellite with inclined north-south orbit track westward in such a rate. It can cover every area of the world in a constant time of the day known as local sun time with turn of satellite from north to south which ensures the same illumination conditions when obtaining data over a particular point on a series of days. During the descending pass from north to south the satellite travels on the sun light side of the earth, whereas on ascending pass from south to north it travels on the shadow side of the earth. These satellites regularly covers whole globe and yields repetitive coverage periodically. All remote sensing resources satellites are grouped in this category (IRS series).

Sensor is the device that collects energy either in EMR or others form changes it into a signal and for obtaining information about target in comfortable form under investigation. Sensors used for remote sensing may be widely categorized as Optical Infrared Region (OIR) and microwave region. OIR and microwave sensors may further be subcategorized into passive and active on the basis of energy source.

Inherent Characteristics and Spectral Signature of objects

The process of image forming for photography fundamentally works on the negative which is composed to tiny silver formed film via various section of fill service amount of light depends on reflection of electromagnetic radiation from various object. After passing light via optical system develops various tones and textures.

Interpretation is primary issue with recognizing change in tonal values under visual image, there after different object look on certain reflective characters of each other spots, is must be matching point for some object, behave different under influence of moisture; illumination conditions and different wavelength of incoming energy can reflect a various wavelength of incident energy and different amount of light is the reason. General key might be on tone characteristics of features/objects, would not be this condition, other characteristics of objects like shape, size and pattern leverages to recognize spectral signature is the measuring parameters decides the characteristics of the wavelength reflected by any object and further this can be categorized in.

I. Spectral variation: differentiation in reflected and emissivity decides the function of wavelength.

II. Spatial variation: differentiation in reflectivity and emissivity with spatial position like shape texture, and size of the materials made in object.

III. Temporal variation: variation of emissivity and reflectivity change the signature according to time and reason.

IV. Polarization variation: variation is introduced by the material of radiation reflected or emitted by it.

All these four features of electromagnetic radiation may be interdependent measurement of variation and correlating them with object. Apart from spectral signature of different object, the knowledge of conditional polarization of reflected radiation in remote sensing, their dimension is for analysis and interpretation of the data. Valuable data may be received by these parameters is useful.

Remote Sensing Applications in Agriculture

Agriculture is dynamic natural resource among other resource and it directly belongs to human sustainability and summerized, reliable and timely suggestive and executable programming are vital tool to recharge agriculture pace. Agricultural survey is frequently conducted by various apex and local level organization to assess status of crop, rangeland, land information, livestock and related issues. These data give valuable information to policy maker, grower and planner for effective management at site, district and state level. In fact, survey is main process of planning and allocation of limited resources to sectoral development of Indian economy.

Importance: Remote sensing is a tools to get the reliable data on targeted feature without may contact to the object it is basically depend on an object by a device utilizing character related to the object with EM energy which is assessed in spectral bands for identification of the object in this kind of study and requires multiple tabular data map which can provide combination with various information from existing map.

- Various platforms provide utility of RS techniques in agriculture survey, which is now-a-day widely used.
- Synoptic view of image/object is obtained by satellite data, which is almost difficult from conventional methods.
- Using geographic information system (GIS), process of data acquisition and its analysis is faster than any conventional methods.
- Expression of ready map is so easy for every man perception to understand, easy digital format map is developed as per need with fine and accurate technology keeping importance to this technique.

Remote sensing tool is unique way of recording data in both visible and invisible forms, in which ultraviolet, reflected, infrared, thermal infrared and microwave are invisible categories in the part of EM spectrum. Due to some phenomenon, it may not be observed, can be obtained with remote sensing techniques, like chlorophyll variation, diseased and insect affected trees, may be identified by remote sensing tools under any weather condition.

Present Status of Data Generations

Under the guidance of Ministry of Agriculture, departments like land record, director of agriculture and district statistical office are responsive agencies for generation of data and district statistical office are responsive agencies in collection of data. generation of data from developed map is a skill work for arrangement and visible format regarding perfect information, meanwhile working with remote sensing errors and fact depends on person's expertize in handing RS software and experience.

Fundamental Problem in Survey

- **Reliability of data:** Man observes data depending on their realistic observation with limited access but almost perfect due to manual process. On other hands, remotely sensed data mainly depends on machine technique, although human error like phenomenon is not associated with remote sensing but some problematic issues are always present while processing remote sensing data, which include distortion, lack of geo-reference or tagging imperfection cause problem in execution of remote sensing FEC and TC are another issue in processing of remote sensing data, whether that are targeted for particular objective to be fulfil the theme. Agriculture data have almost greenery in every aspect of crop and their management. In such cases, it is very difficult task to manage properly.

- **Cost and benefits:** Even remote sensing technique is accurate and easier in obtaining information but involved cost is so high which often distract the human to consider the application. Different types of satellite imageries use for various purposes of obtaining information costs lakh of rupees for small area, therefore it is limited to high level organization and experts.
- **Methods of selection:** Remote sensing is a tool which is used in different disciplines for specific purpose and method dictates how technologies will be taken in consideration depending on depth of work to be performed in deciding the appropriate methods. Data are basically collected differently which may cause the lack of accuracy with mishandling tools.
- **Measurement of area:** Mostly data acquired remote sensing satellite are in different format, later it needs primary processing like orthogonal correction, Geo-tag error these all lead to measurement of error and line data actuality, whether point, polygon and line data are in perfect place or not is a big matter in extracting result. If measurement of polygon deviate from basic ground reality always changes the actual measurement.
- **Non sampling error:** Because the data are obtained from remote sensing techniques i.e., without physical contact to object, so there is issue of non-sampling errors and lacks reality due to no real ground observation unless the ground truthing data is not fortified. Scaling difference play a role in measuring object accurately and process further with right planning in real ground, but it requires more effort to compensate remote sensing perfectly.

Advantages of Remote Sensing Techniques

With the main aim of improving the present tools in generating data related to agriculture, number of specific benefits may result from the use of RS techniques.

1. **Vantage point:** Because the agricultural coverage depends on the sun as a energy source, it is exposed to the aerial view and, consequently, is ideally suited for remote sensing techniques.
2. **Coverage:** By using high elevated sensor platforms, is now possibly panoramic data on a single shot. The advent of high-flying aircraft and satellites, single high quality images covering thousand square miles.

3. **Permanent record:** After obtaining image, it works as a permanent record of a landscape as temporal and spatial data which can be monitored and evaluated the agricultural resources.
4. **Mapping Base**: Specific types of remote sensing imagery are pictorial maps of the landscape and after rectification it can be used, and also allow for accurate measurement to be made on the imagery, discarding time consuming process on the ground surveys. These images can also aid ground data sampling as a base map for site specific agriculture features, and for base of ground sampling areas.
5. **Cost savings:** It is cost saving when compared with the advantages, which may be received from analysis of satellite imagery.
6. **Real-time capability:** The imagery can rapidly be procured and detailed may support to eliminate the lack of timeliness which plagues in several agricultural survey.

Other Advantages of Remote Sensing

- Easy data obtaining over unreachable area.
- Data recording at different scales and resolutions.
- Analysis process is done in lab, thus lowering the amount of field work.
- Colour composites may be produced from three basic band images in further providing better details of the area.
- Stereo-satellite data can be used for 3-dimensional studies.

Satellite Data Acquisition

- Satellite collects remotely sensed data from true ground surface but acquisition of date has many atmospheric obstacles in the way and blurs the images. Different advance satellite is now being used for acquisition of quality data to be used in public domains. Satellite data and scanning mechanism both together works for acquisition of proper quality data.
- Satellite has two types of data acquisition *i.e.* geo-stationery satellite synchronized in orbital plane at 36000 km from earth whereas sun synchronous also sets on satellite orbital place with running 800-900 km from earth. IRS (Indian Remote Satellite/sensing - 1C) set, it in such a way it crosses equatorial at 10:30 a.m. and lathering camera for repeated interval over mean radius of earth (6371 km).
- Scating mechanism works with either across track or optical or whisk. Groom scanners, mostly attached With Landsat USA. Another types of scanning

mechanism is along the track, is push broom mostly Indian satellite found in this categories.

- Characteristics of data: Based on acquisition they are characterized in different form i.e. spatial, radiometric, temporal resolution given below details:

Spatial resolution	Spectral resolution
High resolution - 0.6 to 4 m	Fine wavelength
Medium resolution - 4 to 30 m	Band
Low resolution - 30 to > 1000 m	Multispectral

Radiometric

- 8 bit data $2^8 = 256$, 0 to 256 i.e. more clear picture.
- 7 bit data 27 = 156, 0 to 155 i.e. less clear picture.

Applications in Land Resource Inventory

IRS launched first RS satellite for obtaining remotely sensed data in various resource inventories in1998. Application and validation programme (AVP) involves thematic and software Scientists to process the data basically for crop acreage prediction of estimation, Indian Remote Sensing covers 38 meter dimension in 7A format. CARTOSAT data works under one mission (Carto-DEMs) which is collected stereo data as x, y and dimensions, Digital Elevation Model (DEM) delineates elevational change on surface with spatial resolution (2.5m) and radiometric resolution 10 bits with swath of 30 metres to observe and collect surface situation.

LIDAR System

In Both Coherent and Incoherent LIDAR, there are two Types of Pulse Models

There are basically two types of pulse models (Coherent and Incoherent), regular increase in amount of computer power combined with modern technology have developed micropulse system. This system considerably uses less energy in laser, typically as microjoule which always safer for eyes without safety measures. The high power system is common in research of atmosphere widely used for measuring weather parameters like height, layering and densities of clouds, particle properties of cloud (extinction coefficient, back scatter coefficient, depolarization), pressure of atmosphere, wind, temperature, humidity etc.

Major Components of LIDAR System

1. Laser (600-1000 nm) is very common for non-scientific applications. These are expensive but can be focussed and affordlessly absorbed by our eyes and maximum power is reduced to make eye safety. At much high level power 1550 nm lasers have eye safety since the wavelength is not focussed to eyes. The detector technologies are not so developed and wavelengths are commonly used at longer ranges with less accuracy. Laser setting involves laser repetition rate checks speed of data collection. Laser cavity length, number of passes need via gain materials are attributed by pulse length. Feasible resolution of target is obtained by shorter pulses giving LIDAR receiver detectors and electronics with sufficient bandwith.
2. Optics and scanner: Faster images may be developed having affected too by the speed at scanning rate of system. Scanning of azimuth and elevation alongwith dual oscillating plane mirrors, combined with polygon mirror and dual exis scanner are several options. Range and angular resolution is affected byoptic choices. A return signal is collected via hole mirror/beam splitter are more option.
3. **Photodetector and receiver electronics**: LIDAR uses two main photodetector technologies like silicon avalanche photobodies/ photomultipliers. In RADAR design sensivity of receiver is one parameter balances.
4. **Position and navigation systems**: LIDAR sensors in mobile platforms like airplanes or satellites need setting the absolute position and direction of sensor. This device commonly involves GPS receiver and inertial measurement unit.

Applications of LIDAR

In Agriculture and Allied Sectors

Research scientists of agriculture have already developed a way to include LIDAR for rating yield of field. The technic guide to growers for identifying different land yields prediction. LIDAR helps in determining the precise rate of application of costlier inputs, it can create topological map, slope direction and direction of solar exposure in farms. This technology is valuable for farmers if it is used in field with expensive inputs. Airborne LIDAR systems can be used in canopy height, biomass of plants and area of leaf measurement. Topographical map including resource indication, direction and prediction may also be created from LIDAR.

Geology and Soil Science

Watershed related information like river terraces and river banks, topographical differences beneath the canopy of plants, higher resolve spatial output of elevation and change in landscape. Some important features such as fault and uplift can be detected by aircraft-based LIDAR and GPS together.

List of Top Sources of Free Remote Sensing Data

The high quality remote sensing data are needed for sky rocketing with wave of remote sensing application and several research can be performed day by day. Each RS analysis revolves around the data having specified resolution, portion and sensor which should be free of cost. Below listed some top level remote sensing data.

License, source and operating system support

GIS software	Free software	Open source	Windows	Mac OSX	Linux	Web	Other
ArcGIS	Viewer (s)	No	Yes	No	Yes	Yes	Google Earth Plugin, KML, WMS
Autodesk	Viewer (s)	No	Yes	No	Yes	Yes	No
Cadcorp	Viewer (s)	No	Yes	No	No	Yes	No
CAPAWARE	Yes	Yes	Yes	No	No	No	No
Chameleon	Yes	Yes	Yes	Yes	Yes	AMP	No
Deegree	Yes	Yes	Java	Java	Java	Yes	No
Erdas Imagine	Viewers &	No	Yes	No	No	Yes	No
GeoBase - Telogis	Trial	No	Yes	No	Yes	Yes	Traffic, WMS ADAS, Routing
GeoNetwork	Yes	Yes	Java	Java	Java	Yes	No
GeoServer	Yes	Yes	Java	Java	Java	Java	No
GeoTools	Yes	Yes	Java	Java	Java	No	No
GRASS	Yes	Yes	Yes	Yes	Yes	via py WPS	No
GVSIG	Yes	Yes	Java	Java	Java	No	No
IDRISI	No	No	Yes	No	No	No	No
ILOG J Views Maps	Viewer (s)	No	Java	Java	Java	Java & DHTML /Ajax	No
ILWIS	Yes	Yes	Yes	No	No	No	No
Intergraph	Viewer (s)	No	Yes	No	No	Yes	KML
JUMP GIS	Yes	Yes	Java	Java	Java	No	No

Kosmo	Yes	Yes	Java	Java	Java	No	No
Land Serf	No	No	Java	Java	Java	No	No
Map Dot Net	No	No	Yes	No	No	Yes	
Manifold System	No	No	Yes	No	No	Yes	No
Microsoft Map Point	Discont-inued	No	Yes	No	No	Yes	No
Pitney Bowes MapInfo Pro	Viewer (s)	No	Yes	No	No	Yes	No
MapServer	Yes	Yes	Yes	Yes	Yes	AMP	No
Maptitude Caliper software	No	No	Yes	No	No	Yes	No
MapWindow GIS	Yes	Yes	Yes	No	No	No	No
Oracle Spatial	No	No	Yes	Yes	Yes	Yes	No
Panorama	No	No	"GIS Map 2005"	No	"GIS Pano-rama"	No	No
PostGIS	Yes	Yes	Yes	Yes	Yes	Yes	No
QGIS	Yes	Yes	Yes	Yes	Yes	Yes	Google Earth Plugin, KML, WMS
RegioGraph	No	No	Yes	No	No	No	No
RemoteView	No	No	Yes	No	No	No	No
SAGA GIS	Yes	Yes	Yes	Yes	Yes	No	KLM
SAP HANA	Free Trial	No	No	No	Yes	Yes	No
Small world	No	Yes	Yes	No	Yes	Read-only	OLE, XML, Multiuser, Utility Data Model, Data Translator export/import
SPRING	Yes	Yes	Yes	No	Yes	No	No
Terra Lib Terra View	Yes	Yes	Yes	No	Yes	No	No
TNTmips	Viewer (s)	No	Yes	Yes	Yes	No	No
Trans Modeler Caliper Software	No	No	Yes	No	No	No	No
UDIG	Yes	Yes	Java	Java	Java	No	No

Remote Sensing in Morphology

Surface morphology is a part of study offers direct form of interspectation from satellite images. The aerial photograph with acquired forward overlap generally gives third dimension of height, which supports to perfect interpretation with morphology. Land surface morphology exist and later than geology although geology is combined with many processes of geoscience. Genesis of relief forms on surface of earth crust is dealt with geomorphology, even some natural process are directly responses to farm surface of earth. Remote sensing can be a effective tools in this study, satellite images possesses combined information of whole study which connects ecology and its impact of human activities on natural landscape.

Geomorphology

Basic Concepts

Earth surface differes due to many of the processes of hypogenous or endogenous which include diastrophism i.e. deformation of land surface creates geological structures, techtonic activity and also the process of volcanism in formation of landforms. The present form of modification is due to generation of earth surface by external factors like erosion and sedimentation phenomenon of water, wind and glacier. Apart from these processes, these are governed by gravitational movement and weathering to ocean-land interaction as a result the forms of land owing to waves, tides, current and many physical processes. Climate plays vital role in shaping of earth's surface due to processes these work on surface materials which behave differently with various climatic zones (Van Westen, 1994).

LIDAR utilizes ultraviolet, NIR (Near Infrared) or visible light to image objects and may be associated with wide range of targets, even non-metalic targets, rocks, rain, chemicals, clouds, aerosol and single molecules. The LIDAR technologies have been extremely used in atmospheric and metereological research. From 10 micrometers to 250 nm (Ultraviolet) wavelength are used for targets and backscattering is occurred afterwards typically. Here Rayleigh scattering and flourscence are also used for this purpose. Atmospheric components are mapped using suitable combinations of wavelengths by viewing wavelength based changes of returned signal.

Case Studies using GIS and Remote Sensing Techniques

1. Change study on spatio-temporal dynamics of city environ using remote sensing and GIS

The population data of Jagdalpur city was collected from Municipal Corporation of Jagdalpur city for the year 1981, 1991 and 2011. The Survey of India (SOI) toposheets of 1:50,000 scales for the year 1981 been registered in GIS as referred data and taken to map the extent of urban expansion. Zone maps of urban development by Jagdalpur registered and digitized in GIS analyzing the urban for the year 1990 and 2018. To map and monitor the urban sprawl of the city and its environs, Landsat 5 Thematic Mapper data (30 m) of 9th December 1990 and 15th September 2018 were download from USGS Earth Explorer (USGS, 2018) and analyzed to change dynamics of land use/land cover of Jagdalpur city and its environs for the year 1990 and 2018. For validating the results, survey was planned in the study area during February 2018 and portable Global Positing System (GPS) based field information was collected. The Google earth images were widely used to label the classes and validation with the field survey.

Image Classification Based on GIS Analysis

Prior to analyze, the subset of images for the study area were created from Landsat 5 TM images for the year 1990 and 2018 to categorize. Primarily, the size of the feature is adjusted by the scale parameter, which determines the maximum allowable heterogeneity of the targets and the shape depends on segmentation parameters and smaller objects are merged into larger ones. This continued until the targets reach a maximum allowed heterogeneity. The vector layer of segments generated along with layer of statistics were taken from ArcGIS (ver 10.3) using overlay, integration, change detection, area calculation and land cover classes. Hence, land use refers to the various uses are done on water bodies, habitat, dense forest, low dense habitat, scrub forest, vacant lands, cultivated lands, low dense forest and others resulting due to land use change have been mapped and measured in around the city. In the United Kingdom, residential development with less than 20 dwelling units/ha is considered low density and 60 dwelling units/ha is considered high density (TCPA, 2003). Area analysis for different classes were carried out in ArcGIS to assess the spatio-temporal dynamics of land use classes for the year 1990 and 2018. GPS based field survey was conducted in the study area and collected filed data for about 75 sampling locations covering all land use classes. Kappa coefficient (k), a discrete multivariate technique (Cohen, 1960) was used to assess the accuracy of the results obtained through analysis of Landsat 5 TM data.

Cohen's kappak = Po-Pe/1-Pe

Where: Po = observed agreement and Pe = chance agreement. The Kappa statistic varies from 0 to 1, where 0 = agreement equivalent to chance 0.1-0.20 = slight agreement, 0.21-0.40 = fair agreement, 0.41-0.60 = moderate agreement, 0.61-0.80 = substantial agreement, 0.81-0.99 = near perfect agreement and 1 = perfect agreement.

Status of Urban Sprawl in 1981

Data from City Municipal Corporation, were assessed that the urban area of Jagdalpur city in the year 1981 was about 636.88 ha. The urban spread boundary of 1981 was overlaid on the SOI Toposheet of 1990 in GIS to find the extent of urban sprawl. The map exhibits that the urban area was mainly dwelled to the centre of palace. The development of linear growth has been seen in the eastern part of Jagdalpur city in Adawal towards Jaypore road connects Odisha.

Status of Urban Sprawl in 1990

The analysis of Landsat 5 TM data (30 m) based analysis for the year 1990 clearly denoted about the development of urban spreading at the cost of permanent fallows and out skirt agriculture areas. The extent of urban area in the year 1990 shows that it was in all the directions more specific in southern and western parts of the city. High dense settlements have been mainly observed in southern part of the city. Vacant lands occupied predominantly in western and eastern area of the Jagdalpur city with an area of 19.38 per cent of TGA. Analysis of out skirt cultivated lands of Jagdalpur city, area expansion noticed in northern and southern parts with an area of 10.10 and 8.0 per cent of TGA. The analysis of Landsat 5 TM data of 1990 also indicates that the development of industrial area near new bus station as development of bypass highway in the part. Habitat development might be observed in the western part of Jagdalpur city covering Dharmpura, which has become an educational hub with various new Engineering college came up in this period.

Status of Urban Sprawl in 2018

Vacant lands mainly noticed in western and southern parts with an area of 13.5 per cent and rainfed rice occupied mainly in conjunction of western and southern parts of city with an occupy 8.0 per cent of TGA. 2000 onwards, the western part of city has been developed as educational hub and opening of Medical college in southern part again gained momentum for constructing colonies and purchasing vacant and cultivated lands. Eastern part of the city has been recognized for NMDC at Nagarnar suddenly expanded settlement by covering cultivated lands into godown, market, rental houses etc. The low dense settlements have been developed along Asna area of Jagdalpur city due to Indrawati river as administrative barrier in northern side.

Urban Sprawl of Jagdalpur City between 1990 and 2018

The spatial alongwith temporal change in land use pattern over 1990 to 2018 has been observed that the more area occupied by vacant lands, low dense forest and scrub forest with 19.8, 15.9 and 15.3%, respectively in imageries of 1990 which is changed with 2018, first three classes occupied more area by low dense habitat (21.9%), habitat (19.2%) and vacant lands (13.5%); however, lowest (6.3%) under dense forest. These change in land use due to more colony development and expansion of Jagdalpur city in west and south direction alongwith educational hub as a part transformed large area in residential area tag conversion of cultivated lands over the period of time. Negative change has been mapped in dense forest, scrub forest, low dense forest, vacant lands, cultivated lands, in which high degree of negative change observed with vacant lands (-6.27%) and less in dense forest (-1.29%), low habitat occupied more area of Jagdalpur in all directions of encroachment reaching 7.21%.

Analysis of low dense habitat area shows that significant area has been increased from 14.3 to 21.9 per cent of TGA during 1990 to 2018. It was the expansion in all directions of Jagdalpur city at the cost of vacant land deptation. Analysis shows that dense habitat spread around the Jagdalpur city and predominantly it consists of settlement areas, which are coming up on cultivated areas and vacant lands. Development of new colonies and establishment of educational institutes in out skirt region increased the low dense habitat around the Jagdalpur city. The cultivated area has been reduced significantly from 10.1 to 8.0 per cent of TGA due to development of commercial and residential areas. The vacant lands are main targeted area in western parts of the city occupying 19.8 per cent in the year 1990, whereas, it has been found considerably decreased 13.5 per cent in the year 2018. The degraded scrubland areas have been considerably decreased from 15.3 per cent in 1990 to 12.1 per cent in the year 2018 and confined to southern and northern parts. The area under water bodies occupies 4.9 per cent in 1990 and been slightly increased to 7.3 per cent in the year 2018 and in absolute terms gained the area from digging soil for construction works on vacant lands. It is observed that the eastern and southern sides of the city have recorded more urban growth in 2018 as compared to the urban growth noticed in the year 1990. In the context of upcoming mega construction, many industrial, educational building and residential colonies emerging up, future growth of urban landscape of Jagdalpur city is likely to be rapid in east and west.

Assessment of Urban Sprawl Across Urban Development

The majority of habitats are in core area of city, whereas in the year 2018 area under these settlements has been increased considerably in all directions. Heart of the city is considered as central part near to palace, agglomeration has risen in both 1990 and 2018, but southern-eastern location occupied by low dense habitat and similar change found in south-western parts. In southern-eastern and southern-western part of Jagdalpur city, drastic change have been taken place with habitat from 1990 to 2018, due to more cultivated and vacant lands converted into institutional and habitat rapidly and eastern-southern has newly developed sector curbing most of the area under NMDC (National Mineral Development Corporation) which indirectly increased the habitat, rental houses and purchasing lands for business.

Accuracy Assessment and Validation

Accuracy assessment and validation was done by generating error matrix whether the land use classes of 2018 were correctly classified or not. This process was carried out using 75 field survey points gathered during field survey, which projected to one of eight classes, as summarized. Kappa coefficient value of 0.75 indicates that an observed classification is in near substantial agreement. The overall accuracies were 76.02 per cent. User's accuracy of individual classes was considerably high and it found higher than 64 per cent. Whereas, the producer's accuracy of individual classes ranging from 45.0 to 82 per cent. Analysis shows that the classes like habitat, cultivated area, forest, vacant land and waterbodies were mapped due to their distinct pattern and compactness. Whereas, the classes like low dense habitat, low dense forest, dense forest and scrub forest have shown slight ambiguity in identification of classification. The contributing factors of the misclassification includes similar spectral information, class areas smaller than the spatial resolution have been mapped in detail with survey data.

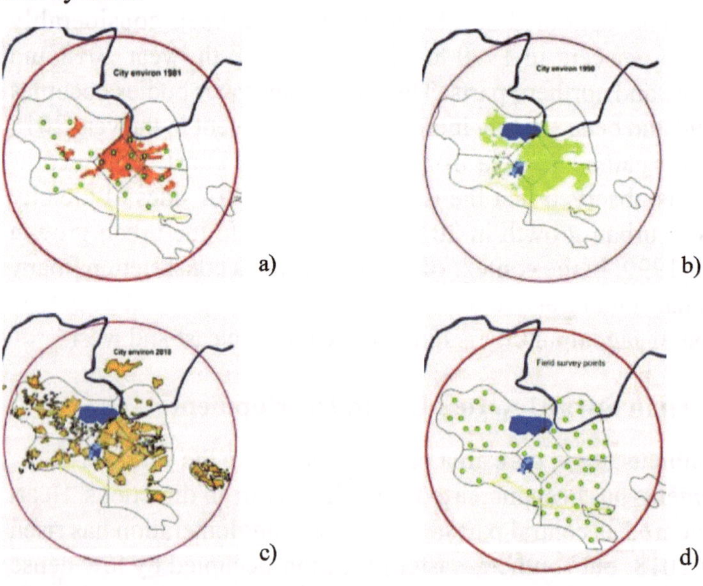

Fig. 5: Spatio-temporal dynamics of urban sprawl of Jagdalpur city during 1981(a), 1990 (b) and 2018 (c) and field survey points (d)

Precipitation

Perfect measurement of precipitation is a prospective goal in meteorological research and regular requirement of hydrology which depends precisely on the obtained data for modeling. The most precise method of determining a real precipitation is ground radar-based radar. Satellite images from GOES, NOAA, TIROS-N, TRMM and NIMBUS explored new types of data on clouds and frontal systems.

A. In thick clouds (1.0km) rain is possible when the upper surface of the cloud is at less that -15°C.

B. The probability of rain is inversely proportional to the temperature of the upper surface of the cloud.

C. Precipitation intensity is directly proportional to the area of the upper surface of the cloud at temperature of less than -15°C.

Surface Water: Best application of remote sensing in water resources is the mapping surface water bodies, like streams, lakes, tank, marshes and bogs, within a given region. The area covered with open water is easily delineated by remote-sensing techniques because of the specific radiation characteristics of water. The delineation of floods in vegetation-covered areas is more difficult, but it can be obtained either with radar or in combination of radiation and topographic information. RS data obtained on flood area is characterized by combining data on flood and flood plain for mapping and delineating flood management. Flood plain projection for assessing damage area in correlation to amount of rain predicted by remote sensing is playing as useful tool through characteristics of river channel width, depth, roughness, degree of tortuousity and braiding can also be available from remote-sensing surveys.

2. Study of groundwater potentiality in rainfed plateau of Chhattisgarh using remote sensing and GIS

Data on underground water is useful in water resource development which includes availability of potential and non-potential aquifers of the region, depth, quantity alongwith quality, recharging rate of particular aquifer, impact of pumping on land scarce, aquifer extent, recharging location alongwith discharge areas and balance between withdrawal and natural discharge into rivers. Basically storage capacity depends on properties of areas. Under ground water creates the base flow for the streams which is source of water for springs and seeps (From seepage of water).

To assess groundwater potential zones, the methodology for the present research work is designed using multi-parametric data set like conventional maps from secondary source *viz.* topographic maps, rainfall data, geological map etc. and RS information. RS information is used directly for thematic map preparation which includes geomorphology, drainage density, rainfall, lithology, lineament density, slope and LULC (Sreedevi *et al.*, 2001). The areas of interest in the present study were marked from the SRTM images, and DEM and topographic sheets of the Survey of India (SoI) using ERDAS Imagine options. The DEM was received from SRTM {(US Geological Survey (USGS) website (www.earthexplorar.usgs.gov update 2016 with 30 m resolution)}. An integrated approach of multi-spectral satellite data, DEM and topographical sheets of the Survey of India are for database preparation and parametric calculation of the tract as geomorphic feature, lithology, LULC (Thomas *et al.*, 2009). Input variables are extracted from RS information and secondary data with GIS software packages (Mark, 1984). The Landsat 8 satellite (November 2018) image was taken to produce and update the thematic information of the tract using Spatial Analyst Tool of Arc GIS 10.3. In the present study of lithology, parent material of soil is considered as an important factor. Hence, geomorphological data are obtained from USGS, and slope values are obtained from SRTM-DEM using spatial analyst tool (Harinarayana *et al.*, 2000). The drainage map is prepared using Topographic Sheets of SoI and DEM from which drainage density is determined by spatial analyst tool in Arc GIS. Inverse Distance Weight (IDW) interpolation of rainfall data from seven rain-gauge stations (RGS) of block level data from Tehsil administrative unit collected for preparation of rainfall map. All analysis is rectified and then geo-referenced by Universal Transverse Mercator (UTM) coordinate projection and the World Geodetic System (WGS84) datum considering the Ground Control Points (GCPs). To determine groundwater potential track of the present study area, each of the six different thematic layers (geomorphology, drainage density, rainfall, lithology, lineament density, slope and LULC) were integrated applying the weighted overly method of ArcGIS software (Fenta *et al.*, 2015; Waikar and Nilawar, 2014 and Rose and Krishnan, 2009). As variables like classes, weights, ranks for the thematic layers have different impacts in delineating groundwater occurrence and movement, so for their computation of GIS-based multi-criteria evaluation based on Analytical Hierarchy Process (AHP) (Eastman, 1996; Flug *et al.*, 2000) is used. The Maximum Likelihood Classification (MLC) method is applied and normal land use categories are identified with reference to their water requirement (cultivated land, settlement and water bodies like wet land, pond, river etc.). Finally, the groundwater potentiality (GP) is calculated as follows (Fenta *et al.*, 2015): Groundwater Potential = 0.31 Lithology + 0.20 Lineament density + 0.15 Geomorphology + 0.14 Slope + 0.10 Drainage density + 0.06 Rainfall + 0.04 Land use/Land cover.

The Weighted Linear Combination (WLC) method approach to club thematic layers is the steps used for delineating groundwater potential zones (Obi Reddy *et al.*, 2000). The relative importance of each class in the same map and thematic maps are analysed to compare with others by pair-wise comparison matrices and each criterion is compared with other on Saaty's scale from 1 to 9, where value 1 for equal, 3 for moderate, 5 for strong, 7 for very strong, 2, 4, 6 and 8 for intermediate, and 9 for extreme importance of one factor compared to the other one. Saaty's ratio indexes (RI) for different n values representing lithology, lineament density, geomorphology etc. are given Table 1. Accordingly to Saaty (1980), the judgments of the pair-wise comparison within each thematic layer are acceptable i.e., less than 0.10.

Table 1: Saaty's ratio index (RI) for different values of n (Saaty, 1980)

n	**1**	**2**	**3**	**4**	**5**	**6**	**7**	**8**	**9**	**10**
RI	0	0	0.58	0.89	1.12	1.24	1.32	1.41	1.45	1.49

In the study, sensitivity analysis for the influence of rates and weights assigned to each class and thematic layer on the output has been performed through map-removal (Lodwick *et al.*, 1990) and single parameter (Napolitano and Fabbri, 1996) techniques. The geomorphology, drainage density, annual rainfall and lineament density classes are given in Table 2 and 3.

Table 2: Comparison matrix classes for geomorphology with consistency ratio (CR)

Geomorphology (CR = 0.002)	**SC**	**DC**	**BSc**	**Co**	**FS**	**MDF**	**Ri**	**VDF**	**Wt**
Structural origin-low dissected hills and valley	1	7	5	7	2	1	5	2	0.27
Structural origin-low dissected hills and valley		1	8	4	8	4	7	8	0.19
Structural origin-moderate dissected hills and valley			1	5	3	6	2	3	0.14
Structural origin-highly dissected hills and valley				1	9	5	3	5	0.14
Denudational origin-pediment pediplain complex					1	7	5	2	0.11
Denudational origin-low dissected hills and valley						1	7	4	0.08
Denudational origin-moderate dissected hills & valley							1	9	0.04
Fluvial origin active flood plain								1	0.03

Table 3: Comparison matrix classes with consistency ratio (CR)

Comparison matrix	L	LD	Ge	S	Dd	Rf	LULC	Weight
Lithology (L)	1	2	3	5	6	8	9	0.31
Lineament density (LD)		1	2	3	5	6	8	0.2
Geomorphology (Ge)			1	2	3	4	6	0.15
Slope (S)				1	2	3	5	0.14
Drainage density (Dd)					1	2	3	0.1
Rainfall (Rf)						1	2	0.06
Land use Land cover (LULC)							1	0.04

Evaluation of Physical Factors Controlling Groundwater Occurrence

Geomorphology

Based on suitability of groundwater occurrence, the ranking of the geomorphological units of the study area is as: smooth plain > smooth to irregular plain > moderately irregular > irregular plain and highly irregular. The geomorphological classes along with rates are given in Fig. 1 and Table 2. The highly irregular to irregular plain mostly covers the study area have less impact in occurrence of groundwater and leads barrier to the delineation of hydromorphological usefulness (Dey, 2014).

Drainage Density (Dd)

The drainage map of the area is prepared with the help of topographic maps (scale: 1:50,000) and SRTM-DEM, and its Dd values ranges from 0.012 to 0.035 km/km^2. The most values of the drainage density ranges from 0.010 to 0.015 km/km^2 indicates inverse function of permeability. The high drainage density value of the area indicates poor potentiality of groundwater prevalence. The Track possesses dendritic and parallel drainage pattern which are generally characterized by a tree like drain channels with less homogeneity and uniformity. Based on cording to Sener *et al.* (2005) and Hammouri *et al.* (2012), the drainage density map is classified into six classes using equal interval and the corresponding rates are shown in Table 4 and Fig. 3. The drainage pattern in this area indicates scope of loss of major portion of runoff water with less infiltration capacity of surface soil to recharge the groundwater, and shows that less potentiality for ground water.

Table 4: Comparison matrix classes for Drainage density with consistency ratio (CR)

Drainage density (CR=0.083)	D1	D2	D3	D4	D5	D6	Weight
0.012-0.050 (D1)	1	1	1	2	3	3	0.54
0.050-0.010 (D2)		1	1	1	1	2	0.36
0.010-0.015 (D3)			1	1	2	3	0.54
0.015-0.020 (D4)				1	2	2	0.36
0.020-0.025 (D5)					1	4	0.72
0.025-0.035 (D6)						1	0.18

Rainfall

The rainfall map of the area taken under study was classified into six categories based on rainfall quantity (Table 5 and Fig 2). In general comparatively less annual amount of rainfall indicates low groundwater potentiality, so the low rainfall area should be given less weighted value than that of the high rainfall while considering the groundwater potentiality.

Table 5: Comparison matrix classes for rainfall with consistency ratio (CR)

Rainfall (CR = 0.081)	A	B	C	D	E	F	Weight
1200-1300 (A)	1	3	1.5	1.5	0.75	0.75	0.24
1300-1400 (B)		1	2	1.5	0.5	0.5	0.15
1400-1500 (C)			1	1	3	2	0.22
1500-1600 (D)				1	2	4	0.2
1600-1700 (E)					1	4	0.19
1700-1800 (F)						1	0.13

Lineament Density

Lineament density map is computed from lineaments produced by edge enhancement of the Landsat ETM+ panchromatic band (band 8) and varies from 0.00 to 0.017 km /km ^{2}. Based on equal-interval classification, the lineament density map is classified into five classes and shown in Fig. 5.

Lithology

The Lithic Ustorthents (LU) lithological unit mainly covers the area, and followed by the Typic Haplusterpts (THp), Typic Haplusterts (THt) and Typic Rhodustalfs (TRh) etc. including water bodies. Based on the hydraulic properties, the lithological classes are ranked as: Typic Haplusterpts (THp) > Lithic Haplustepts (LHa) > Chromic Haplusterts (CHa) and Lithic Ustorthents (LU) > Typic

Haplusterpts (THp) > Typic Rhodustalfs (TRh). The lithology map and rates for lithological classes in the study area are shown in Table 6.

Table 6: Comparison matrix classes for lithology with consistency ratio (CR)

Lithology (CR = 0.093)	THt	THi	THp	LU	TRh	CHa	LHa	Weight
Typic Haplusterts (THt)	1	1	1	2	3	3	4	0.19
Typic Haplustalts (THl)		1	1	1	1	2	3	0.13
Typic Haplusterpts (THp)			1	1	2	3	1	0.21
Lithic Ustorthents (LU)				1	2	2	4	0.30
Typic Rhodustalfs (TRh)					1	4	2	0.17
Chromic Haplusterts (CHa)						1	4	0.14
Lithic Haplustepts (LHa)							1	0.09

Slope

The major part of the study falls under plain to gentle slope. It is observed that the most of the area has slope value of 0-30%, so mostly flat to gentle slope cannot be designated as so 'good' category practically for groundwater occurrence because of less favoured infiltration capacity of top soil with respect to time of retention of runoff water on the other side. Fig. 4 and Table 7 show the classified slope map and the corresponding rates respectively of the area.

Table 7: Comparison matrix classes for slope with consistency ratio (CR)

Slope (CR = 0.059)	01-Mar	03-Aug	Aug-15	15-30	30-50	Weight
01-Mar	1	3	0.8	0.8	0.4	0.24
03-Aug		1	0.5	0.15	0.15	0.12
Aug-15			1	1	0.25	0.21
15-30				1	3	0.15
30 or more					1	0.09

Land use/Land Cover

In the present study, the land use pattern and their spatial variation is assessed from satellite data of Landsat-8 November 2018 (30 m spatial resolution). Here standard approach is applied using Erdas Imagine 9.1 software starting from defining the training sites, extraction of signatures from the image and then classification is made. In present study, the ETM+ image with a band combination of 4 (near infrared), 3 (red) and 2 (green) is used to classify into the LULC classes. The LULCs of the area are identified has 31% cultivated land, 15% concrete, barren scrub and forest scrub covers 12% each with 11% of moderately dense forest and needs extraction of huge amount of groundwater almost round the year (except few 2 - 3 months) in this rainfed area. The crop cultivation in the area is characteristically seasonal due to rainfed system of farming and groundwater based irrigation practice is particularly increases. The classified LULC map and their corresponding rates are shown in Fig. 6 and Table 8. As the major part of the track comes under cultivated land, it needs supports for groundwater abstraction and its sustainable management (Pratap *et al.*, 2000).

Table 8: Comparison matrix classes for LULC with consistency ratio (CR)

LULC (CR = 0.096)	SC	DC	BSc	Co	FS	MDF	Ri	VDF	WB	Weight
Agriculture (SC)	1	1	1	2	3	3	4	5	5	0.16
Agriculture (DC)		1	1	1	1	2	3	4	3	0.15
Barren Scrub (BSc)			1	1	2	3	1	4	3	0.12
Concrete (Co)				1	2	2	4	6	3	0.15
Forest Scrub (FS)					1	4	2	5	5	0.12
Moderately Dense Forest (MDF)						1	4	3	5	0.11
River (Ri)							1	3	3	0.07
Very Dense Forest (VDF)								1	4	0.05
Water Body (WB)									1	0.07

Identification of Groundwater Potential Zones

For the seven thematic layers, the consistency ratio (CR) ranges from 0.002 to 0.096. To achieve the priority thematic layer used for delineation of groundwater potential zones of study area, the pair-wise comparison matrix among the thematic layers are calculated (Table 7). Based on associated weights, four most influencing factors are 31% lithology + 20% lineament density + 15% geomorphology + 14% slope + 10% drainage density + 6% rainfall + 4% land use/land cover were identified. Accordingly, the groundwater potentiality zonation map of the study area prepared from the thematic layers and is classified as very poor, poor, moderate, high and very high GP zones (Fig. 7) which indicate that out of the total study area with very high, high, moderate, poor and very poor groundwater potentiality comprises 2185.43 km^2, 519.35 km^2, 239.98 km^2, 1084.90 km^2 and 0.34km^2 that covers 54.23%, 12.89%, 5.95%, 26.92 and 0.01% area, respectively. The groundwater potentiality zonation map shows that poor to very poor zones prominent in the Tract with highly irregular to irregular plain and high drainage density (Jaiswal *et al.*, 2003; Machiwal *et al.*, 2011). In these zones of less rainfall, mostly flat to gentle slope land area with low surface soil infiltration capacity of runoff water to recharge groundwater has effect on groundwater potentiality. The crop cultivation in the area mainly depends on rainfall where surface lithology is characterized mostly by undulating plain of promotes moderate infiltration to groundwater resource, followed by Lithic Ustorthents (LU) lithological unit mainly covers the area, and followed by Typic Haplusterpts (THp), Typic Haplusterts (THt) and Typic Rhodustalfs (TRh) etc.

Table 9: Statistics of map-removal sensitivity analysis

Sensitivity analysis	Validation index (%)			
	Min	Max	Mean	Std Dev (SD)
Drainage density	0	7	1.086	0.227
Geomorphology	0	8	1.128	2.007
Land use land cover	0	7	2.124	1.224
Lineament density	0	8	1.89	0.125
Lithology	0	9	2.105	0.234
Rainfall	0	9	2.083	0.156
Slope	0	3	1.5	0.135

Table 10: Statistics of single-parameters sensitivity analysis

Single-parameters	Empirical weight (%)	Min	Max	Mean	Std Dev (SD)
Lithology (L)	31	4	60	23.46	14.03
Lineament density (LD)	20	6	59	23.16	13.10
Geomorphology (Ge)	15	3	48	18.84	3.45
Slope (S)	14	6	38	14.91	0.07
Drainage density (Dd)	10	1	27	10.6	2.27
Rainfall (Rf)	6	1.5	19	7.46	7.78
Land use Land cover (LULC)	4.5	1	4	1.57	0.97

The results sensitivity analysis using map removal techniques for groundwater potentiality zonation is highly varied due to possible removal of lineament density from the computation with Mean Variation Index (MVI) value of 1.890% that may be mainly contributed to relatively higher weight assigned to the lithology layer with Empirical Mean Weight (EMW) value of 23.16% (Table 5). The groundwater potential map is moderately sensitive to rainfall with MVI value of 2.083; however, it is less sensitive to LULC, geomorphology, drainage density, slope and lithology with respective MVI value of 2.124, 1.128, 1.086, 1.500 and 2.105, respectively (Table 9). The variation in index of single thematic layer only depends on the rate and weight. The sensitivity analysis using single-parameter map removal techniques shows deviations from the effective weights in comparison to the empirical weights. Similar to the map-removal technique, the single parameter technique indicates lithology as most effective parameter in the groundwater potentiality study in the study area with the Mean Effective Weight (MEW) value of 23.46%, and followed by lineament density, geomorphology, slope, drainage density, rainfall and LULC with EW value of 23.16%, 18.84%, 14.91%, 10.60%, 7.46%, 1.57%, respectively with responding EMW values of 20%, 15%, 14%, 10%, 6% and 4%. The MEW and EMW values of geomorphology, slope and drainage density are close to each other.

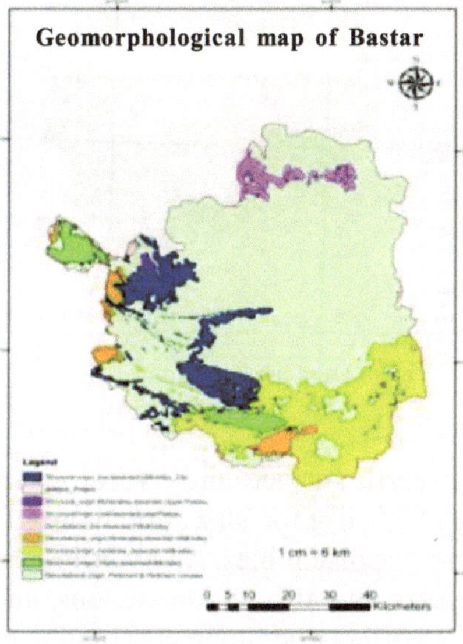

Fig. 1. Geomorphologic Map

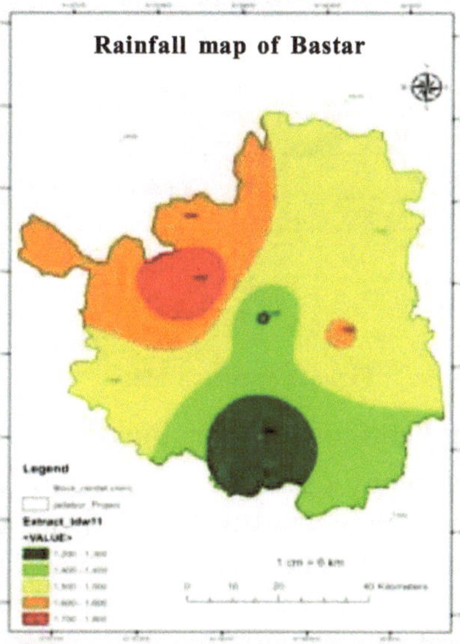

Fig. 2. Rainfall Map

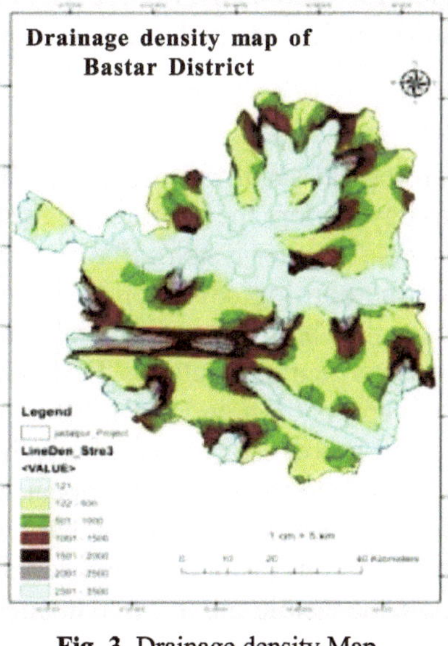

Fig. 3. Drainage density Map

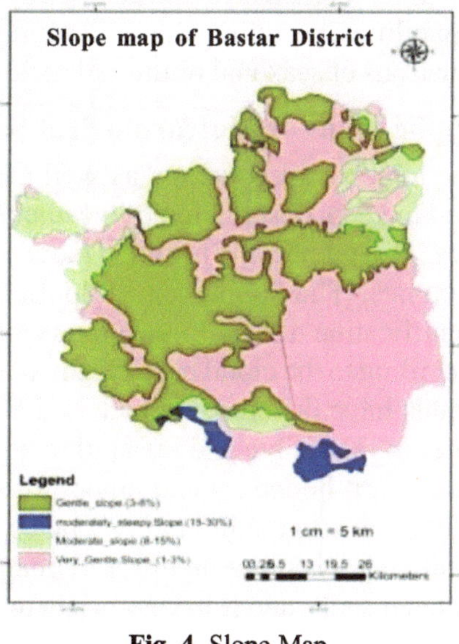

Fig. 4. Slope Map

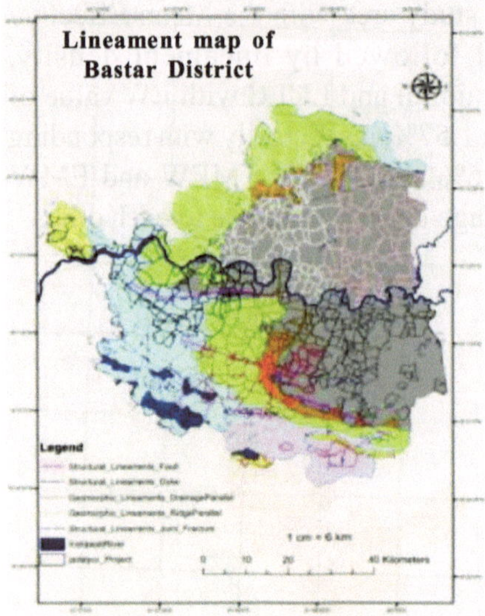

Fig. 5. Lineament Map

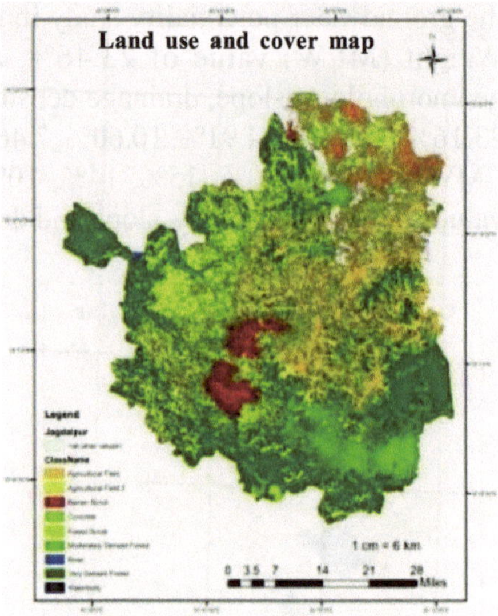

Fig. 6. Land use & Land use Map

Applications in Hydrology

Hydrology deals the water behavior with earth surface and hydrology is prominently concerned to many applications of RS, like forestry, agriculture and land cover, because water is a main factor in these disciplines. All hydrological processes are dynamic, not only between years, but also within seasons, and therefore it requires frequent observations. RS offers a common observation of the spatial distribution of hydrological concept, often enriches ground water resource. Radar has revolutionized hydrological research with its active sensing capabilities, permiting the time window of image to include inclement weather situations or seasonal or diurnal darkness.

Applications of Meteorological Satellites

The huge aerial coverage as well as meteorological satellite images may be used to keep, observation of weather systems days before they come near to an area. This is specially useful in monitoring adverse weather systems like tropical cyclones. The fundamental application of meteorological satellite is for identification of clouds and clouds may be broadly classified into three classes according to the cloud base height, namely, various degrees of clouds. Different clouds have different characteristics in shape and pattern and have different tones in the visible and infrared images. Fog and low dense clouds are seen by their sharp boundary and smooth texture on satellite image. They appear in bright white to medium gray tone on the visible image, but they show dark to medium gray colour on infrared image. Cumulonimbus (Thundery) appears in globular shape and is in very bright tone on both the visible and infrared images. In addition, meteorological satellites are widely used in many areas of applications.

3. Rainfall Variability Study

GIS methodologies

For the preparation of various thematic maps using GIS package, the base maps with correct coordinates were developed the geo-referred places and the errors obtained during the process of digitization were rectified. The map has been projected through geo-referencing techniques. The attribute were created by default for identity of each polygon (blocks). The names of the blocks in the maps entered to facilitate adding the different parameters required to be analyzed. With the help of GIS, the regions have been identified (Singh *et al.*, 2009).

Spatial Interpolation using ArcGIS 10.3

Data on meteorological parameters collected from the blocks were processed in ArcGIS 10.3 for obtaining visual map of rainfall differences. Interpolation was predicted by approximating observation spots. The polygons were interpolated based on data generated through climate analysis in order to obtain reasonable results. The notion of proximity with that of gradual change of the trend surface was used. IDW connected on the assumption that the value at an unsampled location was distance-weighted average of the values from surrounding data points, within a specified window under **Inverse distance weighting (IDW).** The points closest to the prediction locations were assumed to have greater influence on the predicted value than those further away, such that the weight attached to each point was an inverse function of its distance from the target location. Surface interpolation was used for a selected set of all the samples to estimate each of the output grid's cell values in dry spells of the study area (Katyal *et al.*, 1996).

Districts-wise Rainfall of South Chhattisgarh

The water losses from the rice field in the form of evapotranspiration and percolation are to be assumed around 2 to 4 mm/day during the *Kharif* season (Anonumous, 2018). The rainfall accounts about 50 mm/week, which is considered as a stable rainfall period without stress. From mean weekly rainfall of all the seven districts of southern Chhattisgarh for stable rainfall weeks have been computed and depicted in Table 1 and covariance presented in Fig. 1 (b and d). The inception and cessation of such period has been analysed and presented. It is noticed that the duration of stable period varied from 9 weeks in the *Sukma* district to 14 weeks in *Bastar* and *Narayanpur* which were high rainfall region. Rainfall received more than 50 mm/week from 23rd week in Bastar to 26th week in *Kanker* whereas termination started with 38 week in *Dantewada* and 43rd week in *Kondagaon* which are typical rainfed areas (Singh *et al.*, 2008).

Spatial Variability of Crop Productivity

The spatial variability maps of productivity of different districts *viz.*, *Bastar, Sukma, Bijapur, Narayanpur, Dantewada, Kondagaon* and *Kanker* have been prepared and presented as covariance of productivity in Fig.4(a). The coefficient of variability map on productivity shows the regions of sustainable and unsustainable. It is observed from spatial productive map that the lower yields (<2.0 t/ha) has been noticed in the *Dantewada, Sukma* and *Bijapur*, whereas the rest of the districts have high productivity (2.0 t/ha). The coefficient of variability maps indicated that interventions for stable productivity is needed while many of the blocks showed higher variability according to Singh *et al.* (2009). There is a need to develop strategies to make the productivity more sustainable through better management techniques.

The sustainable yield index (SYI) map delineated the sustainable productivity of the blocks shown in Fig. 4(c). It was recorded from plotted map, *Geedam, Jagdalpur, Bastar, Bakawand, Kondagaon, Pharasgaon, Bijapur, Narharpur, Kanker, Bhanupratappur* and *Charama* are sustainable yield index (SYI) in southern part of Chhattisgarh, it may be due to better crop management with extra inputs contributed for enhancing sustainable production. Medium SYI triggered in *Bhopalapatanam, Bijapur, Katekalyan, Dantewada, Tokapal, Lohandiguda, Bhairamgarh, Makadi, Keshkal, Antagarh, Koyalibeda* and *Durgkondal* which are basically pure rainfed blocks and always supported by high rainfall due to surrounding dense forest. *Usur, Konta, Sukma, Chhindgarh, Darbha, Bastanar, Narayanpur* and *Orchha* blocks are remotely located where low inputs based rice cultivation keeps lower the production resulting lower stability yield index.

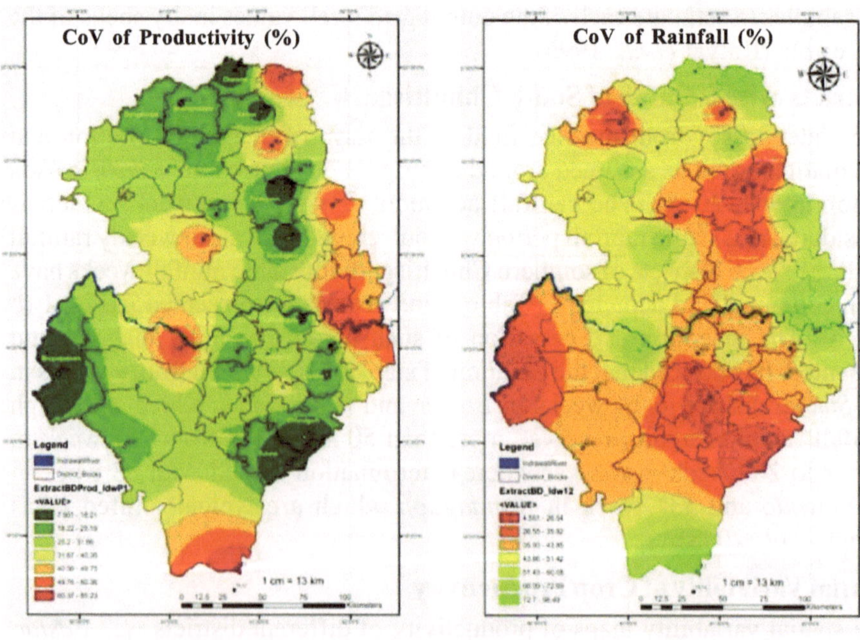

a) b)

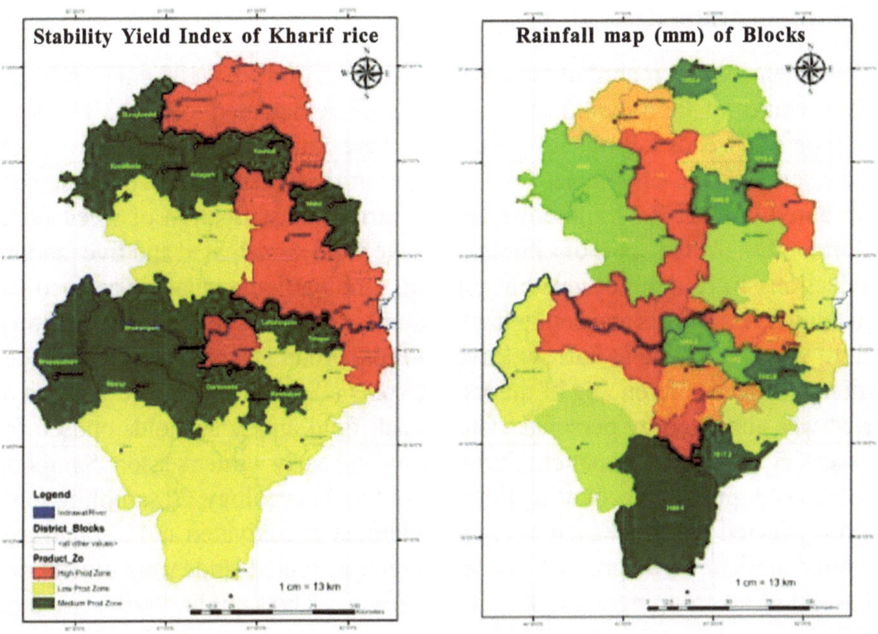

c) d)

Fig. 4. (a-d). Coefficient of variation on productivity (%),rainfall (%), Yield stability index and rainfall map of different blocks of Bastar division in Chhattisgarh

4. Crop, Weeds and Water Resource Planning

Details of the Dam

Kosarteda Medium Irrigation Project (Chhattisgarh) envisaged construction of *Kosarteda* dam across *Kosarted* Nala, a tributary of river Markandi, under Indravati sub-basin of Godavari Basin and is situated near village *Salemeta* in Bastar district of Chhattisgarh, about 54 Km from Jagdalpur in South Chhattisgarh (Fig. 4). The Project began in 1980 but due to non-clearance of forestland falls under submergence it was stopped in 1990-91 from the Ministry of Environment & Forest, Government of India and re-started in the year 2002-03 after approval of diversion of required forestland from Environment & Forest ministry. The Project comprises of an earthen dam 1305 m long with maximum height of 25.60 metres, 155 m long west weir on a saddle on left flank with its crest at 117.70 m is provided with a maximum discharging capacity of 1100 cusec. The canal system has main canal of 24.54 km length with branching of 7.95 km length and head discharge of 10.47 m^3/sec covers area of irrigation in 11120 ha per year with 139% irrigation intensity and 9271 hectare cultivated Command Area, in which Net Irrigated Area is 8000 hectares sprawling in 25 villages.

Sampling Methods

Weed density was recorded by using a quadrat of 100 cm x 100 cm (1 m^2) size from center of the random selected fields of demarcated villages. The total numbers of weeds falling within quadrate were counted species wise from 110 field samples of each villages (n = 22). The entire weed inside the quadrat were uprooted in each field and collected for further classification of weed flora. Randomly selected spots of sampling village were demarcated and five random selections were done by quadrat placing. One particular place was used for placing five quadrats and counted weed number based on species. Further weed flora were classified as narrow leaved weeds, broad leaved weeds and sedges alongwith geo-referencing of the sample spots (Fig. 6). Existing cultivation of rice was surveyed by personal visit to each field and households chosen for assessing diversity and pattern during rainy and early winter season. Sampling method adopted for accounting flora present in that ecology, 22 sampling spots from selected villages which were characterized as cultivated and wetland area from beneficiary villages of Kosarteda dam. Cultivated lands were mostly rice based fallow cropping while kharif-rabi season. The sampling was started on developing as permanent wetlands or crop season wetlands (Fig. 7). Due to rice cultivation, development of wetland area in low lying farming, were isolated by image analysis. According to the shape counting with location of dam covered area and matched the area converted in wetlands (Fig. 8).

Image Analysis

For studying the wetlands scenario of Kosarteda dam, particularly the area of influence under Kosarteda Dam, KOMPSAT 2 high resolution multispectral optical satellite imagery has been used. Four visible optical bands i.e., Blue, Green, Red and Near Infrared were in 4m resolution and one panchromatic band of 1m resolution supplied for developing map. To get the maximum data, we first stacked all the individual spectral bands in a single image file then with help of pan sharpening method in ERDAS Imagine software, generated high resolution (1m) multispectral color imagery merging 4m multispectral imagery with 1m panchromatic imagery. This helped for easier identification of target objects in the imagery. As the RPC data available in the imagery for Geometric correction was not accurate enough, we used external source of GCPs to achieve required accuracy then all the images are mosaicked for the whole area. Actual area of interest (AOI) was clipped from the whole imagery using AOI vector shape file in ERDAS. Further, accuracy of land features is checked with Google Earth images. Attribute fields are populated with appropriate land feature types. Simultaneously scouting to the surveyed and sampled fields were crossed check using prepared map to set the accuracy, which provided reliability of works.

Effect of Land Use

Land use change in dam area comprising catchment, command and storage, further developed wet area and cultivated area in Fig. 7 and 8 depicted about descriptive statistic of land use change and shifting of weed diversity after dam construction. the area of villages was influenced by irrigation and rainfall in expansion of wetlands from 3.14 to 90.75 ha with average of 44.49 ha per village with standard deviation 24.947 ha indicated wide range of variation. Similarly, the change in weed diversity, considering broad leaved, narrow leaved and sedge, over all scenario showed that the composition of weeds changed by population dynamics. Moreover, broad leaved and sedge increased approximately three times than narrow leaved after construction of dam. These features expressed about shifting of narrow leaved weeds by broad leaved weeds as increased wet area cultivation and favoured much to remaining two categories of weeds (Table 2 and 3). The cultivated lands converted into wetland were noticed with drastic change in broad leaved and narrow leaved weeds after dam construction. The all nine variables were varied differently with change in land use pattern after villages came under dam. The high degree of variation was observed in variables of area plots among nine ranging from 5.21 (BLWs) to 36.57 (Cultivated areas). The higher variation was noticed with cultivated area followed by sedge population after dam (31.31).

Covariance matrix among area, wetland, cultivated land and weed composition indicated that the effect of land use change on broad leaved, narrow leaved and sedges (Table 4) were apparent, it is obvious as the wetland increased and decreased in dry aerobic lands over the villages. There were much negative inverse relation between sedge and wetland (before dam); cultivated lands and broad leaved (after dam); cultivated lands and sedge (after and before dam); cultivated land and narrow leaved (after dam); broad leaved weeds and sedge; broad leaved (after dam) and area; cultivated lands and sedge (before dam); narrow leaved weeds (after and before dam) and sedge; sedge and cultivated lands; sedge (after dam) and sedge (before dam).

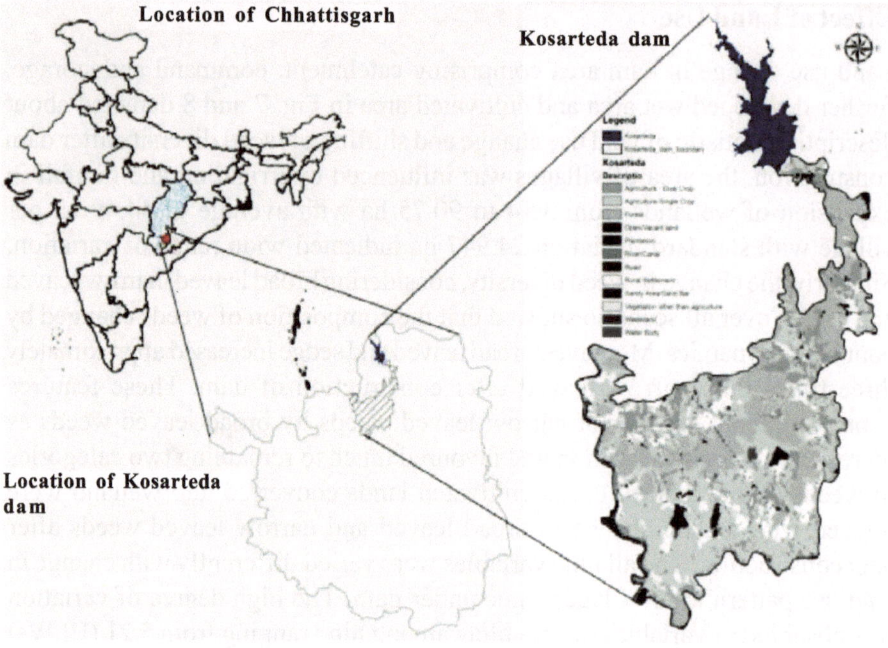

Fig. 5: Study Area of *Kosarteda* Dam in District Map

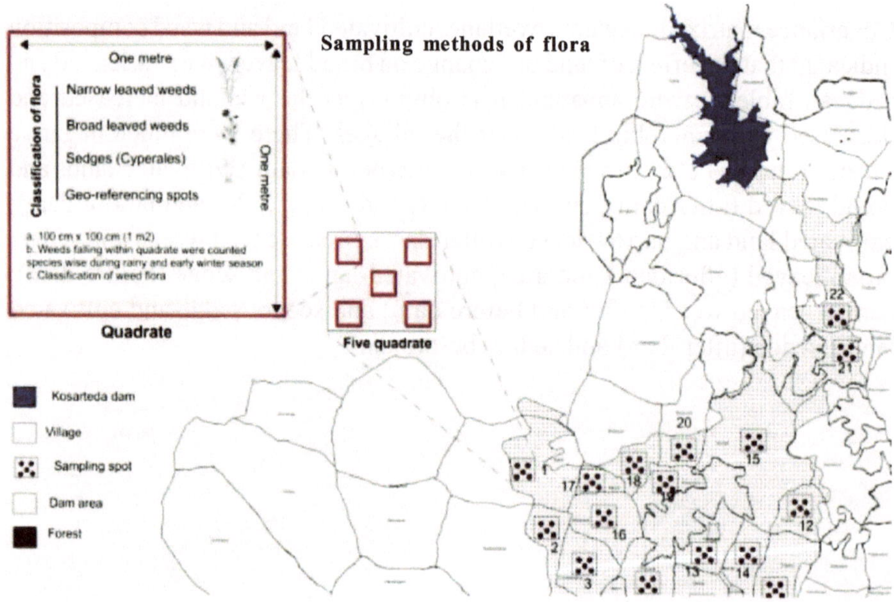

Fig. 6: Sampling Method of *Kosarteda* Dam

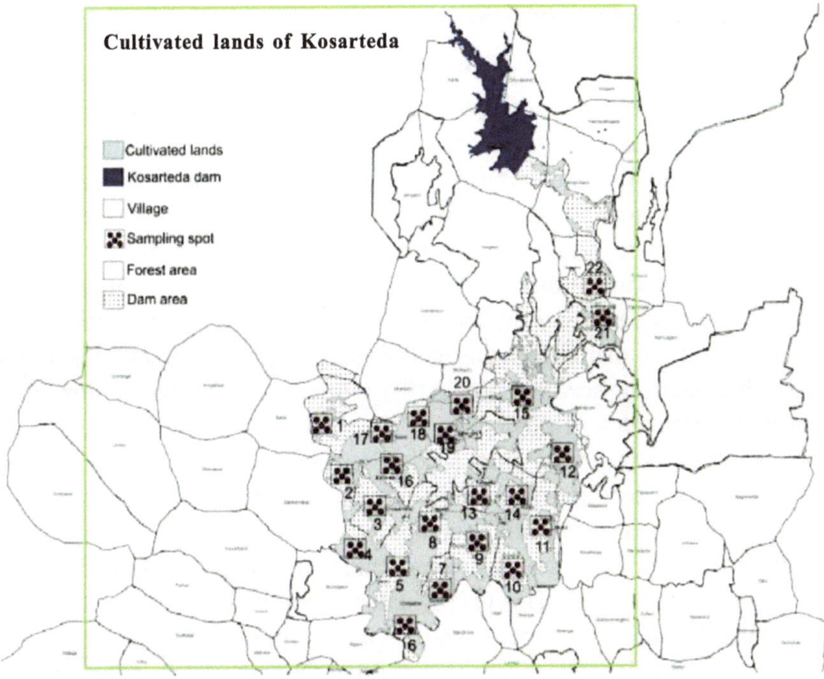

Fig. 7: Cultivated Lands of *Kosarteda* Dam

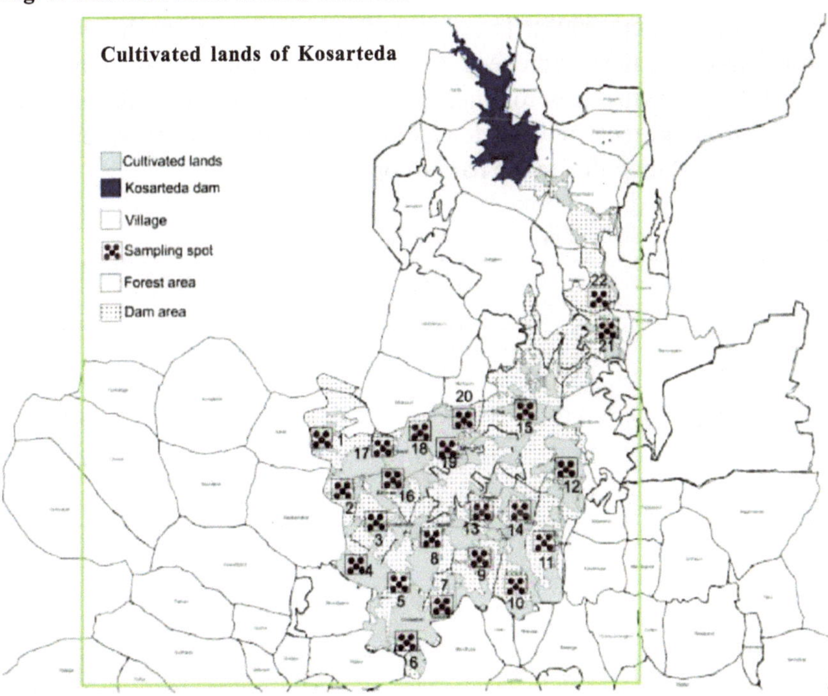

Fig. 8: Wetlands of *Kosarteda* Dam

5. Rice Cropping and Landforms

Transplanting in lowland was kept as fixed variable and compared with remaining methods of crop establishment on two farming *i.e.* upland and lowland in five combinations under either between and within groups of crop establishments and landscapes. The lowland was used for direct seeding provided more prone to have wild rice because sowing in lowland is congenial for higher rate of seed establishment as sowing prefers early in May and June, the light shower support to tilling and early germination but upland sowing begins later with onset which leads to flow surface seeds to lowlands. These all favour the conditions for more density and dry matter of wild rice, another supportive practice is direct seeding by broadcasting seeds on proper tillage operation, so, germination takes place in haphazard manner cultivated one. The shelter of wild by cultivated rice, with rice cannot be identified within group leads to higher infestation. The midland farming with direct seeding ranked second position after lowland plus DSR. Significant differences were found in comparison of between and within groups. Model fit statistics for direct seeding rice on three farming situations had similar stationary R^2, whereas, Ljung-Box Q (18) statistics was highest in lowland which was significantly superior to upland and lowland farming (Table 6 and Fig. 9). Knowledge of weed dispersal mechanisms allows the formulation of preventive measures that can avert the entry of the most dreaded species into agro-ecosystems (Benvenuti, 2007). The plenty of wild rice seeds might remain in filed after harvesting and that the seeds remaining vival with high mobility. From above results, on average, approximately 30% of the wild rice seeds remained in the harvested field, most of which fell far from their mother plants and extended their area of infestation due to the harvest operation.

Table 6: Descriptive Statistics of pairwise comparison

Parameter	Pair 1		Pair 2		Pair 3	
	DSR-U	**DSR-M**	**DSR-L**	**Trans.-U**	**Trans.-M**	**Trans.-L**
Min	5	10	31	4	7	20
Max	10.7	21	67	9	16	44
Mean	7.23	14.31	45.13	6.02	10.9	29.61
Std Dev.	1.53	3.05	9.57	1.38	2.17	6.22

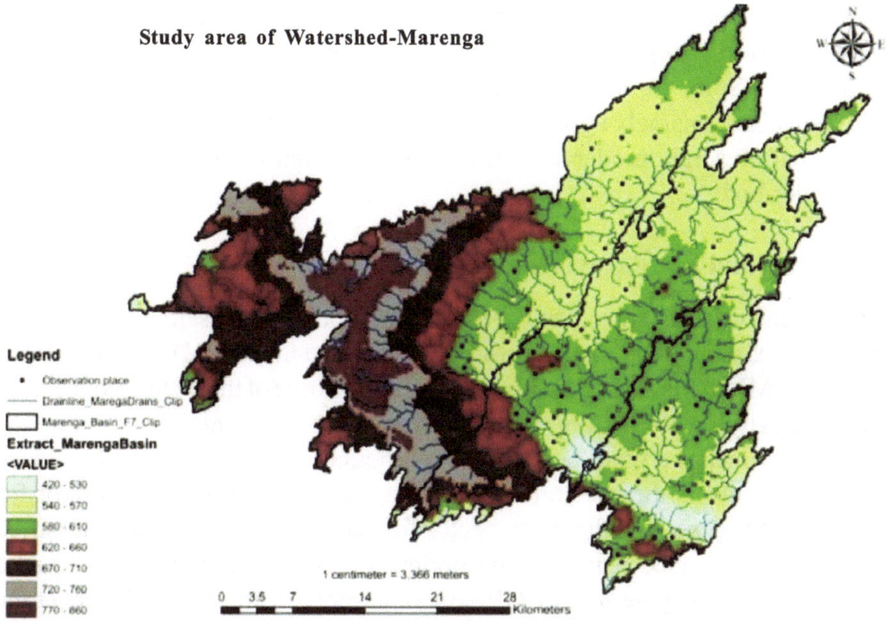

Fig. 9. Location map of upland, midland and lowland in study area

6. Change Study on Land use and Land Cover

In the present study, nine land use and land cover (LULC) categories were identified namely agriculture field, agriculture field (double crop), forest scrub, barren scrub, moderate dense forest, very dense forest, concrete, river and water body. Description of these land cover classes are presented with the main objective of the present study was to analyse and identify the nature and extent of land use and land cover changes.

Database Preparation

These data sets were imported in image processing software *i.e.* ERDAS Imagine version 9.3 (Leica Geosystems, Atlanta, U.S.A.) to create a false colour composite (FCC). The layer set option in image interpreter tool box was used to generate FCCs for the study areas. The sub-setting of satellite images were performed for extracting area from both images by geo-referenced outline boundary. Multi- temporal satellite data set observed by LISS - III, Multi spectral scanner (MSS), LISS - III, were used for the analysis. The remote sensing data used for this study include: LISS - III (2005) and LISS-III (2015) and other materials used were topographic maps. The change detection techniques by using multi-temporal satellite imagery improve the knowing landscape dynamics. The present study illustrates the spatio-temporal dynamics of land use and land cover of seven blocks of district Bastar, Chhattisgarh, India. Supervised classification technique has been chosen using maximum likelihood technique in ERDAS 9.3 Software. The images of the study area were categorized into nine different classes namely agriculture field, agriculture field (double crop), forest scrub, barren scrub, moderate dense forest, very dense forest, concrete, river and water body.

Land Use and Land Cover Detection and Analysis

For the land use and land cover classification, supervised classification, method having maximum likelihood algorithm was applied in the ERDAS Imagine 9.3 Software. MLC (Maximum likelihood algorithm) is one of the wide used methods like supervised classification with remote sensing data which is based on the probability means a pixel belongs to a particular class. The spectral distance method calculates the spectral distance between the measurement vector for the candidate pixel and the mean vector for each signature. The misclassified areas were corrected using recode option in ERDAS Imagine after ground truthing. Erdas imagine and Arc GIS software were constructive tools for getting out the land use and land cover layers, toposheets and satellite imageries of Survey of India also used in study of land use and land cover classes including agriculture field, agriculture field (double crop), forest scrub, barren scrub, moderate dense forest, very dense forest, concrete, river and water body. Image processing techniques was used to make visual explanation of land use geometric correction, radiometric correction, mosaicing and clipping of the images.

Land use and Land Cover Change Detection and Analysis

For performing land use and land cover change detection, a post-classification detection method was employed. A pixel-based comparison was used to produce change information on pixel basis. Thus, interpret the changes more efficiently taking the advantage of "-from, -to" information. A change matrix (Weng, 2001) was produced with the help of ERDAS Imagine software. Quantitatively a real data of the overall land use and land cover changes as well as gains and losses in each category between 2005 and 2015 were then compiled. Analysis of remote sensing imagery includes the identification of different marks in image. Visual interpretation using elements (tone, shape, size, pattern, texture, shadow, and association) were used for interpretation. Digital image classifications techniques were grouped pixels represent to land cover features. This area was classified into nine classes: agriculture field, agriculture field (double crop), forest scrub, barren scrub, moderate dense forest, very dense forest, concrete, river and water body.

Findings

Image analysis and accuracy assessment was corrected contract amongst a standard assumed to be correct and a classified image of unknown class accuracy assessment of image classification was approved using 150 points, 100 points since field survey data and 50 points current topographic maps and helped the ISRO Bhuvan land use and land cover maps. The land cover and land use representing of the LISS-III image, auxiliary data and the result of visual explanation was combined with the classification outcome using GIS in instruction to progress the classification accuracy of the classified images.

Land Use and Land Cover of District

Accuracy assessment of the land use and land cover classification result obtained and exhibited an overall accuracy of 89.25% for 2005 and 93.51% for 2015. Fig. 10-11 depicts spatial distributional pattern of land use and land cover of the seven blocks for the year 2005 and 2015. These data reveal that in 2005, area of seven blocks were under unban built up 0.05% (3.10 sq km), rural built up 0.10% (6.63 sq km), agricultural plantation 0.05% (3.54 sq km), agricultural crop land 28.89% (1905.22 sq km), agricultural fallow 3.81% (251.63 sq km), very dense forest 57.95% (3822.30 sq km), moderate forest 7.74% (510.35 sq km), barren scrub-I 0.76% (50.02 sq km) and barren scrub-II negligible (0.20 sq km) and water bodies 0.65% (42.60 sq km) as given in Table 1). Whereas decreasing trend of land use was observed in agricultural fallow land (-187.29 sq km), very dense forest (-582.31 sq km), moderate forest (220.63 sq km) and barren scrub-I (-19.06 sq km) and remaining land uses were increased. The higher degree of increment in rural built up area and less increment was seen under wetlands/water body. The decreasing trend was in land use of ten year span was due to conversion of vacant lands into different human activities as increasing family size and separation.

Land Use and Land Cover Change

During the last one decade, built up area both in urban (6.23 sq km) and rural (143.05 sq km), agricultural plantation (0.79 sq km), cropland (634.18 sq km) and barren scrub-II (0.61 sq km) supposed to be increased showing more intense in agricultural crop lands in last decade but same time agricultural fallow (-96.34 sq km), very dense forest (-582.31 sq km), moderate forest (-102.10 sq km) and barren scrub-I (-19.05 sq km) were decreased due to harvesting of forest illegally and encroachment with felling activities expanded the existing land covers. Many of the abandoned lands are being converted in commercial crop and vegetables which resulted as increased in land use for Built up area both in urban and rural, agricultural plantation, crop land and barren scrub. To assess land encroachment for different land categories during the last two decades, a change detection matrix was prepared which shows that.

i) Built up urban as well as rural, agricultural plantation and cropland and barren/unculturable/wastelands/sandy area were increased in land use of 2015 as compared to 2005.

ii) Agricultural fallow, very dense forest, moderate forest and barren scrub-I were decreased due to harvesting of forest illegally and encroachment with felling activities expanded the existing land covers.

iii) The highest positive change in built up rural and the lowest change was recorded in water body.

iv) The higher degree of increment in rural built up area and less increment was seen under wetlands/water body.

v) The decreasing trend was analysed in barren/unculturable/wastelands, agricultural fallow, forest deciduous and forest scrub in 2015 as compared to 2005.

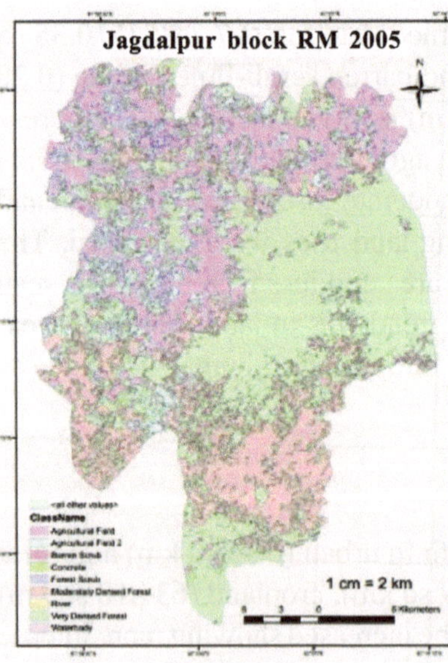

LULC-2005

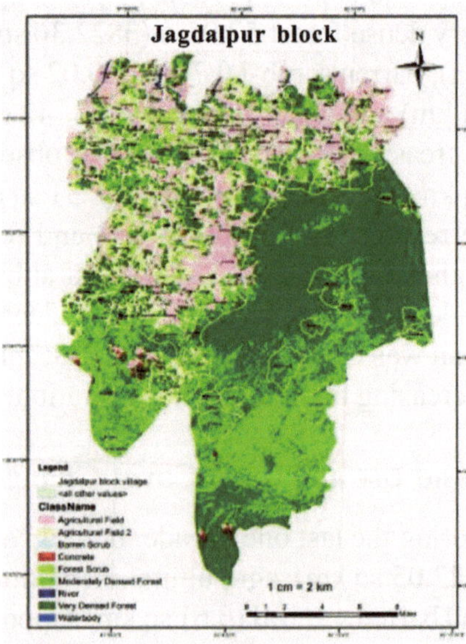

LULC-2015

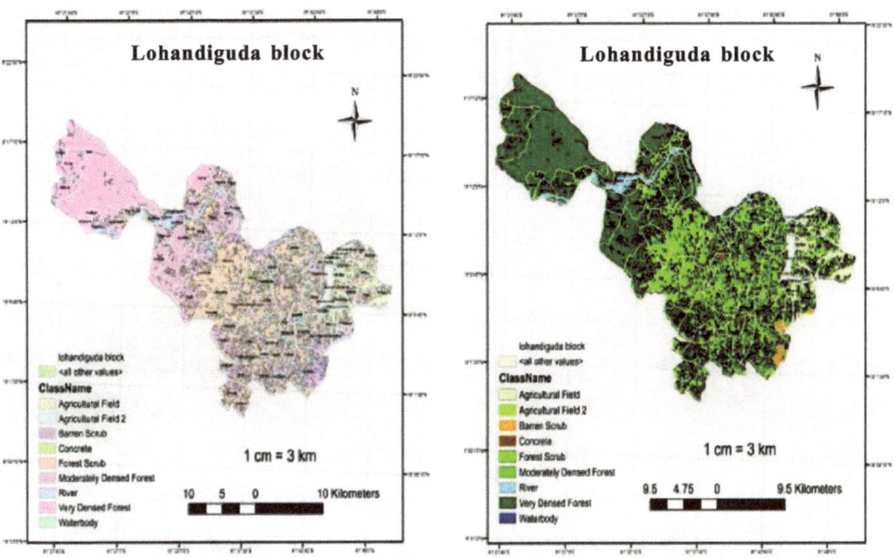

LULC-2005 LULC-2015

Fig. 10: LULC Maps of Jagdalpur and Lohandiguda Blocks in 2005 and 2015

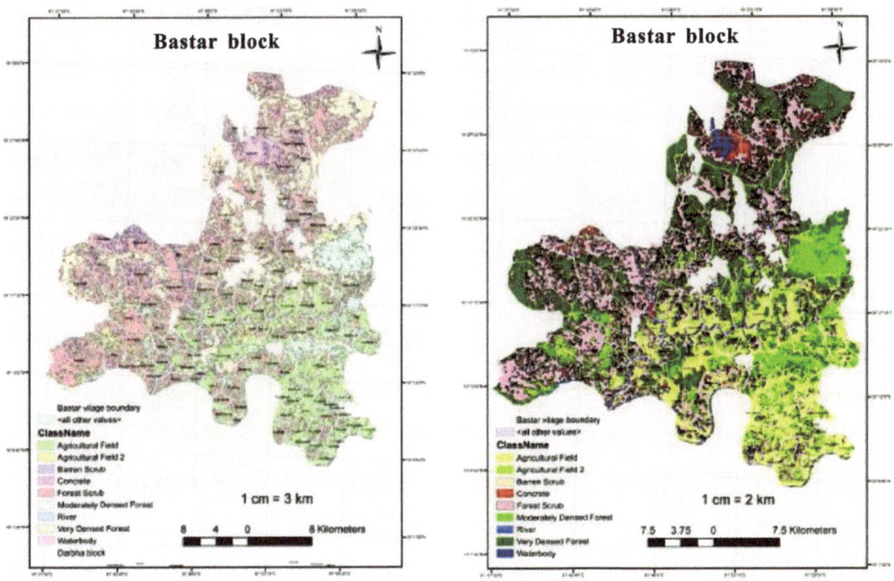

LULC-2005 LULC-2015

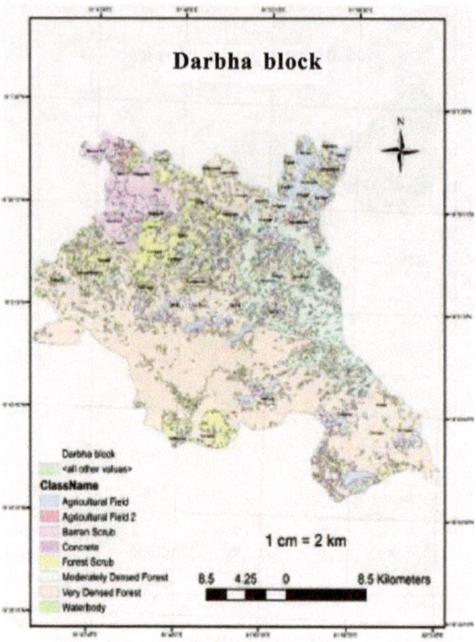

LULC-2005

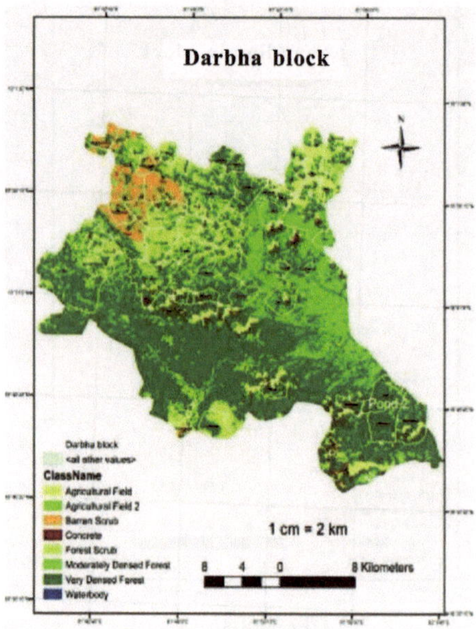

LULC-2015

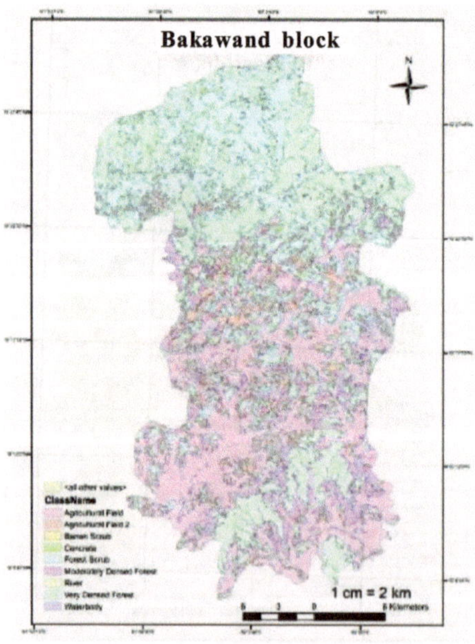

LULC-2005

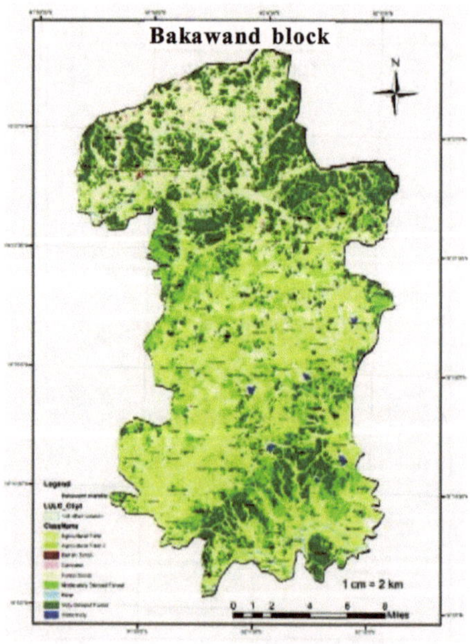

LULC-2015

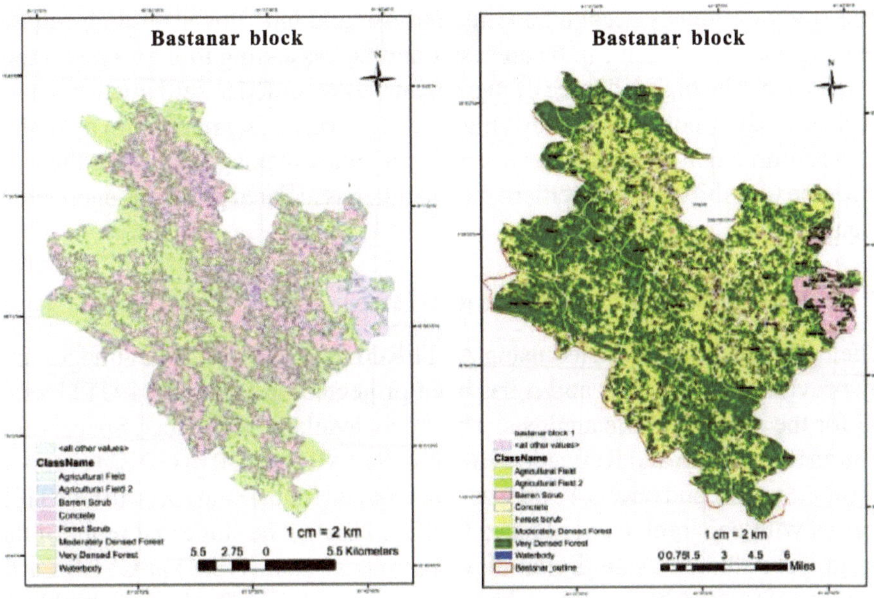

LULC-2005 LULC-2015

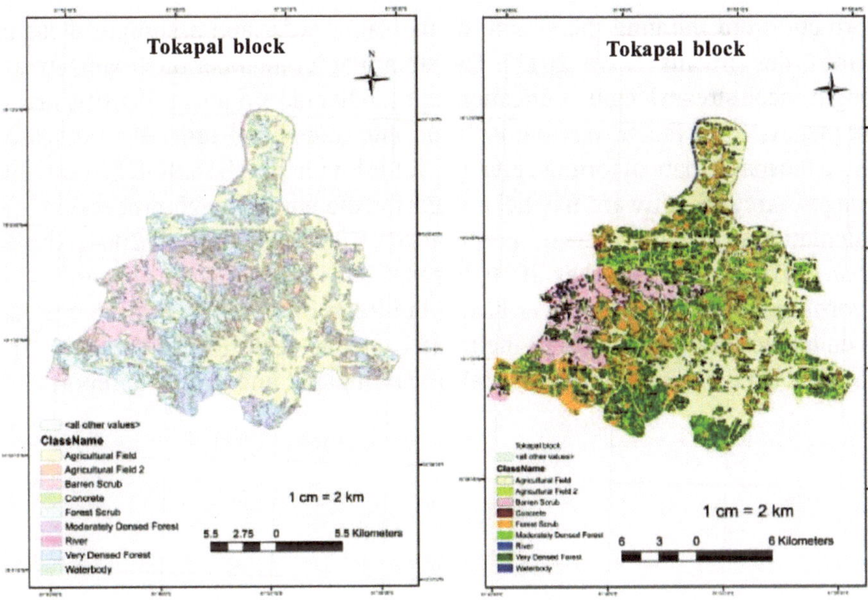

LULC-2005 LULC-2015

Fig. 11: LULC Maps of Tokapal Block in 2005 and 2015

The study obviously recognized the land use and land cover through remote sensing and GIS which can be an easier and fast assessing tool for assessment of land use. The higher degree of increment was recorded in settlement because ever increasing population is driving force for converting maximum available land resource that needs special attention in policy making, otherwise the land resource will shift towards settlement and other associated problems encounters regularly.

7. Basic Characteristics of Indrawati River

The basin has been extracted using ASTERGDEM (USGS, 2012) images and by providing pour points and it has been projected on WGS 1984 UTM zone 45 for the morphometric analysis. The freely available Advanced Spaceborne Thermal Emission and Reflection Radiometer (ASTER) 30 m GDEM (version 2) of one arc second (arcsec) grid was downloaded for the study area in GeoTIFF format with geographic coordinates (USGS, 2012). The slope and relief of the basin were studied using digital elevation model data (DEM) at USGS Earth Explorer for river basin and make the stream analysis. The law of Strahler's method of stream ordering adopted for ordering the streams (Strahler, 1964). The result of the stream order converted from raster to feature. A manual correction did merging the stream of the same order and assigning these as same order streams (Dave, 2011). The stream order, number of stream, stream length, mean stream length, bifurcation ratios, relief ratio, drainage density, stream frequency, form factor, circulatory ratio and elongation ratio were assessed using the mathematical formula given in Table1 with the ASTERGDEM satellite images. ArcGIS software has been used for the entire image processing and calculation of all parameters of morphometry study [Vittala *et al.*, 2004; Ahmed *et al.*, 2010; Patel and Sarkar, 2010, Biswas, 2014]. To show the changes in the hydrology of the Indrawti river basin, the trend of water flow discharge has been analysed. The changes in the trend exert the peak flow of the river. The data has been collected from several research paper and available reports.

Table 1: Mathematical formulae for analysis of basin characteristics

S.No.	Parameters	Formulae	References	Results
1.	Stream order (u)	Hierarchical rank	Strahler (1)	8
2.	Stream number	Based on stream order	Strahler (1)	85636
3.	Stream length (Lu) (km)	Length of stream	Horton (1945)	42259.3
4.	Mean Stream length (Lsm)	Lu=SL/Nu	Strahler (1964)	0.493
5.	Bifurcation ratio (Rb)	Rb=Nu/Nu+1	Schum (1956)	3.144
6.	Length of overland flow (Lg)	Lg=1/Dx2	Horton (1945)	0.002
7.	Drainage density (Dd)	Dd="Lu/Au	Horton (1945)	1.041
8.	Stream frequency (Fs)	D="Nu/Au	Horton (1945)	3.088
9.	Form factor (Ff)	$Ff=A/LP^2$	Horton (1945)	1.22
10.	Circulatory ratio (Rc)	$Rc=4"A/P^2$	Strahler (1964)	2.634
11.	Elongation ratio (Re)	Re=D/Lb	Schum (1956)	0.901
12.	Leminscate method (k)	K=L2/4A	Chortey *et al.* (1957)	6.348
13.	Reliefratio	Rh=H/Lb	Schum (1963)	1.758

Indrawati River Basin

Linear Aspects of Morphometry

Stream order (u): Stream order is defined as a measure of the position of a stream in the hierarchal of tributaries (Leopold *et al.*, 1964, Horton, 1932 and Strahler, 1952), have developed stream ordering system. The *Indrawati* River, which is a main stream of the study area, is the eight stream orders (Based on Strahler's method of stream order). The variation extends order and size of the tributary basin is due to physiographic and structural conditions prevailing in the basin. The river basin develops over the shale, sandstone, gneiss and slate as major rock and thereby the number and order of streams are more. Total stream number is 85636 showing value 31.023 and 8179.61 as minimum and maximum, respectively from total mean length of 0.493 km and standard deviation of 692.83 while study of the *Indrawati* basin. The highest number of first order streams are 600150 followed by second order stream of 308424 and lowest was 3035 expressing initiation and formation of new stream apparently.

Stream number: The total stream segments in each order are known as stream number. R.E. Horton states that the number of stream segments of each order from an inverse geometric sequence with the order number. The number of stream orders has been counted with the help of ArcGIS software. A total number of streams in the basin are 85636. The underlying tender rocks and undulating plain favour a large number of streams further more initiation. In the *Indrawati* basin, the first order of the streams is associated with the highest number of streams and remaining are gradually decreased.

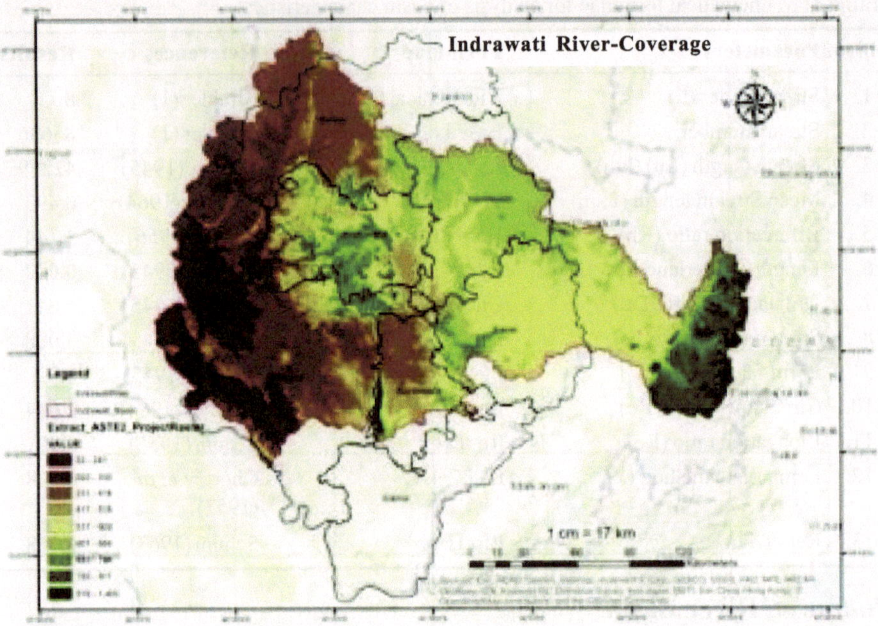

a) Basin Coverage of Indrawati River

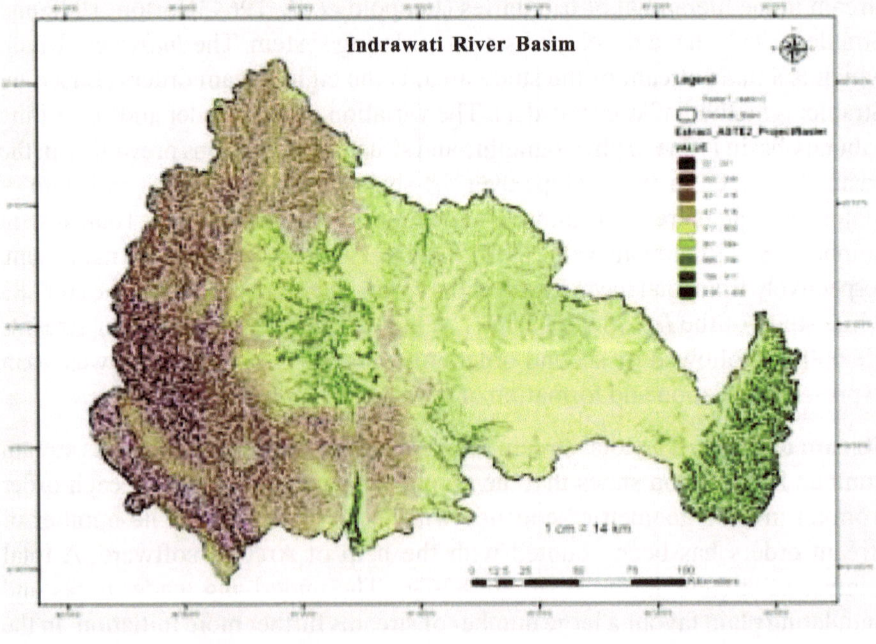

b) River Basin of Indrawati

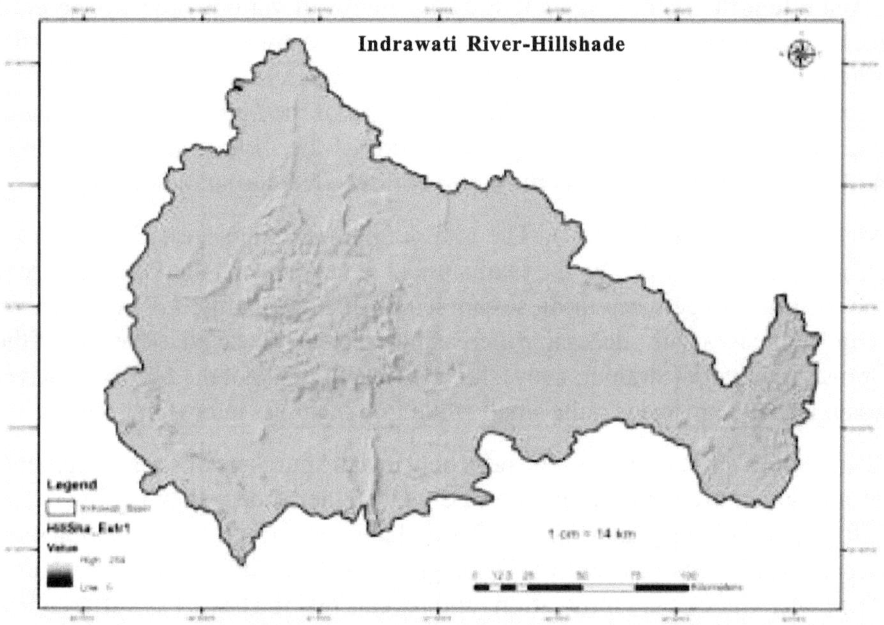

c) Hillshade of Indrawati River

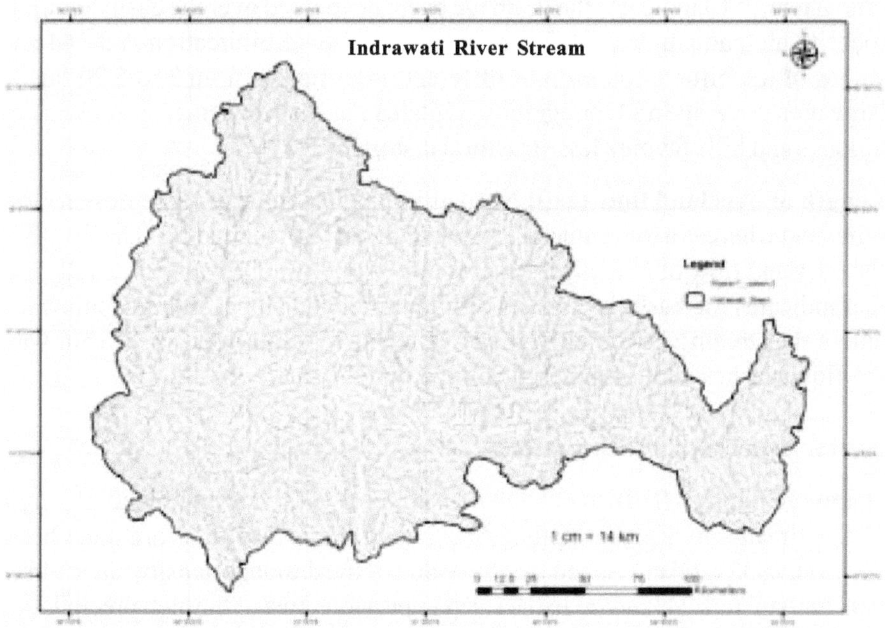

d) Stream Networks of Indrawati Basin

Fig. 12: Basin Characteristic Map of Indrawati River

Stream lengths (Lu): The total streams lengths of various orders have been measured with the help of calculate geometry of GIS tools. It is indicative of the chronological development of streams and derived from source to mouth of the streams (Magesh *et al.*, 2013). The total length of the *Indrawati* river is about 535 kms, and the length of the total streams of the *Indrawati* River basin is 42259.27 km as length of treams increase flow coverage automatically.

Mean stream length (Lsm): The total length of stream measured and total stream length is divided by the total number of segments in that order. There is the relationship between mean stream length and basin order *i.e.* mean stream length increases with successive increasing orders. It is related to the size of the drainage network (Strahler, 1964). Mean Stream Length of the *Indrawati* River basin is 0.493 km and is quite small while flowing takes many things away.

Bifurcation ratio (Rb): It is the ratio between the numbers of stream segments of any given order to the number the next higher order (Singh, 1971). The bifurcation ratio ranges in between 3 to 5. The irregularities of bifurcation ratio depend on the geological and the lithological development of the drainage basin. The lower value of the bifurcation ratio reveals that the basin has suffered less structural disturbances and the higher values of the bifurcation ratio indicate strong structural control on the drainage pattern (Strahler, 1964). Bifurcation ratio having >10 indicates the drainage basin developed over the easily erodible rocks (Kale and Gupta, 2010). The average value of bifurcation is 3.144 and values of the bifurcation ratio of different order ranges from 2 to 5.26 due to large area coverage and topography of plateau as district demarcation lines by hillocks and hills favours less structural disturbances.

Length of overland flow (Lg): Normally, a higher value of Lg represents low relief and whereas a low value of Lg is an indicative of high relief. The length of the overland flow of *Indrawati* River is 0.002 km/km^2. The value is usually low that indicates the basin is consists of high relief and slope, and thus rainwater enters the stream very quickly, meanwhile entry of rain water in stream way, the flow washes a lot of materials on the way.

Aerial Aspects of Morphometry

Drainage density (Dd): Drainage density (Dd) is the ratio of the total length of the streams in a given drainage basin and the area of that drainage basin (Horton, 1932) and envisaged that the value of the drainage density ranges from 0.93 km/km^2 to 1.24 km/km^2 in the steep impervious area of the high precipitation region and zero for the permeable basin with high infiltration rate. Langbien considered that the drainage density is ranged from 0.55 to 2.09 for the humid region with the average drainage density of 1.03. Low drainage density indicates permeable subsurface and coarse drainage (Magesh *et al.*, 2013). Drainage density of the *Indrawti* River Basin is 1.041 km/km^2, and it means weak subsurface material, belongs to medium texture of the basin with steep impervious.

Stream frequency (Fs): It is expressed as the ratio of a total number of channels cumulated for all orders within a given drainage basin and the area of that drainage basin (Horton, 1932). It indicates the index of various stages of landscape development and depends on the nature and amount of rainfall, the nature of rock and soil permeability of the region. Stream frequency of the *Indrawati* River basin is 3.088/km^2, which indicates high relief and high infiltration of the basin because of compartmentation. Hence, both the drainage density and the stream frequency are the parameters for measuring the spacing of stream channel in the basin.

Form factor (Ff): The value of the form factor varies from 0 (highly elongated shape) to 1 (perfect circular shape). The value of form factor of the *Indrawati* River basin is 1.22 which depicts that the basin form perfectly circular shape and cause flood situation in the district in rainy season, and it is the indication of high peak flow of the basin.

Circulatory ratio (Rc): The Circulatory ratio is to provide a quantitative index of the shape for the basin. He had defined circulatory ratio as the ratio of basin area to the area of the circle having the same parameter as the basin. A circular basin has a maximum efficiency of the movement of runoff, whereas an elongated basin has the least frequency. This information is very significant in forecasting of drainage discharge, particularly in a time of the flood (Jha, 1996). The value of the circulatory ratio is 2.364 which explain high circular shape and high run off flow of discharge of the *Indrawati* River basin while heavy down pour.

Elongation ratio (Re): This ratio usually runs from 0.6 to 1.0 over a broad range of climatic and geological type. Values near 1.0 are a typical region of low relief while values from 0.51 to 0.94 are associated with strong relief and steep ground slope. The ratio is a meaningful index for classifying drainage basins into vary shapes as circular (above 0.9), oval (0.8-0.9), less elongated (0.7-0.8) and elongated (below 0.7). The value of elongation ratio of the *Indrawati* River basin is 0.901. So, the basin has a circular in shape and associating strong relief of surface and low peak flow.

Leminscate method (K): It is the comparison of the basin with the leminscate curve. The high value of K indicates elongated shape and on the contrary, a little value indicates the circular shape of the basin. The K value of *Indrawati* river basin is 6.348 that depicts that the river is a perfectly circular and it indicates high peak flow of discharge of the basin. *Indrawati* basin has higher K means high order stream is present and further it will increase with progress.

Relief Aspects of Morphometry

Relief Ratio: The Relief ratio is the ratio between the total relief of a basin and the longest dimension of the basin parallel to the main drainage line (Schumm, 1956). According to Schumm, a dimensionless height-length ratio equal to the tangent of the angle formed by two planes intersecting at the mouth of the basin, one representing the horizontal, the other passing through the highest point of the basin. It denotes the overall steepness of a drainage basin and is an indicator of the intensity of degradational processes operating on slopes of that basin. The relief ratio of the river basin is 1.758 that indicates this basin is composed of more resistant in flow by hindrance of hills and hillocks of basin, and the basin is under intense relief and steep slope.

Drainage Patterns of the *Indrawati* River Basin

In the *Indrawati* river basin, Tree-like dendritic type of drainage pattern mainly develops over the existing rocks apart from the dendritic pattern also exhibits the Herringbone, parallel and centrifugal type of drainage pattern. The parallel drainage pattern, where the control of the regional slope, parallel faults and lineaments predominate, is discernible too. In this drainage pattern, parents and tributaries flow in right angle to meet. In some peak of the ridges, Centrifugal drainage pattern, where streams radiate in all directions from a common centre, is significant feature of the hillocks.

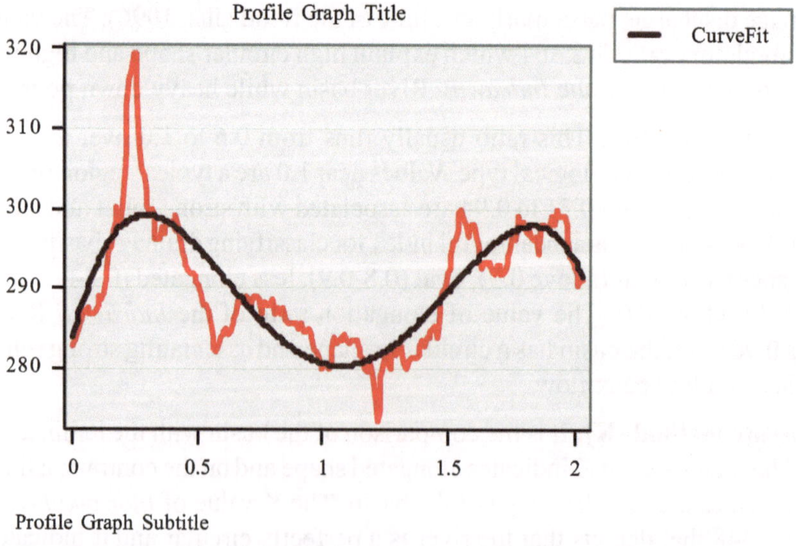

Fig. 13: Long Profile of Indrawati Basin

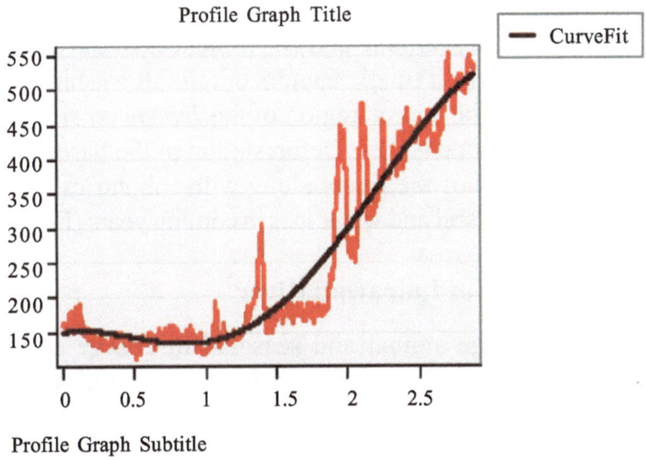

Fig. 14: Cross Profile of Indrawati Basin

Long profile of the river: It is generally concave to the sky, but the slope is decreasing rapidly at first and then gradually (Knighton., 1998). The River originates at 688 m above mean sea level and runs 535 km. The long profile of a river is dependent upon the lithology of the underlying structure, stream flow, discharge, the amount and texture of the channel load, flow resistance, flow velocity, width and depth of the channel, and regional slope (Kale and Gupta, 2010). The *Indrawati* River has a different channel slope and concavity. The regular concave profile is interrupted by the convex profile at about 20-30 kms from the origin. The convex slope is between 1500-3000 metres due to plateau shortly change in movement on structural differences and concave in between 1000-2000 metres above meaning sea level having sharp turn due to landforms. The irregularities are due to the presence of the more resistance hillocks and change in slope (Figure 3).

Cross profiles of the river: The cross profile varies from the narrow, steep-sided trenches to gentle open form, ultimately depends on the resistance offered by the undulating plateau slopes and the erosive capacity of the water during rain. Cross profile of the *Indrawati* River in different regimes exerts the processes and dominant controlling factor. Most of the cross profiles are 'U' shaped in nature and it represents lateral cutting rather than down erosion. Near the source, the dominance of hills and river has more stream power for lateral cutting, thus flat 'U' shaped profile is significant (Figure 4).

Recent Hydrological Changes in *Indrawati* River Basin

The significant changes have been observed in the *Indrawati* River Basin mainly due to climatic and anthropogenic causes. The climatic variability leads to heavy and erratic rainfall of the region which induces soil loss and thereby retreat of sedimentation of the river basin is discernible and consequences of the events are shallow depth, diversion, flood with small quantum of rainfall washing out top agriculturally important soil. The source region of the *Indrawati* river, is eastern ghat experienced with abrupt changes. Deforestation in the basin area also increases the erosion capacity of the rivers along with tributaries. As a result, basin might be more prone to soil and water loss in coming years (Fig. 3).

Temporal Changes in Discharge of Indrawati River

A tendency of decrease in average annual and seasonal discharge of the *Indrawati* River has been experienced. It is significant from the several studies that the decline of discharge is also experienced. The flow characteristic is controlled by variability of rainfall. The gradual decrease of discharge in winter onwards is noticed due to less flow and uneven distribution between states like Odisha and Chhattisgarh during lean periods. Simultaneously, the irregularity of the Monsoon disrupts the average discharge of the river in a lesser extent. The present study on drainage basin has been done on the basis of geo-morphological perspective. Study of the morphometry is concerned with the genesis, development and distribution of landforms (Yellappa *et al.*, 2011). An important property of the drainage basin is its hierarchical in nature, each tributary in a drainage system has its basin area. In any drainage basin, there are several variables which always interacting with other variables and give birth to particular types of landforms. The study reveals that the drainage basin is associated with the early stage of drainage development, and high order of stream dominates the river basin. The circular shape of the basin reveals high runoff and low infiltration capacity and uncontrolled flow of river water with disturbing dependent factors of basin. Recently, several anthropogenic activities like house construction on banks, fast deforestation, siltation and climatic variability (erratic rainfall and rising temperature) caused the several hydrological changes in the *Indrawati* River basin. Recent changes in discharge can affect the agradational and degradational processes that also affect the overall welfare of society.

8. Water Storage Structure Study

Four hundred eighteen open dug well data were collected by survey of the region in cluster of Jagdalpur, Bastanar, Bakawand, Lohandiguda, Darbha, Tokapal and Bastar blocks in this study. The present study explores the status of the open dug wells in region by surveying villages by villages at pre- and post-monsoon period as in a case study from seven blocks of Bastar district. The study area comprised of seven blocks (*Bakwand, Bastar, Tokapal, Darbh, Bastanar, Jagdalpur* and *Lohandiguda*) lies in the southern most part of

Chhattisgarh, India. It extends between 81°27'03 N to 82°7'58 N latitudes and 18°40'25 E to 19°38'45 E longitudes and encompasses an area of 10470.00 km^2. Geologically, the blocks are made-up of laterite, basalt, sandstone, shale, limestone, granite, quartzite, charnokite, and gneiss. On an average, the study area receives about 1404.80 mm of rainfall annually. The annual mean maximum, minimum and average temperature of the study area stands at 42°C, 18°C and 28°C, respectively. The master stream of block is Indrawati river which flows from east to west and divides the blocks into two halves.

We surveyed and collected data on number of dug wells, dimension, depth, strata of site, level of water in wells, appearance, usage, drying time, nearby stream, water. The water samples were also collected randomly from 10% of total surveyed open dug wells, analysed for sodium, nitrate, phosphorus content, pH, electric conductivity at laboratory, S.G. College of Agriculture & Research Station, Jagdalpur. Data were collected approaching individual open dug wells at each selected villages of the blocks. Surveyors were appointed for mentioned period with hand held GPS (Mak-Garmin) to perfectly note the geo-referred locations using developed proforma. Owner's view also noted meantime to know the perception on wells. The collected data on the wells were imported on GIS platform (ArcGIS 10.3) with geology, drain line, topography under administrative boundary of the blocks alongwith reference data.

Findings

Drastic change and unscientific land-use pattern were noticed over the region. These age-old structures are ill-maintained, and the dumping of non-degradable waste inside chokes the air vents and restricts the natural inflow of water. Most of the wells are unlined structure and have the innate strength to withstand with subsoil flow. The average diameter of the wells is 0.8 to 3.0m. The depth varies from 3 to 20 m depending on the availability of subsurface water flows under gravity; it is common practice of removal deposited mud annually to open natural vents for recharging the wells through surface flow. The higher number of open dug wells (179) was recorded in Jagdalpur block including 121 dug wells from Jagdalpur city alone followed by Bastar (76) and Tokapal (77), all the mentioned dug wells were randomly selected to know the status of these wells at present. Among the blocks, availability of dug wells showed standard deviation of 59.15 and mean of 59.71. Mostly stream recorded with Bastanar block (619) due to higher degree of geo-morphological variation led to provide wider movement while rainfall on undulated ground surface, where lowest number of stream was in Lohandiguda, the whole Lohandiguda block has hilly track that's why formed less streams, but second largest area coverage (2640.7 ha) next to Bastar. The highest stream area covered by Bastar (5068.9 ha) then Lohandiguda (2640.7

ha) and Bakawand (1318.3 ha) with standard deviation of stream and its area were highly fluctuated value of 143.77 and 1761.56, respectively.

Detailed inventory of 418 open dug wells was made during pre-monsoon (May) and post-monsoon (October) 2017-18. The data showed that the yield of the tunnel wells had reduced considerably over the years. Similarly, it was observed that all the wells in and around localized water sources or river or stream was discharging huge quantities of subsurface water during rainy season and this water reached the *Chua* or *Kunwa*. To prevent undesirable loss of water, we recommend that the mouth of the wells be fenced with 3 feet retaining wall around the well to protect mud flow from surface, an engineering structure designed in this study, having a control valve at the bottom. The inlets of the pipes should have sieves to prevent leaves and other solids from entry.

Construction of new tunnel wells should be discouraged in the region. The *Panchayat* authorities should collect details of all the existing wells in their respective *Panchayats*, and the data should be brought to a digital (spatio-temporal) platform. There is a pressing need to create awareness about restoring and reviving these traditional water harvesting structures. These are not only for more sustainable in the long run as compared to bore wells, but also carry age-old wisdom for future natural resources.

Jagdalpur Block

Locations of open dug well were identified by personal survey to the points at pre and post-monsoon period for measurement of total depth and water below ground level. The whole Jagdalpur is set on shale geology which is basically identified as Jagdalpur formation, sedimentary rock composed of mud that is mixture of flacks of clay minerals and tiny fragments of quartz and calcite. Most of the open dug wells are clay based which recharges fast with augment of rainfall and fall fast with retreating rainfall. This is a characteristic feature of shale based open dug wells, subsurface water inflow through vents found around the well inside with porous composition after rain. On the basis of survey, the maximum depth of open dug wells was noticed in Babusemara and Dhanpunji village with 30-40 m having drying time of March and water is used for drinking, whereas minimum depth 0-5m rarely noticed while survey but some interesting feature was seen in headquarter of Jagdalpur block. Jagdalpur city has 121 open dug wells itself and 70% are not in use due to contamination by sewage water or no maintenance regularly, otherwise two large rainwater harvesting structures constructed in Jagdalpur city namely Gangamunda and Dalpatsagar, wells present in vicinity of flow line between the structures has hardly 0.5-1.0 m water level below ground level (bgl) throughout year and the open dug wells are situated away from the basic catchment get dried even depths are more than

20m (Pradhan *et al.*, 2019). The whole Jagdalpur block is characterized with more number of dug wells been excavated in between 16-20m depth. The most of the wells found dry in March and April month, rarely 7% wells are dried in May, 1-3% of wells are still use for drinking, domestic as well as irrigation purpose. Panwar and Chakrapani (2013) suggested the way for recharge of wells and ground water. Dwindling of ground recharge also accelerated by diversion of natural flow as explained by Mishra *et al.* (2009) results drought phenomenon.

Location of maximum wells located to residential area is purposely built terrain top and lowering sides are used for cultivation that is a reason wells get dried in March, some of the well located in low lying area or near to stream flow or internal connection with hard porous media provide survivability of open dug wells. The storage structures like dug wells in urban and rural area might be a stalwart mechanism in ground water recharge since high rainfall always moves quickly to main drain line like river system no longer retain rainwater which could be a part of infiltration more in below ground. Although, sandy loam soils are in large area which has 20-30 mm/hr infiltration rate can enhance infiltration during rainy season onwards.

Bastanar Block

Total 36 dug wells were surveyed and recorded data on prescribed format to collect information pertaining to open dug wells. Undulating and rocky geomorphology do not allow digging much deeper. Depth of maximum wells ranged within 5-10m, in which 24 open dug wells across the locations were found under rain water fed due to undulating plain, whereas limited number of wells (05) found in 6-10m depth and higher depth was 30-35m drying in April and May of 10 and 15 open dug wells, respectively. Another important aspect is use of these wells, all wells are being used for domestic purpose and upto some extend irrigation to backyard crops is common adoptional practice in this block. Most of the villages surveyed were align to drainage parallel, dyke and fault, was the major reason to dry up in April and in some cases February and March, due to structural lineament features take water deeper to contribute aquifers. Among these dug wells, 3 wells have been identified as perennial water retaining open wells situated at Jamgaon, Turangur and Sadra villages on shale and sandstone formation, but Jamgaon is located away from lineament features dyke and drainage parallel, some of the local specific individual character like impermeable layer of bottom like humus content and regular oozing water from vents might be strong consideration of the open dug wells supported to retain water throughout year. Apart from individual specificity, geological formations are mostly governed to storage of rainwater. Diversified geological setting in

Bastanar block contains shale and sandstone (Abujhmar group and sandstone formation) with structural drainage parallel, dyke and fault support for recharging ground water, which is influenced largely to surface water retaining infiltration of rainwater into subsurface (Hussain, 2004).

Lohandiguda Block

Most of the open dug wells found on Abujhmar group. Two wells at Matnar and Mardum on sandstone (Tirathgarh group). Depth of open dug wells was shallow *i.e.* 0-5m in Karekot, Binta, Sataspur, Bheja, Chandela, Kaknar (Karekot cluster) are in Indrawati river basin confined around by hills and valley type topography helps in remaining water. In contrast, Mardum, Matnar, Parapur, Kasturpal, Badrenga are in hilly plateau, which are rainfed wells drying fast with cessation of rainfall and these villages prefers little higher depth than Karekot cluster to extend water availability month. Lohandiguda block is rarefied populated area and villages are located away from each other due to high dissected and various groups of geological settings have been identified features of shale banded iron and shale (Jagdalpur group) in western part, centrally it is composed of shale sandstone Arcosic (Abujhmar group) which is larger coverage of this geology (Dora, 2011, Dora, 2014), whereas northern parts comprised of sandstone (Tirathgarh groups). Apart from hilly track toward Jagdalpur almost flat topography again forces to dig more deeper to hold water long. The geological setting is greatly influenced by ground morphology like hilly track, valley and undulating hillocks superimposed on geological setting that not supported directly for retaining water into open dug wells. The regions is quite unique in surface features than remaining blocks of Bastar characterized the water storage structures. In valley region of Lohandiguda, long period of clay deposition in lower valley promoted settlement with developing open dug wells digging the clay to inflow water through small vents into the dug wells.

Bastar Block

Bastar block imposed on two geological sandstone formation as Tirathgarh group and other shale (Jagdalpur formation), sporadic shale geological setting found in villages like Bhanpuri, Badejirakhal, Jaibel, Chhindgarh on joint fracture of structural lineament finds in northern. Khokhaseoni village situated near *Narangi* river is completely flood plain area and during kharif inundation is common feature which hardly allows to grow rice crop on such adverse situation (Mishra *et al.*, 1984). The village has 30 open dug wells having depth of 0-5m from the cultivated lands to backyards, after back flow of flood water keeps the wells filled till May and farmers use to fit shallow drill bore wells in bottom of dug well and extracts water from lower strata for irrigating the vegetables as well as rabi crops. Among the surveyed open dug wells, 30 wells are in 0-5m depth even they dry in January to March, less number of the wells retain water till April due to complete plain area and slight depression do not affect much to the drying time. Sandstone based open dug wells of Kungarpal, Mandlapal and Kawadgaon are dried in January and March due to shortfall of recharging capacity and the basin plain contribute much to Indrawati river system without staying longer in such situations. Whereas same situational setting with Jamgaon lasts till May, it may be due to near sloppy side of hillocks where water stores in gap of hillock seepages slowly to down side. Bodanpal, Basoli, Amaguda and Kungarpal are either 0-5m or 6-10m depth gets dried in January, even they are near to river flow or sandstone formation, both has their non limitation being sandy loam soil which holds water till saturation with rain water, if there is some depletion in saturation starts loosing moisture. Sandstone is deeper and after definite range, water presents surely, which is rarely reached to open dug wells (Crookshak 1963), this might be reason for drying early than rest of the wells. No deeper (>10m) dug well has been noted from Bastar block. In Vishrampuri, wells get dried in May month may be joining of two geological units sandstone (Tirathgarh group) and shale (Jagdalpur formation) for retaining longer. It was observed from collected data that 32 dug wells were used for irrigation purpose whereas 23 dug wells were in domestic use.

Bakawand Block

The block completely falls under expansion of shale (Jagdalpur formation) having almost plain topography and intensive vegetable growing area demand more water for irrigation which influenced more to traditional open dug wells. Now hardly we found open dug wells in the block because of high degree of tube wells are being drilled, even some of the zone showing depletion of ground water owing higher exploitation, no strong aquifer system finds in the block. All wells were in range of 10-20m depth and dried in March and April due to lack of recharging system and hard strata of soil along porous confined zone (*Murum*) below limit the support much longer (Sarkar *et al.*, 1994). There might be so many reasons for drying of dug wells, one of them is no regular maintenance associated with high water demand at regular interval perpetuating spots, draw more water depletes underground water. Bakawand is only block that may be strongly fallen in danger zone in coming years due unmannerful expansion of land use with high water use.

Depth of Open Dug Wells

The depth wise observations recorded on open dug wells, the data shows that maximum number of dug wells were in range of 5 to 10m depth then 11 to 15 m category regardless the blocks. As depth increased, number of dug wells decreased due to higher cost of construction and availability of hand pump or bore wells at village level. Hence, positivity of dug wells is not only serving water to people but sometime recharge ground water through rainfall in underground structures as compared to drilling bore wells, even the bore wells exploited more groundwater rather recharge. Tokapal block had higher number of dug wells in the depth of 21 to 25m (21) otherwise remaining blocks hardly increased the depth beyond 20m except Jagdalpur and Bastanar where finger count open dug wells constructed with more than 25m (Table 2). The depth is directly correlated with strata of particular blocks, Tokapal and Bastanar are over hard geology of granites and gneisses in deeper layer purposely forces them to dig deeper. In case of Jagdalpur, there are mostly old dug wells which were deeper (Srivastava *et al.*, 1996). Now a day government schemes are only hope to excavate open dug wells for irrigation purpose otherwise people diverted to bore wells. Ultimately water table went down sharply due to lack of rainwater storing structures, this alarms us how the future situation will, sustain under depleting such ensured water harvesting structures in the region, the prospect might be thrown light on this valuable aspects.

Drying Time

Drying time of open dug wells are curious features of the study. The most of the rain fed dug wells were found drying in March and April, possessing little more with April drying. This is because of either the wells are deep or stream fed, which supplies oozing surface water to open dug wells and lasting till April or May until the stream flow get dried. In vice-versa, block wise observations expressed that categorized two group of drying i.e. early (February-March) and late drying (April-May) (Table 3). In this aspect, Tokapal and Jagdalpur had maximum wells with drying in March, although Tokapal had still some wells drying in April but that was less than March drying. Bastar and Darbha were also May drying wells, Tokapal seemed to be variable rate of drying, some dug wells dried in January and February month due to surface morphology is highly undulating across the Tokapal block as a result high degree of variation was seen. Instead of early and late drying of the dug wells were still possessed water throughout year with faster recharge capacity in Jagdalpur and Lohandiguda.

Usage and Appearance

Usage of open well water in different blocks comprised domestic, irrigation and drinking purpose, and appearance of wells were dirty, green, muddy and oily as parameters. Domestic use of open wells were higher in Bastar (23), Tokapal (25), Darbha (12) and Jagdalpur (15), and 33 dug wells noticed for irrigation use at Bastar block followed by Tokapal (11); drinking purpose was generally less, only single digit because of well water is not maintained by villagers annually for drinking before onset of monsoon. The availability of hand pumps in the villages discouraged the drinking water from open dug wells, which were only source of drinking earlier. Overall 94, 57 and 16 dug wells were under domestic, irrigation and drinking purposes, respectively. Appearance is primary focus point to accept or reject, on the basis of colour, odour and dirty appearance recorded higher number of open wells in Bastar block (12), Tokapal (15) and Bastanar (29) comparatively green appearance which was higher with Jagdalpur (8) and Bastar (8). Lohandiguda had zero well in green appearance. Muddy appearance is common in all blocks of the district. Tokapal (21) and Bastar (25) had higher number of wells followed by Darbha (10) detailed in Table 4.

Water Quality

Water quality assessment of purposely selected 45 water samples from open dug wells was done by analysing pH, EC, carbonate and bicarbonate. Out of 418 sampled dug wells, 45 dug wells were purposely selected to assess quality of the water. The pH ranged from 6.33 to 9.18, in open dug wells of Karanpur, Alnar, Rampal, Upanpal, Bilauri and Jiragaon were found more than 8 pH, only one wells had 9.18 pH and remainings were within 7 to 8. The dug wells from Dondawal (6.33) and Bhaisabandha (6.83) were hardly crossed 7.0 pH. Among the samples, 2 wells had 6-7 pH, 7 wells were more than 8 pH, and highest number of wells (38) found under 7-8 pH.

Similarly EC (electric conductivity) also analysed and found much different in electric conductivity, 11 wells were in 0.05-0.10 EC, 8 wells in 0.10-0.15 EC, 4 wells in 0.15-0.45 EC. The highest numbers of open dug wells were found in 0.15-0.30 EC. Carbonate presents in 19 water samples, ranging 0.4 to 6.8 the higher carbonate which was recorded with Bastar sampled wells (6.8 meq per litre) and lower with Karanpur (0.4 meq per litre). It was below the non-permissible limit but some of the wells may be increased their carbonate content due to adding carbonate water from outside sources. Bicarbonate presents in all samples except one sample from Kurandi (0.00), otherwise it had wide range of carbonate presence in 0.2 to 28.8 meq per litre, sparsely distributed sampling indicated that most of the wells showed 1 to 3 meq per litre. Bijaput's open dug well was observed 7.2 meq per litre bicarbonate which was markedly higher than remaining except Bastar sample (Table 5). Depth and construction of concrete wall around inner wall depends on profile characteristics as compact profile finds in early depth did not go for concrete wall construction but collapsing strata reach up to certain depth, it needs construction of retaining wall around to check collapsing of wells. Most of the wells were found with 2-3m wall construction (Figure 7) ultimately leads to sustainability of open dug wells.

Rainfall and geology decide how much quantity of surface water moves into ground storage, the Bastar district has diverged form of geology alongwith surface morphology that provides faster movement and higher storing capacity. In this connection, net ground water availability (ham) is more in Jagdalpur (9855.28 ham) followed by Bastar block (8152.44 ham), Lahandiguda (8107.67 ham), Darbha (6921.27 ham), Bakawand (6291.61 ham),Tokapal (5814.21 ham) and Bastanar (4920.07 ham), whereas ground water draft highly varies among blocks, high ground water draft blocks are Bastar (1656.59 ham), Jagdalpur (1448.84 ham), and Tokapal (1035.14 ham). Some of the blocks are below 500 ham viz., Lohandiguda (315.105 ham), Darbha (276.98 ham) and Bastanar (139.72 ham). Bakawand ranges 500 to 1000 ham. The higher degree of settlement and cultivation of more water demanding crops are main reason for high ground water draft, sometimes plain surface morphology also insists to people for mentioned task. Low ground water draft in Lohandiguda, Darbha and Bastanar envisaged by undulating plain and ridge-valley topography, it limits to the process of settlement and agricultural allied activity, which are more prominent in these blocks due to more forest cover than rest of blocks.

Another aspect is stage of ground water development, due to basin like plain presents in Bastar, Tokapal, Jagdalpur and Bakawand, rainwater remains longer period has high potential of ground water development curbing 20.30, 17.80, 14.7 and 14.14% in respective blocks in rain water harvesting structures, otherwise remaining three blocks namely Lohandiguda, Bastanar and Darbha have 3.89, 2.84 and 4.00%, respectively. Future prospect of ground water resource is high in Jagdalpur (8775.54 ham) followed by Lohandiguda (7766.67 ham) and lower in Tokapal (4738.59 ham) and Bastanar (4763.77 ham).

Area Suitable for Dug Wells

All blocks fortunately possess significant area suitable for dug wells. The more area of Jagdalpur, Lohandiguda, Tokapal, Bastanar and Bakawand blocks falls under suitable for dug well construction due to the area prone to basin of Indrawati river, so subsurface collection in dug wells are perpetuated whereas less area in Bastanar. The dug wells lies in juncture of Bakawand, Jagdalpur, Bastar, Tokapal and eastern part of Lahandiguda are suitable for artificial ground water recharge, might be possibility of increasing dug well to contribute more ground water. With age old wisdom of local people and experience made the system vital till date. The higher number of vital dug wells was recorded in Jagdalpur (179), Tokapal (77), Bastar (76) (Table 2) which are still under use with drying in March and April which was 26.50 and 27.69%, respectively in the mentioned months (Table 3) under influence of river basin flow and regulate subsurface flow till raising temperature and high evapotranspiration.

Matrix Calculation

The correlation and covariance among the factors remained negative with each others. Correlation matrix ranged from -0.10 to -0.40 with linearity of R^2 value 0.061 and means of 6.10% variability. The covariance had higher degree of variability among the factors with linearity of 0377 (R^2) showing 37.7% variability (Figure 4 and 5). The basic difference of the analysis on different factors had increasing trend with correlation and declining trend with linearity of the factors.

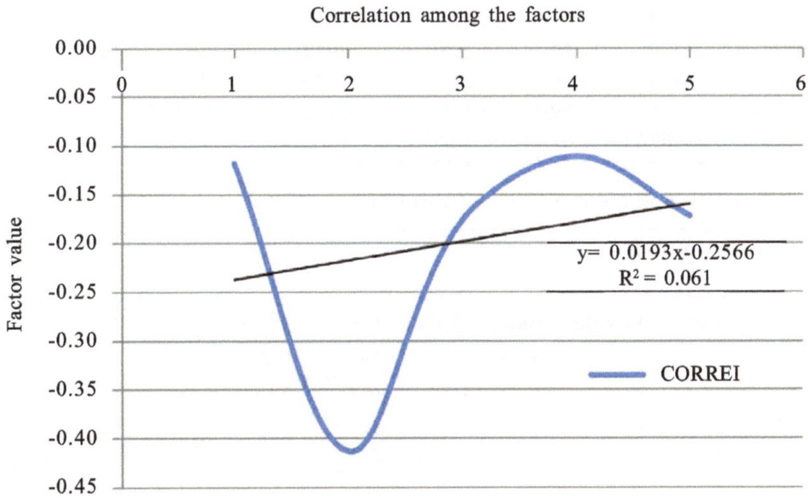

Fig. 4: Correlation between fectors :*1-Area and wells, 2- Area and number of stream, 3- Wells and number of stream, 4- Wells and Stream area, 5- Stream and stream area*

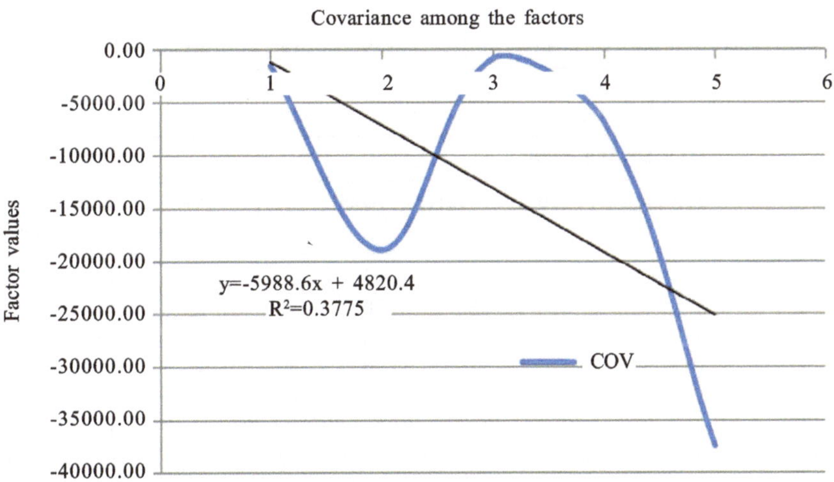

Fig. 5: Covariance between factors: *1- Area and wells, 2- Area and number of stream, 3- Wells and number of stream, 4- Wells and Stream area, 5- Stream and stream area*

Table 1: Number of observed wells in different blocks

Block	Area (km^2)	No. of well	Stream		Depth (m)		
			Number	Area (ha)	Max	Min	Mean
Bastar	1225	76	279	5068.9	19	5	12
Darbha	979	24	318	735.3	16	2	9
Bakawand	1180	13	242	1318.3	20	9	14.5
Tokapal	354	77	254	344.5	28	7	17.5
Jagdalpur	720	179	224	39.4	42	2	22
Lohandiguda	596	13	198	2640.7	20	2	11
Bastanar	320	36	619	778.9	33	7	20
STDV	371.28	59.15	143.77	1761.56	9.38	2.91	4.85
Mean	767.71	59.71	304.86	1560.86	25.43	4.86	15.14

Table 2: Number of observed wells in different blocks

Range of depth (m)	No. of well								
	Bastar	Darbha	Baka wand	Toka pal	Jagdal pur	Lohan diguda	Bast anar	Total	Percent
5 to 10	40	8	9	12	49	7	26	151	36.12
11 to 15	21	6	3	24	45	5	1	105	25.12
16 to 20	15	10	1	15	32	1	7	81	19.38
21 to 25				21	21			42	10.05
26 to 30				5	15			20	4.78
31 to 35					8		1	9	2.15
36 to 40					9		1	10	2.39
41 to 45					0			0	0
	76	**24**	**13**	**77**	**179**	**13**	**36**	**418**	**100**

Table 3: Open dug well drying time

Block	Well Drying in month							
	January	February	March	April	May	No drying	Total	Per cent
Bastar	0	15	7	25	21	5	73	**17.4**
Darbha	3	3	8	20	5	12	51	**12.26**
Bakawand	0	3	3	13	2	0	21	**5.14**
Tokapal	18	28	35	30	15	0	125	**30.02**
Jagdalpur	0	0	48	8	0	25	81	**19.38**
Lohandiguda	0	2	8	3	0	0	13	**3.16**
Bastanar	2	0	2	17	25	8	53	**12.66**
Total	23	51	111	116	68	50		
%	5.49	12.26	26.5	27.69	16.22	11.87		

Table 4: Usage and appearance of well water

Block	Usage			Appearance			
	Domestic	**Irrigation**	**Drinking**	**Dirty**	**Green**	**Muddy**	**Oily**
Bastar	23	33	0	12	8	25	1
Darbha	12	8	3	9	2	10	0
Bakawand	5	3	1	5	1	6	0
Tokapal	25	11	3	15	5	21	0
Jagdalpur	15	0	7	7	8	3	2
Lohandiguda	5	2	1	3	0	6	0
Bastanar	9	0	1	29	1	5	0
Total	94	57	16	80	25	76	3

Table 5: Water quality analysis of sampled wells

Geology, Stream and Wells

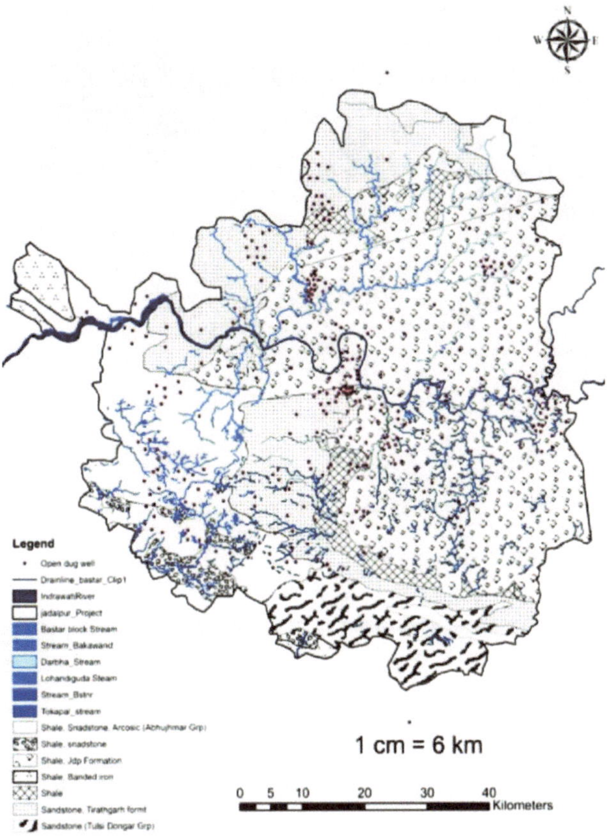

Fig. 2: Geology, Stream and Open Dug Wells Location of Bastar District

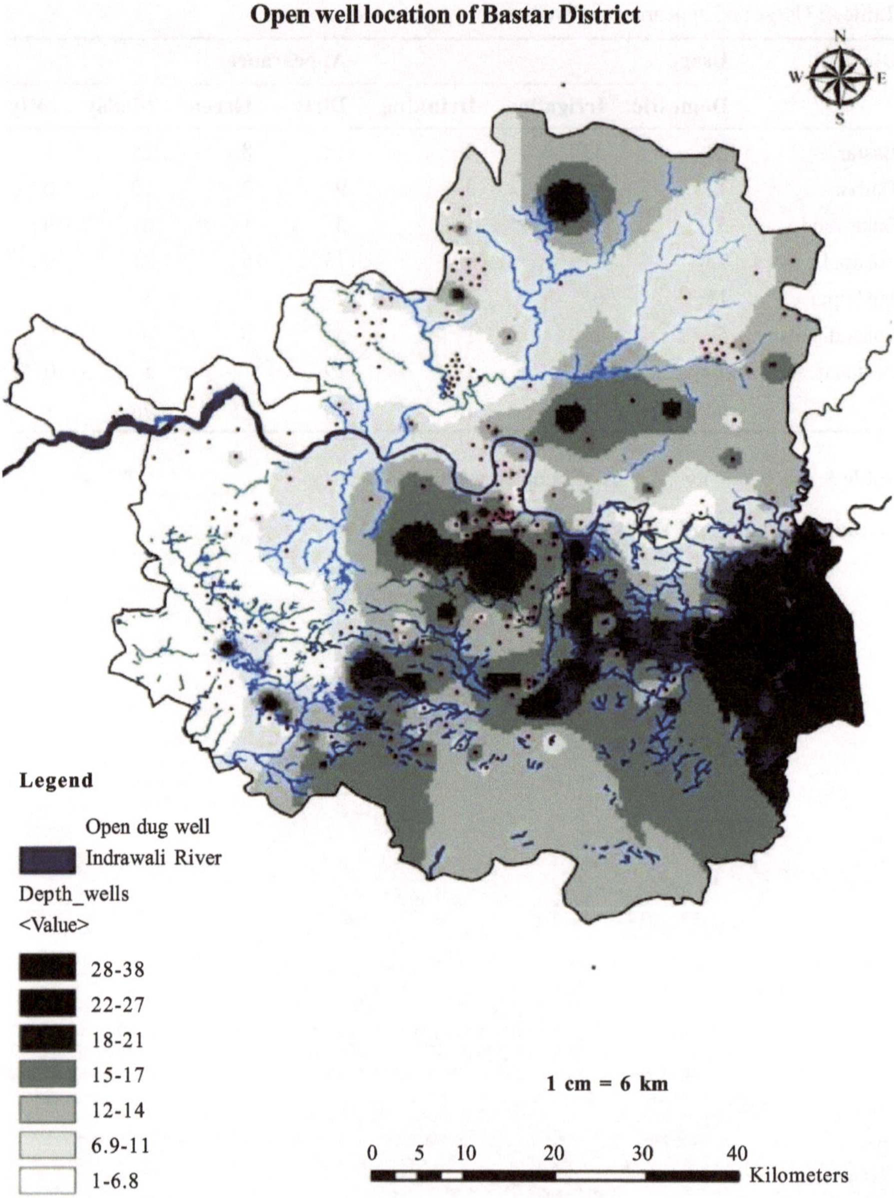

Fig. 3: Open Dug Well Location and Depth of Bastar District

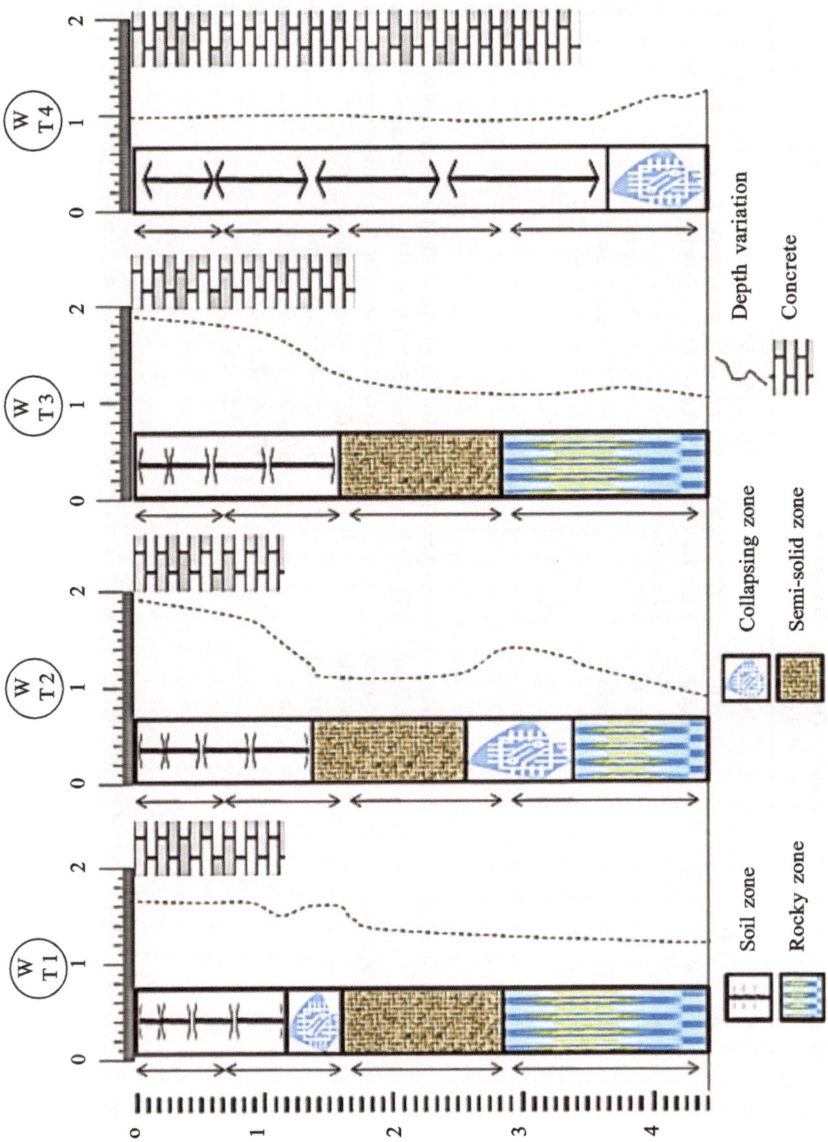

Fig. 7: Schematic Diagram of Open Dug Well Construction

Table. Satellites and their specification

Data Product	Provider	Orbital Height	Spatial Resolution	Swath Width	Pass Over Time	Date Range of Acquisition	Spectral Coverage	Access and Restrictions	Data Use
Landsat 5 TM	NASA/ USGS	705 km Sun-synchronous	30m 120m	185 km	Every 16 days Equator at ~ 09h 45 (local time)	since March 1,1984 *Note*: First Landsat Mission in 1972	B1: 0.45-0.52 μm (30m) B2: 0.52-0.60 μm (30m) B3: 0.63-0.69 μm (30m) B4: 0.76-0.90 μm (3m) B5: 1.55-1.75 μm (30m) B6: 10.4-12.5 μm (120m) (IR) B7: 2.08-2.35 μm (30m)	Free access, use and redistribution;	oceanography, aerosols, bathymetry, vegetation type, peak vegetation, biomass content analysis, moisture analysis, thermal mapping, mineral deposit identification
Landsat 7 ETM+	NASA/ USGS	705 km Sun-synchronous	15m 30m 60m	183 km	Every 16 days Equator at ~10h 00 (local time)	since April 15, 1999	B1: 0.45-0.515 μm (30m) B2: 0.525-0.605 μm (30m) B3: 0.63-0.69 μm (30m) B4: 0.75-0.90 μm (30m) B5: 1.55-1.75 μm (30m) B6: 10.4-12.5 μm (60m) B7: 2.09-2.35 μm (30m) B8: 0.52-0.9 μm (15m)	Free access, use and redistribution;	oceanography, aerosols, bathymetry, vegetation types, peak vegetation, biomass content analysis, moisture analysis, thermal mapping, mineral deposit identification
Landsat 8 OLI (B1-B9) TIRS (B10-B11)	NASA/ USGS	705 km Sun-synchronous	15m 30m 60m 100m	185 km	Every 16 days Equator at ~ 10h	since February 11, 2013	B1: 0.433–0.453 μm (30m) B2: 0.450–0.515 μm (30m) B3: 0.525–0.600 μm (30m) B4: 0.630–0.680 μm (30m)	Free access, use and redistribution;	oceanography, aerosols, bathymetry, vegetation types,

					00 (local time)		B5: 0.845–0.885 µm (30m) B6: 1.560–1.660 µm (60m) B7: 2.100–2.300 µm (30m) B8: 0.500–0.680 µm (15m) B9: 1.360–1.390 µm (30m) B10: 10.6-11.2 µm (100m) (IR) B11: 11.5-12.5 µm (100m) (IR)		peak vegetation, biomass content analysis, moisture analysis, cloud cover analysis, thermal mapping, soil moisture estimation
AVHRR/3 Advanced Very High Resolution Radiometer	NOAA/ USGS	830–870 km Sun-synchronous	1090m	833 km	Twice daily; entire planet	since May 1998 AVHRR/ 1/(1978) AVHRR/ 2 (1981; continuous date since 1981)	B1: 0.58-0.68 µm (1.09km) B2: 0.725-1.00 µm (1.09km) B3A: 1.58-1.64 µm (1.09km) B3B: 3.55-3.93 µm (1.09km) B4: 10.30-11.30µm (1.09km) B5: 11.50-12.50µm (1.09km)	Free access, use and redistribution;	cloud and surface mapping, land-water bounds, recognition of snow and ice, sea surface temperatures and cloud cover analysis at night
MODIS Moderate Resolution Imaging Spectroradiometer	NASA	705 km Sun-synchronous	250m (B1-B2) 500m (B3-B7) 1000m (B8-B36)	2330 km	Daily; equator at ~10h30 and 13h30 (local time)	Terra: December 18, 1999 Aqua: May 4, 2002	B1: 620 - 670 nm B2: 841 - 876 nm B3: 459 - 479 nm B4: 545 - 565 nm B5: 1230 - 1250 nm B6: 1628 - 1652 nm B7: 2105 - 2155 nm B8: 405 - 420 nm B9: 438 - 448 nm B10: 483 - 493 nm B11: 526 - 536 nm B12: 546 - 556 nm B13: 662 - 672 nm B14: 673 - 683 nm	Free access, use and redistribution;	aerosols, land and cloud boundaries and properties, ocean biology, biogeochemistry, atm. water vapour, sea surface and atmospheric temperature, cloud analysis

							B15: 743 - 753 nm B16: 862 - 877 nm B17: 890 - 920 nm B18: 931 - 941 nm B19: 915 - 965 nm B20: 3.660 - 3.840 μm B21: 3.929 - 3.989 μm B22: 3.929 - 3.989 μm B23: 4.020 - 4.080 μm B24: 4.433 - 4.498 μm B25: 4.482 - 4.549 μm B26: 1.360 - 1.390 μm B27: 6.535 - 6.895 μm B28: 7.175 - 7.475 μm B29: 8.400 - 8.700 μm B30: 9.580 - 9.880 μm B31: 10.780 - 11.280 μm B32: 11.770 - 12.270 μm B33: 13.185 - 13.485 μm B34: 13.485 - 13.785 μm B35: 13.785 - 14.085 μm B36: 14.085 - 14.385 μm		
Quick Bird	Digital Globe	482 km 450 km Sun-synchronous	65 cm B/W 2.62 m RGBiR 61 cm B/W 2.44 m RGBiR	16.8 km 18 km	Every 2.4-5.9 days, equator at 10h30 (local time)	since October 18, 2001	B/W: 405-1053 nm R: 430 - 545 nm G: 466 - 620 nm B: 590 - 710 nm NIR: 715 - 918 nm	Data needs to be purchased from Digital Globe or a commercial reseller; if imagery is not available in archive, special	mapping, change detection plannig (engineering, natural resources urban, infrastructure), land-use, EIA, tourism, military, crop management,

								request can be made	environmental monitoring
GOES Geostatio--ary Operational Environmental Satellite	NOAA	35 790 km Geostatio-nary	1 km 4 km 8 km	Pacific Ocean, americas and Atlantic (160°E to 20° W)	captures and sends data at various intervals; up to 8 per hour in the Contine-ntal US	First Mission 1978	B1 (Visible) (1 km) B2 (Shortwave) (4 km) B3 (Moisture) (8 km (4 km GOES 12/13/14/15)) B4 (Longwave 1) (4 km) B5 and 6 (Longwave 2) (4 km) GOES also has remote sensing equipment to detect space weather.	Free access, use and redistribution;	weather tracking, water vapour analysis, meteorology and atmospheric science
Ikonos	Digital Globe	681 km Sun-synchron-ous	80 cm B/W 3.2 m RBGiR	11.3 km	every 3 days	launch September 24, 1999	B/W: 445-900 nm B: 445-516 nm G: 506-595 nm R: 632-698 nm NiR: 757-853 nm	Data needs to be purchased from Digital Globe or a commercial reseller; if imagery is not available in archive, special request can be made	mapping, change detection, planning (engineering, natural resources, urban, infrastruct-ure), land-use, EIA tourism, military, crop management, environmental monitoring
SPOT Satellite pour l' Observat-ion de la Terre	EADS Astrium	694 km Sun-synchron-ous	2.5 m 5 m 10 m 20 m	60 km	every 1–3 days	SPOT1 launched in 1986 SPOT6 launched in 2012	B/W: 0.450-0.745 µm R: 0.625-0.695 µm G: 0.530-0.590 µm B: 0.450-0.520 µm NiR: 0.760-0.890 µm	Data needs to be purchased from EADS Astrium; if imagery is not available in archive, special request can be made	mapping, change detection, planning (engineering, natural resources, urban, infrastruct-ure), land-use, EIA tourism, military, crop management, environmental

									monitoring
RADARSAT	Canadian Space Agency MDA	RADARSAT1 793–821 km RADARSAT-2 798 km *RADARSAT Constellation* 592,7 km	8–100 m 3x1m – 100 x 100m *3x1m – 100 x 100 m*	45–500 km 18 – 500 m *5-500 km*	14 (14,92 Constellation) orbitsper day; at equator: 6h00 and 18h00 (local)	RADARSAT 1 launched on November 4, 1995 RADARSAT-2 launched on December 14, 2007 RADARSAT Constellation to be launched in 2018	Synthetic Aperture Radar (SAR)	Data needs to be purchased from MDA for commercial purposes; available for research througth the SOAR partnership from MDA and the Government of Canada	environmental monitoring, ice monitoring, marine surveillance, disaster management, hydrology, mapping, geology, agriculture and forestry
ASTER Advanced Spaceborne Thermal Emission and Reflectance Radiometer	NASA Government of Japan	705 km Sun-synchronous	15–90 m	60 km	Daily; equator at ~10h 30 (local)	since December 18, 1999 (on Terra)	B1: 0.520-0.600 µm (15m) B2: 0.630-0.690 µm (15m) B3: 0.760-0.860 µm (15m) B4: 0.760-0.860 µm (15m) B5: 1.600-1.700 µm (30m) B6: 2.145-2.185 µm (30m) B7: 2.185-2.225 µm (30m) B8: 2.235-2.285 µm (30m) B9: 2.295-2.365 µm (30 m) B10: 2.360-2.430 µm (30m) B11: 8.125-8.475 µm (90m) B12: 8.475-8.825 µm (90m) B13: 8.925-9.275 µm (90m) B14: 10.250-10.950µm (90m) B15: 10.950-11.650µm (90m)	Data needs to be purchased for commercial purposes; Educational use and NASA-supported research permitted	vegetation, ecosystem dynamics, hazard and disaster monitoring, change detection, earth science, land cover analysis

10

Remote Sensing Imagery

Remotely gathered data are available from a range of sources and data collection techniques is often one type of tool that is not always found within the public domain easily. This is larger due to the fact that most of the data are acquired by equipment is expensive to build and maintain. However, there are many types of basic imagery, high-quality imageries are readily available widely at subsidized costs, particularly the purpose intented.

Image Classification

Two major categories of image classification techniques are **unsupervised** (calculated by software) and **supervised** (human-guided) classification.

i) **Unsupervised classification** where the outcomes (groupings of pixels with common characteristics) are based on the software analysis of an image without user providing sample classes. The computer uses the techniques to determine and pixels are related and grouped them into classes. The user can specify algorism software which will be used desire number of output classes, otherwise it does not aid in the classification process. However, user must have knowledge of the area being classified when the groupings of pixels with common characteristics produced by the computer being related to actual features on the ground (such as wetlands, developed areas, coniferous forests, etc.).

ii) **Supervised classification** is based on the idea that a user can select sample pixels in an image these are representative of specific classes and then direct the image processing software to use these training sites as references for the classification of all other pixels in image. Training sites (also known as testing sets or input classes) are selected based on the knowledge of the user. The user also sets the bounds for how similar other pixels must be grouped them together. These bounds are often set based on the spectral characteristics of the training area plus or minus a certain increment (often based "brightness" or strength of reflection in specific spectral bands). The user also designates the number of classes where the image is classified into. Many analysis use a combination of supervised and unsupervised classification processes to develop final output analysis and classified maps.

Satellite Types

Satellites can be classified by their functions. Satellites are launched into space to do a specific job. The type of satellite that is launched to monitor cloud patterns for a weather station may be different than a satellite launched to send television signals across country. The satellite must be designed specifically to fulfill its function.

Below these are the names of nine different types of satellites. You can click either on the picture or on the name to learn more about that type of satellite, and its example.

1. Astronomy satellites - Hubble Space Telescope
2. Atmospheric Studies satellites - Polar
3. Communications satellites - Anik E
4. Navigation satellites - Navstar
5. Reconaissance satellites - Kennan, Big Bird, Lacrosse
6. Remote Sensing satellites - Radarsat
7. Search and Rescue satellites - Cospas-Sarsat
8. Space Exploration satellites - Galileo
9. Weather satellites - Meteosat

Aerial Photography

Aerial photography has two uses that are of interest in class exercises: (1) collection of detailed measurements from aerial photos in the preparation of maps; and (2) to determine land-use, environmental conditions, and geologic information (outcrop locations, lineation, etc). It should be noted that aerial photographs are not maps. Maps are orthogonal representations of the earth's surface, means they are directionally and geometrically accurate. Aerial photos often display a high degree of radial distortion that must be corrected. Most GIS packages have some mechanism or work flow for correcting this distortion (see georeferencing) or you make an effort to find corrected data online.

Types of Aerial Photography

- Black and White: Older and lower cost surveys are collected on black and white media and coverage over is essentially complete. Multiple generations are ideal for comparing for recent change detection of the land surface.
- Color: More recent or higher cost aerial photo surveys are on color media and coverage over most key areas are available but not always at zero cost.
- Infrared: Primary use is vegetation studies as vegetation is a very strong reflector of infrared radiation.

Sources of Aerial Photography

Imagery is ready to load means it generally comes in the form of Digital Orthophoto Quadrangle (DOQ) or Digital Orthophoto Quarter Quadrangle (DOQQ). These are available from many sources including the US Geological Survey DOQ online order site. There are also a range of commercial organizations that provide low-cost downloads of individual and regional DOQQ sets (e.g., Geocommunity).

Satellite Imagery

Satellite imagery is collected by a host of national and international government, and private agencies. Most of this data is protected by copyright and use access has to be negotiated individualy or institutionally. Free access is possible through collaboration with NASA and NASA funded institutions. Data products span the useful electro-magnetic spectrum in a variety of resolutions and it falls upon the instructor to consider the utility of this data in the instructional environment. In many cases, free or low-cost data has a resolution cell size greater than 100m/pixel thus this type of imagery often provides a big-picture regional view but may not provide detailed insight to geologic features found on the ground. Nonetheless, this type of data can be very useful in multi-scale analysis and to help students gain an appreciation for the scale of features on the ground that can have a substantial influence on the bulk reflectivity collected during satellite flyovers.

Types of Satellite Digital Imagery

Remotely sensed satellite data come in two basic types, passively collected data and actively collected data. Passive data collection focuses on acquiring intensities of electromagnetic radiation generated by the sun and reflected off the surface of the planet. Active data collection is largely restricted to devices that send and generate a pulse of energy to that is reflected back to the satellite to be recorded.

Most of the readily available data is passively collected and is limited to energy not absorbed by the Earth's atmosphere. Satellite imagery based on passive reflectivity comes in 4 basic types, which are visible, infrared, multispectral, and hyperspectral.

The type and resolution of the data collected is generally keyed to the mission of the satellite. Visible data consists of pixels composing color values of red, green, and blue to make three bands of data on a raster image. Infrared imagery usually consists of the images that include the visible channels as well as some range of the infra-red spectrum. Multispectral data include up to 7-12 channels of data and hyperspectral can be up to 50 bands or more of data collected over discrete bandwidths of the electromagnetic spectrum. How all of the data is used beyond the scope of this view, but it's worth keeping in mind that there are a range of available products and it may require a great deal of research to determine what type of data is useful in context of field based exercise.

As of the spring of 2007, NASA lists over 100 satellites providing imagery for viewing from various online image repositories. Images from Landsat-1, -2, -3, -4, -5, and -7 are by far the most common satellite sources used by geologists in conducting field based research. Landsat-5 and -7 are the only two satellites still in service where the instruments on board consist of a multi-spectral scanner (MSS) and an "Enhanced Thematic Mapper-plus" instrument, respectively. Specific details regarding these instruments and their imagery can be found at the GeoCover Tutorial Site hosted by NASA.

Sources of Satellite Digital Imagery

Much of the available data can be purchased from a number of commercial sources. One of the best way to have wide ranging access to NASA related imagery is to collaborate with a NASA scientist. The Jet Propulsion laboratory offers a range of educator resources for individuals who participate in their Higher Education Faculty Program. Other sources suitable for field mapping exercises include the NASA hosted GeoCover Site, which provides imagery through the MrSid format. The National Geologic Map Database provides a help page for working with MrSID images. Additional information on using imagery from the GeoCover site (a.k.a. Zulu) can be found at a GIS online tutorial hosted by the Rocky Mountain Mapping Center of the U.S. Geological Survey. The US Geological Survey provides a informative site dedicated to the Landsat program. Scenes can also be ordered from the USGS EROS site.

Data Preparation for Geologic Mapping

Preparing data for a digital geologic mapping project generally involves three steps:

1. Preparing digital base map data (i.e. downloadable or previously stored thematic, topographic, or remotely sensed data, or data that you digitize, scan and geo-reference);
2. Creating a database and/or individual files to store data that will be gathered in the field (e.g. the locations and descriptive attributes of rock units, rock unit contacts, and measured attitudes);
3. Creating a map that is ready for editing in the field.

What follows is discussion and instructions for completing these steps with ArcGIS 9.x and ArcPad 7.x software. Design of GeoPad projects can take several tracts, from those that fully implement all of the features of digitizing in a field environment, to those that implement only a subset (e.g. collection of linear e.g. faults, unit contacts) and/or point (strike/dip, station observations) features; or simply constructing sketch maps on spatially referenced base maps. The techniques discussed below might be tested first with a pilot project done in a local setting.

The following steps illustrate the preparation of a GeoPad field mapping project, once a field area has been selected (a second option yet to be created, is the download of a map document template and geodatabase for a prototypical map area that can be used a model to be modified as needed):

Base Map Preparation

Preparation of base map data requires familiarity with GIS data formats and spatial references (i.e. datums and coordinate systems/projections) so that all base map layers properly co-register and have adequate resolution. For base map data obtained from different sources, preparation may be example, involve projecting datasets to a common spatial reference, defining a spatial reference for data that lack such, clipping to an area of interest and/or preparing derivative base map layers, such as those that portray slope or topography in shaded relief. Detailed procedures for scanning, georeferencing and digitizing paper maps are beyond the scope of this discussion but are available at the GIS and GPS Applications page at the University of Texas.

1. Define region of interest for current project
2. Decide which datasets are valuable to your project
3. Identify sources of datasets and download to local computer
    - Topographic
    - Thematic
    - Imagery

4. Identify and georeference any additional non-digital sources of spatial data
   - Compile tabular data with x,y location information into a spreadsheet and add to GIS application
   - Scan paper map products
   - Clip scanned image to area of interest and save as compatible file format (tiff, jpeg)
   - Georeference scanned image
5. Confirm that all datasets are in the same coordinate system, projection and datum.
   - If coordinate system is undefined, find original coordinate system and establish spatial reference
   - If not all the same, project to a common coordinate system and datum
6. Prepare topographic derivatives such as slope or hillshade layers
7. Clip all spatial data to a common project area extent

Databases and Editable Files

Creating a database and/or stand-alone files to store data gathered in the field is less straight-forward and can take several tacts, depending on the degree of sophistication desired, the software available in the office and field, and one's facility with database design and implementation. At the simplest level, the sticky issues of structuring and creating files for field editing could seemingly be avoided entirely by simply drawing geologic line, point, and polygon features directly on base map layers using the tablet drawing tools available, for example, in ArcMap software. This intuitive approach is unfortunately unsatisfactory from several standpoints, not the least of which is an inability to also capture and store descriptive data (a.k.a. "attributes", e.g. strike and dip measurements, inferred vs. exposed contacts, formation names, etc.) associated with each feature that, at a minimum, are needed to symbolize and annotate a geologic map. GIS software is designed with precisely this consideration in mind, and ESRI "feature classes" provide the file structure for storing such attributes for each and every feature mapped. Feature classes that hold digital data come in two flavors: those that reside within a geodatabase environment and those that stand-alone (i.e. shapefiles). Feature classes within geodatabases have two principle advantages over stand-alone shapefiles for field mapping:

1. The capability of applying a "domain" to each attributes to be collected. A domain is predefined list of all possible values for an attribute (e.g. the

domain for the attribute "line type" might have the values solid, dashed, dotted, or queried). When entering or editing attribute data, domain values appear as selectable options in a list. Domains can be text or numeric values, like strike, dip, line type, formation name, etc., allowing simple and rapid data entry in the field. A similar ability to pick attributes values from a list can be created for shapefiles, but requires custom forms built with ArcPad Studio or by hand coding.

2. If shapefiles are required, for example for use with ArcPad software, then they can be created from geodatabase feature classes with the domains intact. An export tool is available in ArcMap to create shapefiles from geodatabase feature classes that simultaneously creates forms for attribute entry. The forms contain domain values in selectable lists, again obviating the need to peck in letters or numbers with a stylus. Once edited in the field, shapefiles created this way can be imported back into the geodatabase, updating the original feature classes from which they came.

Project Design

1. **Feature classes that hold digital data come in two flavors**: those that reside within a geodatabase environment and those that stand-alone (e.g. shapefiles). Feature classes within geodatabases have two advantages: predefined attribute domains allow rapid entry of data either within forms in ArcPad or when editing directly within ArcMap. Below are examples of each of these approaches.
   - **Geodatabases**: Tutorials exist to help you create your own geodatabase
   - **Shape files**: Tutorials exist to help you create your own shape files
2. **Create a map project within ArcMap that contains base map layers and newly created feature classes**
   - Set the 'Map Properties' for the ArcMap project to always use relative paths to locate data sources
   - Load all base map layers and geologic feature classes into ArcMap
   - Create/download symbology (i.e. layer files) for the feature classes line data, point data
   - For ArcPad projects, export feature classes and base layers to shapefiles and MrSid rasters with the ArcPad export toolbar in ArcMap. With an ArcMap project that uses geodatabase feature classes with defined domains, this automatically creates data entry forms like those that can be created manually with ArcPad Studio. Clipping data sets to project area boundaries can be done at this stage as well.

3. **Customizing the mapping software interface**
   - Customize toolbars (ArcPad, ArcMap): A custom geologic mapping toolbar greatly simplifies the process of mapping
   - Integrate external data collectors into the ArcMap environment, for examples: GPS, laser range finders, magnetometers, field microscopes, digital cameras

Information Management

Because of the large number of files created during fieldwork, it is important to have a plan for how to organize and backup your files.

- Backup techniques—thumb drive
- File structures for storing field notes (e.g. OneNote or Journal files), digital photos
- Standard file storage structure for all GeoPads
- Scheme for management of geospatial data of project that involves compiling a map from several individuals vs individual mapping exercises

Geo-referencing

Geo-referencing is the process of taking a digital image, it could be an airphoto, a scanned geologic map, or a picture of a topographic map, and adding geographic information to the image so that GIS or mapping software can 'place' the image in its appropriate real world location. This process is completed by selecting pixels in the digital image and assigning them geographic coordinates. In rare instances, one may already know the geographic coordinates of certain pixels in an image; more frequently, a non-georeferenced image is georeferenced to an existing image that already has embedded geographic information, such as a DRG, DLG, or DEM.

Specialized software is generally necessary to complete the process of geocoding. ArcGIS has functionality for this procedure, as do many remote sensing software packages, such as ENVI. For the purposes of GeoPads, the most pressing need for georeferencing are the digital images of geologic maps available from the National Geologic Map Database. The USGS provides a comprehensive tutorial on georeferencing in ArcGIS. Other programs will follow a similar procedure.

Logistics

Below are some of the logistical issues and solutions one will typically encounter using GeoPads.

- **Loading GeoPads** – standard approaches to loading and maintaining the operating system and software applications on Windows computers are directly applicable to the GeoPads. Common approaches include Ghosting or Microsoft Sysprep

- **Distributing Projects** – a variety of approaches can be used to distribute projects to students' GeoPads, such as:
- **USB Flash Drives** – Students can be given a flash drive with the contents of the project on it. This can be a time-consuming process, if there a lot of thumb drives to load, or one needs to be passed around a large group. (The students can also carry these in the field as a back-up option.)
- **Bulk Distribution** – Applications, such as Ghost, can be used to bulk distribute files and folders to students' GeoPads over a network.
- **Network File Sharing** – A shared network drive can host projects for students to copy to their GeoPads.
- **Backups**

USB Flash Drives

Network File Sharing – Provide students with network file storage to copy backups of their work. Automatic copying is also an option. Network file sharing can also be used by instructors to remotely copy data from students to their own computer or a network drive.

- **Power**: If you're spending time in the field away from the grid, you need to consider how you will recharge the GeoPads and related peripherals, such as using a generator. A good choice is an electronic-equipment sensitive, ultra quiet model, such as the Honda 2000i. Make sure the generator has sufficient output and you bring enough fuel to meet your charging needs. You'll also likely need power strips and extension cords to distribute the power.

Safety

- **Hands-free Harness:** Using hands-free harnesses helps to promote a safe environment for both students and GeoPads. Clipping GeoPad up tight against the body increases stability when scrambling about on rough terrain. Using the hands-free harness decreases the odds of accidentally dropping the GeoPad and causing damage through repeated picking up and setting down or taking in and out of backpacks.
- **No Cable Policy**: Avoid attaching peripherals (e.g., GPS, camera, audio headset) through cables to eliminate incidences of snagging and possible damage to the GeoPad and/or the peripherals.

Applications of Satellite Imagery and Remote Sensing Data

Remote sensing data provides essential information that helps in monitoring various applications such as image fusion, change detection and land cover classification. Remote sensing is a key technique used to obtain information related to the earth's resources and environment. What popularized satellite imagery data, is that they can be easily accessed online through various mapping applications like Google Earth and Bing Maps. From being simply able to find, "where is my house" these applications have helped the GIS community in project planning, monitoring disasters and natural calamities and guiding civil defense people.

Remotely sensed satellite images and data include spectral, spatial and temporal resolutions. Spectral statistics involves elements of remotely sensed image classification. The main aspect which influences the accuracy of ground object is spatial resolution. Temporal resolution helps in generation of land cover maps for environmental planning, land use change detection and transportation planning. Data integration and analysis of urban areas using medium resolution **remote sensing** imagery mainly focuses on documentation of built up areas or is used for differentiating between residential, commercial and industrial zones.

1. Providing a base map for graphical reference and assisting planners and engineers

The amount of details that an orthoimagery produces using high resolution satellite imagery is of immense value as it provides a detail image of the selected area along with its surrounding areas.

As maps are location-based they are specifically designed to communicate highly structured data and to give a complete picture about the whole world. There are numerous applications of satellite imagery and remote sensing data. Today nations use information derived from the satellite imagery for government decision making, civil defence operations, police and Geographic Information Systems (GIS) in general. These days, data captured through **Satellite Imagery** has become mandatory and all government plans are to be submitted on the basis of Satellite Imagery data.

2. Extracting mineral deposits with remote sensing based spectral analysis

During the pre-feasibility and feasibility stages of the mineral exploration, it is important to know about the mineral potentiality of the area to be considered for mineral extraction. In such scenarios, satellite remote sensing based mapping and its integration in a GIS platform help geo scientist to map the mineral potential zones easily by saving time. With the help of spectral analysis of satellite image bands the scientist can quickly identify and map mineral availability through special indicators. This will enable exploration geologist to narrow his geo physical, geo chemical and test drilling activities to high potential zones.

3. Disaster mitigation planning and recovery

The result of a natural calamity can be devastating and at times difficult to assess. But disaster risk assessment is necessary for rescue workers.This information has to be prepared and executed quickly and with accuracy. Object-based image classification using change detection (pre- and post-event) is a quick way to acquire damage assessments data. Other similar applications using satellite imagery in disaster assessments include measuring shadows from buildings and digital surface models.

4. Agriculture development

With increasing population across the world and the need for increased agricultural production there is a certain need for proper management of the world's agricultural resources. To make this happen it is first necessary to obtain reliable data on not only the types, but also the quality, quantity and location of these resources. Satellite imagery and GIS will always continue to be a significant factor in the improvement of the present systems of acquiring and generating agricultural maps and resource data. Agriculture mapping and surveys are presently conducted throughout the world, in order to gather information and statistics on crops, range land, livestock and other related agricultural resources.

This information collected is necessary for the implementation of effective management decisions. Agricultural survey is needed for planning and allocation of the limited resources to different sectors of the economy.

5. 3D GIS

3D city models: The models are digital models of urban areas that represent Terrain surfaces, sites, buildings, vegetation, infrastructure and Landscape elements as well as related objects belonging to urban areas. Their components are described and represented by corresponding two-dimensional and three-dimensional spatial data and geo-referenced data. 3D city models support presentation, exploration, analysis, and management of tasks in a large number of different application domains. 3D GIS is the instant and effective Solution for larger and remote locations where manual survey is next to impossible. Various urban/ rural planning departments require 3D GIS data like, Drainage, Sewerage, **Water supply,** Canal Designing BIM and may more.

Geographic Information System (GIS) and Digital Image Analysis

In order to meet the demand of scientists, students and participants of various sponsored training programmes in the field of Geographic Information System (GIS) and digital image analysis in natural resource management, a user friendly 'Training Manual on GIS and Digital Image Processing' has important aspects of hands-on exercises of the user requirements. The training provides enough information and guidance for the practitioners to perform various GIS and image analysis applications. The important topics of hands-on practical in GIS and remote sensing applications to get overall knowledge in the practical exercises using GIS and digital image processing software's. The researchers have some familiarity with GIS and image analysis software's, they should read those which address their specific concerns. The set of step-by-step procedures/instructions with suitable graphics for the important GIS and image analysis softaware's i.e., ArcGIS.

GIS is a tool to efficiently capture, store, update, manipulate, analyze and display all forms of geographically referenced data. GIS is being widely used as spatial analysis tool for effective and efficient means of data generation and management, analysis and display. The true value of GIS can only be realized if the proper tools to collect spatial data and integrate them with attribute data are available. Data used in GIS often come from many types, and are stored in different ways. GIS provides tools and a methods for the integration of different data into a format to be compared and analyzed. Data sources are mainly obtained from remote-sensing satellite imageries, GPS surveys, manual digitization, scanning of aerial photographs, paper maps, and existing digital data sets are promising sources for data input in GIS. Before generation of any spatial data one has to understand the available data types, data formats, data analysis procedures and their capabilities in GIS to get realistic outputs.

Remote sensing (RS), also called earth observation, refers to obtaining information about objects or areas at the Earth's surface without being in direct contact with the object or area. Remote sensing techniques allow taking images of the earth surface in various wavelength region of the electromagnetic spectrum (EMS). One of the major characteristics of a remotely sensed image is the wavelength region it represents in the EMS. Some of the images represent reflected solar radiation in the visible and the near infrared regions of the electromagnetic spectrum, others are the measurements of the energy emitted by the earth surface itself i.e. in the thermal infrared wavelength region.

Geomatica, one of the latest products from PCI Geomatics, is a blend of EASI/ PACE, SPANS, PAMAP, ACE, and OrthoEngine. It has been produced to develop a completely new functionality framework for producing a single, tightly integrated product i.e. Geomatica. The development of custom applications is facilitated through the PCI Visual ModelerTM graphical programming environment, PCI AuthorTM GUI builder, and developer programme. It is highly customisable such that users will be able to select from various components that best fit their needs, create precise end-to-end process solutions using a wide range of tools.

IGIS is geomatics application software that gives the power to visualize the spatial data (Raster & Vector) geographically and to manipulate data (raster and vector) for standard analysis. It facilitates the end user to create maps, images and provides all the tools needed to put data on a map and display it in an effective manner. It helps to solve the geo-location and attribute based queries, present the results of work in the form of publication-quality maps and to create interactive displays that link reports, graphs, tables, drawings, photographs, and other elements to the data. It can be easily customized in order to tailor the interface to suit the needs of the organization, build new tools to automate the work, and develop standalone applications based on mapping components.

The instruction mainly covers the topics on principles and concepts in GIS, digital image analysis, image registration, digital terrain analysis, assimilation of input datasets in digital terrain analysis, processing of digital elevation datasets in GIS, organization of geospatial datasets in GIS, spatial data integration techniques in GIS and visualization techniques. Authors of this publication believe that the contents of training manual are well structured to match the requirements of the users in GIS and digital image processing in ArcGIS, Geomatica and IGIS software's. The manuscript would like to state that it does not promote any software, but made an attempt to provide the details on GIS and digital image processing tools to help the training participants and answer their common questions of exercises. Keeping the needs of the new covers in GIS and digital image processing, every effort has been made to cover all the important aspects, however, if any topics is not cover or partially covered in the training manual, reader's are advised to referred the alternative reference material for detailed information.

GIS and Digital Image Processing Software's

Many GIS and digital image processing software's like VI ArcGIS, eCognition, ERDAS, ENVI, Geometica, Geomedia, IGIS, TNT, Scanex,, etc., provide GIS and digital image processing functionalities based on operating system, versions, augmented by additional programming tools and standards. Some of the open source software like SAGA, GRASS, ILWIS, etc. were freely accessible to the users. A brief note on major image processing and GIS packages were given below.

ArcGIS

ArcGIS is an integrated collection of GIS software products (Arc Objects) for building a complete GIS. It consists of a number of frameworks for deploying GIS, such as, ArcGIS Desktop, ArcGIS Engine, Server GIS, and Mobile GIS. ArcGIS Desktop includes a suite of integrated applications including ArcCatalog, ArcMap, ArcGlobe, ArcToolbox, and ModelBuilder. Using these applications and interfaces, any GIS task, simple to advance, including mapping, geographic analysis, data editing and compilation, data management, visualization, and geo-processing can be performed. ArcGIS Desktop is scalable - from ArcView to ArcEditor to ArcInfo to meet the needs of users.

ERDAS Imagine

ERDAS Imagine comes in three tiers. IMAGINE Essentials is the entry level ERDAS IMAGINE product, with IMAGINE Advantage building upon IMAGINE Essentials, and IMAGINE Professional building upon both IMAGINE Essentials and IMAGINE Advantage. While the basic data creation and visualization tools are available in all the IMAGINE products, the other advanced capabilities, such as, a powerful ortho-rectification capability, mosaicing, image enhancements and terrain analysis. GIS analysis is limited to IMAGINE Advantage and Professional.

ENVI (Environment for Visualizing Images)

ENVI supports imagery types gathered from today's popular satellite and airborne sensors including panchromatic, multi-spectral, hyperspectral, RADAR, thermal, LIDAR, and soon. The robust functionality of ENVI can even be further extended by adding modules, like Orthorectification module, DEM extraction module, Atmospheric correction module with FLAASH and QUAC algorithms, and SARscape module, which provides a unique set of functionality to read, process, analyze and output SAR data and integrate results with other remotely sensed data.

eCognition Developer

eCognition Developer is a powerful development environment for object-based image analysis. It is used in earth sciences to develop rule sets for the automatic analysis of remote sensing data. The object-based approach facilitates analysis of all common data sources, such as medium to high resolution satellite data, high to very high resolution aerial photography, Lidar, radar and even hyperspectral data. eCognition Developer offers a comprehensive collection of algorithms tailored to the different aspects of image analysis.

Geomatica

Geomatica, another advanced image processing software aimed primarily at raster data processing and allows users to load satellite and aerial imagery where advanced analysis can be performed. Geomatica offers solutions for all of geomatics processing needs while maintaining complete interoperability with outside software packages. Geomatica product includes many built-in capabilities to support basic and advanced image processing, classification, and cartographic analysis. Geomatica Prime include all the capabilities of Geomatica Core as well as robust spatial analysis to visualize, analyze, and model geographic information.

IGIS

IGIS is Geomatics application software that gives the power to visualize the spatial data (Raster & Vector) geographically and to manipulate data (raster and vector) for standard analysis. IGIS includes image processing tools for automated feature extraction, object segmentation, change detection and time series analysis. Classification tools include supervised and unsupervised multi-spectral and hyper-spectral classifiers. Class include fuzzy and convolution based modules. All web services are available as standard modules and are compliant to OGC standards.

TNTmips

TNTmips provides, at a single platform GIS, image processing, CAD, desktop cartography, electronic atlas preparation, and other spatial database management and visualization applications, TNTmips has three license levels. TNTmips Pro (professional license), TNTmips Basic and TNTmips Free (freeware). TNTmips can import all kind of data formats into its native format i.e., '.rvc' It is having a very user friendly digitization, terrain and watershed analysis modules. It supports point, line and polygon, all three on a single vector layer.

Open Source Software Packages

Many software's like ILWIS, GRASS Geographic Resources Analysis Support System), SAGA System for Automated Geoscientific Analyses), JUMP GIS. Quantum GIS, and Map Window GIS are nowadays available in public domain for the users to analyze and handling of geospatial data.

Glossary of GIS

Addition: A point process that blends the values of corresponding pixels in two input images. A single parameter controls which input image dominates the output image.

Albedo: Ratio of the amount of electromagnetic energy (solar radiation) reflected by a surface to the amount of energy incident upon the surface.

Arc: a line connecting a set of points.

Area Processes: A category of image processing techniques that calculate the value of each outputimage pixel from the corresponding input-image pixel and its neighbours. Examples include halftoning, sharpening and median filtering.

Aspect Ratio: The ratio of the width of an image to its height. Examples include 4:3, the aspect ratio of a standard TV, and 16:9, the aspect ratio of a widescreen TV.

ASTER: Advanced Spaceborne Thermal Emission and Reflection Radiometer. **AVHRR:** Advanced very high-resolution radiometer.

Attribute: a characteristic which describes a feature. Attributes can be thought of as questions which are asked about the feature.

Average Greyscale: The shade of grey produced by adding the brightnesses of the RGB components of a color pixel and dividing by three. Backward Mapping: The technique geometric processes use to calculate output-image pixel values from input-image pixel values.

AVIRIS: Airborne visible-infrared imaging spectrometer.

Band: Broadcasting frequency within given limits.

Bandwidth: The total range of frequency required to pass a specific modulated (spectral resolution) signal without distortion or loss of data.

Bayer Filter: Enables a CCD to capture color by covering 2x2 blocks of CCD-sensor elements with one red, one blue and two green filters, which makes color CCDs more sensitive to the green wavelengths of light, just like our eyes.

Bi-linear Interpolation: A method of calculating the value of a pixel with fractional co-ordinates that lies in between a 2x2 neighbourhood of pixels.

Bitmap Image: An image composed of black and white pixels.

Blurring: An area process that produces an effect similar to an out-of-focus photograph. Blurring removes the detail in an image by making each pixel more like its

Bounding Box: The smallest rectangle that encloses a shape so that each of the four sides touches an extremity of the shape.

brightness over a small number of pixels. High-pass Filter: A filter that preserves or amplifies the high frequency information in an image. Sharpening is implemented by a high pass filter.

Brightness Transformation: A point process that maps input brightnesses onto output brightnesses with a linear or non-linear mathematical function.

Brightness: Determines the intensity of the color presented by a pixel in a color image, or the shade of grey presented by a pixel in a greyscale image.

Buffer: A zone of a specified distance around coverage

CAD: Computer Aided Design. An automated system for the design, drafting and display of graphically oriented information.

Cadastre: Public record of the extent, value and ownership of land within a district for purposes of taxation.

Capture: The process of measuring and visualising physical phenomena such as visible and non-visihin electromagnetic radiation. Examples include takin photograph and scanning a document.

Cartesian coordinate system: A two dimensional coordinate system in which x measures horizontal distance and y measures vertical distance. An x,y coordinate defines every point on the plane.

CCD: A charge-couple device is an imaging sensor that contains a rectangular grid of light-sensitive capacitors. Each capacitor accumulates a charge proportional to the brightness of the light it detecte the brighter the light, the higher the charge.

CEO: Center for Observing the Earth from Space at Yale University

Clip: The spatial extraction of those features from one coverage that reside entirely within the boundary defined by features in another coverage. Clipping works much like a cookie cutter.

Closing: A morphological operation produced by following a dilation by an erosion. Often used for filling holes in bitmap images.

COGO: Abbreviation for the term Coordinate Geometry. Land surveyors use COGO functions to enter survey data, to calculate precise locations and boundaries, to define curves, and so on.

Color Model: Determines how the color in a digital image is represented numerically. Examples include the RGB and HSB color models.

Composition: A point process that overlays the pixels of a foreground input image onto the pixels of a background input image.

Contour line: An imaginary line joining points of equal elevation.

Contrast Expansion: An image-processing technique that re-distributes the brightness in an image to eliminate regions that are either too dark or too light. Examples include basic and ends-in contrast expansion.

Contrast: The difference between the lightest and darkest regions of an image.

Control points: A set of points on the ground whose horizontal and vertical location is known. Control points are used as the basis for detailed surveys.

Convolution: A method of calculating the new value of a central pixel in a neighbourhood by multiplying each pixel in the neighbourhood by a corresponding weight; the new value of the central pixel is the sum of the multiplications.

Coordinate: An xy location in a Cartesian coordinate system or an x,y,z coordinate in a three dimensional system. Coordinates represent locations on the Earth's surface relative to other locations.

Corrupted Pixel: A pixel value altered by noise.

Coverage units: The units (e.g., feet, meter, inches) of the coordinate system in which a coverage is stored.

Coverage: A digital version of a map forming the basic unit of vector data storage in ARC/INFO. A coverage stores map features as primary features. A coverage usually represents a single theme, or layer, such as soils, roads, or land use.

Cropping: A geometric process that reduces the size of an image by discarding the pixels outside a specified region called the crop selection.

Data conversion: The translation of data from one format to another. ARC/INFO supports data conversion from many different geographic data formats in addition to routines for converting paper maps. Those data formats include DLG, TIGER, DXF, and DEM.

Data: raw collection of facts.

Database management system: a set of programs for features drawn and characterized with scale and direction to represent the real world.

Database: A logical collection of interrelated information, managed and stored as a unit. A GIS database includes data about the spatial location and shape of geographic features recorded as points, lines, and polygons as well as their attributes.

Datum: A set of parameters and control points used to accurately define the three dimensional shape of the Earth. The corresponding datum is the basis for a planar coordinate system.

DBMS: Data Base Management System. Software that manages, manipulates and retrieves data in a database.

DGPS: Differential Global Positioning System. A positioning procedure that uses two receivers, a rover at an unknown location and a base station at a known, fixed location. The base station computes corrections based on the differences between its actual and observed ranges to the satellites being tracked.

Diagonal Axis: The line that runs from the top-left corner of an image to the bottom-right corner, or from the top-right corner to the bottom-left corner.

Digital Camera: An imaging device that focuses visible light onto a CCD.

Digital Elevation Model (DEM): Terrain elevation data organized by quadrangle and provided in digital form.

Digital Image: An image captured by an imaging device and represented in a computer as a rectangular grid of pixels.

Digital map library: A series of directories and subdirectories designed to uniformly organize a collection of spatial data. Map libraries organize geographic data spatially as a set of tiles and thematically as a set of layers.

Digital Terrain Model (DTM): A three-dimensional model of the Earth's surface, provided in digital form.

Digitize: To encode map features as x,y coordinates in digital form. Lines are traced to define their shapes. This can be accomplished either manually or by use of a scanner.

Dilation: A morphological operation that increases the sizeof objects in an image by adding a layer of foreground pixels around each object.

Dissolve: The process of removing boundaries between adjacent polygons that have the same values for a specified attribute.

DLG: Digital Line Graph files from the U.S. Geological Survey

DXF: Data Exchange Format. A format for storing vector data in ASCII or binary files; used by AutoCad or other CAD software and convertible to ARC/INFO coverages.

Edge Detector: An image-processing routine that flags the large changes in pixel brightness that indicate potential edges. Edge detectors often visualise their results in edge maps. Examples include the Sobel, Prewitt, Kirsch and Laplacian edge detectors.

Edge Direction: The angle that specifies the direction of an edge. The angle is perpendicular to the direction of the large change in brightness that indicates the edge.

Edge Map: A greyscale output image that visualises the magnitude of the edge found at each pixel in an input image; the greater the magnitude, the brighter the corresponding edge-map pixel. Thresholding an edge map highlights the strongest edges.

Edge Mask: A set of convolution weights that highlight the size and direction of the edges in an image. Electromagnetic Spectrum: The complete range of electromagnetic radiation from short wavelength gamma radiation to long wavelength radio waves.

Edge matching: An editing procedure to ensure that all features that cross adjacent map sheets have the same edge locations.

Edge: Edges mark the boundaries between the objects in a scene. A large change in pixel brightness over a small number of pixels often indicates the presence of an edge.

EM: Electromagnetic

Erosion: A morphological operation that decreases the size of objects in an image by removing a layer of foreground pixels around each object. Often used for removing projections and blobs in bitmap images.

ETM+: Enhanced Thematic Mapper Plus

Feature attribute table: A table used by ARC/INFO to store attribute information for a specific coverage feature class. Feature attribute tables supported include:

Feature class: The type of feature represented in a coverage. Coverage feature classes include arcs, nodes, label points, polygons, tics, annotation, links, boundaries, routes, and sections.

Features: Both constant and variable width buffers can be generated for a set of coverage features based on each features attribute values.

Flipping: A geometric process that swaps the pixels in an image across the horizontal, vertical and diagonal axes.

Forward Mapping: The technique point and area processes use to calculate output-image pixel values from input-image pixel values. Forward-mapping processes start with a pixel in the input image, calculate a new pixel value, and assign the new value to the corresponding pixel in the output image.

Frame Averaging: A point process that removes noise from a series of input images taken of the same subject. Each output-image pixel value is the average of the corresponding input-image pixel values.

Geocode: The process of identifying a location by one or more x,y coordinates from another location description such as an address.

Geographic Information System (GIS): Geographic Information System. An organized collection of computer hardware, software, geographic data, and personnel designed to efficiently capture, store, update, manipulate, analyze, and display all forms of geographically referenced information.

Geometric Process: A category of image processing techniques that change the size and shape of an image rather than its contents. Examples include cropping, scaling and rotation.

GIS: Global Information System

Global Positioning System (GPS): A satellite based device that records x,y,z coordinates and other data. GPS devices can be taken into the field to record data while driving, hiking, or flying. Ground locations are calculated by signals from satellites orbiting the Earth.

GPS: Global Positioning System

Greyscale Image: An image composed of pixels that present shades of grey.

Halftoning: An area process that simulates shades of grey in bitmap images with patterns of *bitmap pixels. The* density of each 2x2-pixel pattern depends on the ratio of black to white bitmap pixels.

High Frequency: The high frequency information in an image is represented by large changes in pixel

High-contrast Image: An image with large numbers of pixels in the shadows and highlights.

High-key Image: An image that represents a naturally light subject

Highlights: The range of pixel brightnesses that represent the lighter regions of an image.

Histogram Equalization: An image-processing technique that reveals detail hidden in images with a poorly distributed range of brightesses.

Histogram: The histogram of an image visualises the distribution of the brightness in the image by plotting the number of occurrences of each brightness.

Horizontal Axis: The line that runs through the centre of an image from the left of the image to the right.

HSB; A color model that represents each color with three numbers that specify the hue (H), the saturation (S) and the brightness (B) of the color.

Hue: The color in the HSB color model.

IFOV: Instantaneous field of view: the solid angle through which a detector is sensitive to radiation

Image Processing: The field of computer science that develops techniques for enhancing digital images to make them more enjoyable to look at, and easier to analyse by computers as well as humans.

Image: An image records a visual snapshot of the world around us.

Imaging Device: A piece of equipment that captures an image. Examples include digital cameras, side-scan sonar systems and scanning electron microscopes.

Impulse Noise: Also called salt and pepper noise, impulse noise introduces very light (salt) and very dark (pepper) pixels that stand out from their neighbours.

INFO: A tabular DBMS used by ARC/INFO to store and manipulate feature attribute and related tables.

Input Image: The image transformed by an image processing routine.

Interpolation: A method of creating new pixel values from existing pixel values. Examples include nearest neighbour and bi-linear interpolation.

Intersect: The topological integration of two spatial data sets that preserves features that fall within the spatial extent common to both input data sets.

Inversion: A point process that produces an effect similar to photographic negatives: dark pixels become light and light pixels become dark.

Item: In an attribute table, a field of information commonly displayed as a column. A single attribute from a record in an INFO data file.

Kernel: A rectangular grid of convolution weights.

Latitude-longitude: A spherical reference system used to measure locations on surface. Latitude measures angles in the north south direction and longitude measures angles in the east west direction.

Laver: A logical set of thematic data described and stored in a map library. Layers organize a map library by subject matter, e.g., soils, roads, wells, and extend over the entire geographic area defined by the spatial index of the map library.

Line Edge: A line chain of pixels that separates a region of light pixels from a region of dark pixels.

Line: a geographic feature defined by connecting at least two points.

Linear Brightness Transformation: A category of brightness transformations that lighten and darken images using mathematical functions with curved graphs.

Line-in-polygon: A spatial operation in which arcs in one coverage are overlaid with polygons in another to determine which arcs, or portions of arcs are contained within the polygons. Polygon attribute are associated with corresponding arcs in the resulting line coverage.

Logical selection: The process of selecting a subset of features from a coverage using logical selection criteria that operate on the attributes of coverage features (e.g., area greater than 500 m). Only those features whose attributes meet the selection criteria are selected. Also known as feature selection by attribute.

Look-up Table (LUT): A data structure that minimises the number of calculations required to process an image with a point process. The brightness of each outputimage pixel is found in a LUT at the entry indexed by the brightness of the corresponding input-image pixel.

Low Frequency: The low frequency information in an image is represented by small changes in pixel brightness over a small number of pixels.

Low-contrast Image: An image that uses only a small range of the available brightness. Low-contrast images are mostly dark, mostly dull or mostly light.

Low-key Image: An image that represents a naturally dark subject.

Low-pass Filter: A filter that discards or attenuates the high frequency information in an image and preserves the low frequency information. Removing the high frequency information from an image removes the detail and blurs the image. Blurring is implemented by a low pass filter.

Many-to-one-relate: A relate in which many records in one table are related to a single record in another table. A goal in relational database design is to use one to many relates to reduce data storage and redundancy.

Map extent: The rectangular limits (xmin,ymin,xmax,ymax) of the area of the Earth's surface, which user want to display using ARC/INFO. The geographic extent specified by the minimum bounding rectangle of a study area.

Map projection: A systematic conversion of locations on the Earth's surface from spherical to planar coordinates. Several of the more popular projections are: State Plane Coordinates (SPC) which uses feet for units of measure; Universal Transverse Mercator (UTM) which uses meters for units of measure; and latitude and longitude which uses degrees, minutes, and seconds of arc for units of measure.

Map scale: The extent of reduction needed to display a representation of the Earth's surface on a map. A statement of a measure on the map and the equivalent measure on the Earth's surface, often expressed as a representative fraction of distance, such as 1:10,000 (one unit in the map equals 10,000 units on the ground).

Median Filtering: An area process that removes noise by replacing the central pixel in a neighbourhood with the median pixel value of the neighbourhood.

Mid-tones: The range of pixel brightnesses that represent the regions of an image in between the shadows and highlights. Morphological Operation: A category of image

Nearest-neighbour Interpolation: A method of creating values for pixels with fractional co-ordinates that duplicates the value of the pixel with integer co ordinates nearest to the fractional co-ordinates.

Neighbourhood Averaging: An area process that removes noise by replacing the central pixel in a neighbourhood with the average pixel value of the neighbourhood.

neighbours.

Noise: Unwanted changes to the values of the pixels in an image, often introduced by the imaging device during capture. Examples include impulse noise and Gaussian noise.

Non-linear Brightness Transformation: A category brightness transformations that change the brightness of an image using mathematical function with straight-line graphs. Examples include inversion and posterisation

Non-primary color: A color created by mixing the red *green and blue primary colors of the RGB color* model.

One-to-many-relate: A type of relate connecting a unique value in one file to many records (that have the same value) in another file.

Opening: A morphological operation produced by following an erosion by a dilation. Often used for filling holes in bitmap images.

Orthophotography: The process of aerial photographs that have been rectified to produce an accurate image of the Earth by removing tilt and relief displacements which occurred when the photo was taken.

Outlying Pixel: A pixel with an extreme brightness that is much higher or lower than the brightnesses of the other pixels in the image.

Output Image: An image that contains the results of applying an image processing routine to an image.

PAT: Point Attribute Table. Polygon Attribute Table. A coverage can have either a point attribute table or a

Photo Restoration: The application of a series of image processing routines to enhance a damaged photograph.

Photogrammetry: The science of deducing the physicaldimension of objects from measurements on photographs.

Pixel Depth: The number of colors or shades of grey a pixel can present. Bitmap pixels have depth two. typical greyscale pixels have depth 256, and typical color pixels have depth 16, 777, 216.

Pixel Neighbourhood: A region of pixels processed by an area process. Typical neighbourhood dimensions are 3x3 pixels and 5x5 pixels.

Pixel: A square unit of visual information that represents a tiny part of a digital image.

Planimetric: The horizontal (x,y) locations of nontopographic features, such as rivers, lakes, buildings. roads, etc.

Point Processes: A category of image-processing techniques that calculate the value of each outputimage pixel from the value of the corresponding input-image pixel. Examples include inversion and pseudo-color.

point-in-polygon: A spatial operation in which points from one coverage are overlaid with a polygonal coverage to determine which points fall within the polygon boundaries. Points assume the attributes of the polygons within which they fall.

Polygon overlay: A process that merges spatially coincident polygons from two coverages, and their attributes, to create a third coverage, that contains new polygons and describes new relationships.

polygon: A multisided figure that represents area on a map. A feature defined by the arcs that make up its boundary. Every polygon contains one label point within its boundary. Polygons have attributes that describe the geographic feature they represent.

Potential Edge: Edge detectors flag all large changes in pixel brightness over a small number of pixels as a potential edge. An edge-analysis system then decides whether the change in brightness represents the border of an object - a real edge - or some other feature of the object, such as its texture.

Primary colors: The colors red, green and blue from which all other colors in the RGB color model are mixed.

processing techniques that operate on the structure of the objects in an image.

Pseudo-color: A point process that divides the range of brightness in a greyscale input image into groups and assigns each group a color. Each output-image pixel is assigned the color that represents the group into which falls the brightness of the corresponding input-image pixel.

Quadrangle (quad): Typically refers to a map sheet published by the U.S. Geological Survey, a 7.5 minute quadrangle series or the 15 minute quadrangle series. Also known as a topographic or topo map.

Quantization: The calculation that maps the fractional measurements made by imaging devices onto proportional integer pixel brightnesses.

Ramp Edge: A region of pixels that separates a region of light pixels from a region of dark pixels. The pixels in the region change gradually from light to dark.

Raster: Data displayed as discrete picture elements (pixels).

Raw color: The color of the pixels in an image captured by a color CCD before the two unknown RGB component brightnesses of each pixel have been interpolated from the known brightnesses of the corresponding components of neighbouring pixels.

Relate key: The common set of columns used to relate two attribute tables.

Relate: An operation that establishes a temporary connection between corresponding records in two tables using an item common to both. A relate gives access to additional feature attributes that are not stored in a single table.

Remote sensing: Any of the technical disciplines for observing and measuring the Earth from a distance, including satellite imaging, Global Positioning Systems, RADAR, SONAR, aerial photography, etc.

Resolution: Measures the sharpness of an image.

Resolution: The number of pixels available to represe present the details of the subject of a digital image.

RGB color Cube: Visualises the amounts of red, green and blue required to produce each color in the RGB color model as a point in a cube at co-ordinates (x, y, z).

RGB: A color model that represents each color with three numbers that specify the amounts of red (R), green (G) and blue (B) that produce the color.

Roof Edge: A region of pixels that separates a region of light pixels from a region of dark pixels. The pixels in a roof edge increase in brightness to their maximum at the apex of the roof and then decrease to meet the region of pixels on the other side of the edge.

Rotation Hole: An output-image pixel not assigned a value when the input image is rotated with forward mapping.

Rotation: A geometric process that turns an image about its centre by a specified angle.

Row-Column Co-ordinates: The pair of numbers that locate a pixel in the rows & columns of the rectangular grid of pixels that represent a digital image.

Sampling: The process of mapping a continuous quantity of electromagnetic radiation, such as light or X-rays falling on a sensor, onto a discrete, rectangular grid of pixels.

Saturation: The component of the HSB color model that controls the amount of white mixed into the hue.

Scale Factor: A fractional number that controls whether a scaling process enlarges or reduces an image. Scale factors between zero and one reduce images; scale factors greater than one enlarge images.

Scaling: A geometric process that changes the size of an image.

Scanner: An imaging device that focuses light reflected from a document onto a CCD that moves across and down the document.

Sequential-index Co-ordinate: The number that locates a pixel in an image when the pixels in the image are laid end to end in a sequence.

Shadows: The range of pixel brightnesses that represent the darker regions of an image.

Sharpening: An area process that emphasises the detail in an image.

Slope: A measure of change in surface value over distance, expressed in degrees or as a percentage. For example, a rise of 2 meters over distance of 100 meters describes a 2% slope.

Spatial modeling: Analytical procedures applied with GIS. There are three categories of spatial modeling functions that can be applied to geographic data within a GIS: geometric models, such as calculating the distance between features, generating buffers, calculating areas and perimeters, and so on; coincidence modeling, such as polygon overlay; and adjacency modeling such as redistricting and allocation.

Spatial analysis: The process of modeling, examining, and *Interpreting model results. Spatial analysis is the process of extracting or creating new information abo*ut a set of geographic features. Spatial analysis is useful for evaluating suitability and capability, for estimating and predicting, and for interpreting and understanding. In GIS there are four traditional types of spatial analysis: spatial overlay and contiguity analysis, surface analysis, linear analysis, and raster analysis.

SQL: Structured Query Language. A syntax for defining and manipulating data from a relational database. Developed by IBM in the 1970s, it has become an industry standard for query languages in most relational database management systems.

State Plane Coordinates (SPC): A map projection that measures distance in feet. By providing an SPC easting (x) and northing (y), the state name, and the zone number, any location in the United States can be identified by a unique coordinate value.

Step Edge: The ideal edge shape characterised by a large, immediate change in pixel brightness from a region of light pixels to a region of dark pixels.

Structuring Element: The rectangular grid of binary values used by morphological operations to assign a new value to a pixel in a bitmap image.

Subtraction: A point process that identifies the pixels that differ between two input images.

Thresholding: A point process that produces a bitmap version of a greyscale image. Black bitmap pixels represent greyscale pixels darker than a threshold brightness: white bitmap pixels represent grayscale pixels lighter than the threshold.

Thermal Camera: An imaging device that measures the amount of infra-red light emitted by the subject of the image. Hotter objects emit more infra-red light, which show up as the brighter regions of a thermal image.

Thermal Image: A greyscale image captured by a thermal camera. Often enhanced with pseudo-color to assign the same color to regions of pixels that represent similar temperatures.

TIN: Triangulated Irregular Network. A series of triangles constructed using elevation data points taken from coverages. These triangles are used for surface representation and display.

Topography: Shape or configuration of the land surface; represented in map form by contour lines.

Topology: The spatial relationships between connecting or adjacent coverage features.

Transformation: The process that converts coordinates from one coordinate system to another through translation, rotation, and scaling.

Triangulation: A method of surveying in the location of an object may be calculated from the known locations of two other objects. Creating a triangle from the three items, the angles and sides of the triangle can be measured and the location of the unknown object is calculated algebraically.

Vector: A geometric element, stored as a point with x,y coordinates within a computer database

Vertical Axis: The line that runs through the centre of an image from the top of the image to the bottom.

IKONOS: A high-resolution earth observation satellite launched in 1999, which occupies a 682-km sun synchronous orbit and employs linear array technology collecting data in four multispectral bands at a nominal resolution of 4 m, as well as a 1-m-resolution panchromatic band.

Landsat: A series of unmanned NASA earth resource satellites that acquire ultispectral images in the visible and IR bands.

NAD: North Atlantic Datum

NDVI: Normalized Difference Vegetation Index

NIR Near Infrared Remote sensing of energy naturally reflected or radiated from the terrain.

Radiation: Act of giving off electromagnetic energy.

RGB: Red, Green, and Blue-the colors used in constructing visible and false color image representations.

MIR: Mid Infrared

Spatial Resolution: The ability to distinguish between closely spaced objects on an image. Commonly expressed as the most closely spaced line-pairs per unit distance distinguishable.

Spectral Reflectance: Reflectance of electromagnetic energy at specified wavelength intervals.

Spectral Resolution: Range of wavelengths recorded by a detector.

SWIR: Short Wave Infrared

TM: Thematic Mapper

UTM: Universal Transverse Mercator

VI: Vegetation Index

VNIR: Visible Near Infrared

WGS: Worldwide Geographic System

WRS: Worldwide Reference System

ArcGIS related terminology

ArcGIS provides a scalable framework for implementing GIS for a single user or many users on desktops, in servers, over the Web, and in the field. ArcGIS is an integrated family of GIS software products for building a complete GIS. It consists of several primary frameworks for deploying GIS (ESRI, 2010):

- **ArcGIS Desktop** – An integrated suite of professional GIS applications. Most users recognize this as three products: ArcView, ArcEditor, and Arcinfo.
- **ArcGIS Server -** Publishes GIS information and maps as Web services, provides a series of Web GIS applications, and supports enterprise data management.

- **ArcGIS Mobile** - Provides mobile GIS tools and applications for field computing.

ArcGIS Online - Delivers online GIS capabilities that user can access over the Web plus useful maps and data published by ESRI and partners that user can use in their own Web GIS applications.

ArcGIS Engine - Provides a software component library for ArcGIS developers who use C++, .NET, or Java.

- **ArcGIS Desktop** is the primary product used by GIS professionals to compile, use, and manage geographic information. It includes comprehensive professional GIS applications that support a number of GIS tasks, including mapping, data compilation, analysis, geodatabase management, and geographic information sharing.

ArcGIS Desktop includes a suite of applications - ArcMap, ArcCatalog, ArcGlobe, ArcScene, ArcToolbox, and Model Builder. Using these applications and interfaces, user can perform any GIS tasks from simple to advanced.

ArcGIS Desktop, provide number of elements of GIS information, such as the following:

- Map documents, globe documents, and layers
- Geodatabases
- Geoprocessing toolboxes
- Other data files such as imagery

ArcGIS Desktop is scalable and can address the needs of many types of users. It is available at three functional levels:

- **ArcView** focuses on comprehensive data use, mapping, and analysis.
- **ArcEditor** adds advanced geodatabase editing and data creation.
- **Arcinfo** is a complete, professional GIS desktop containing comprehensive GIS functionality and rich geoprocessing tools.

A number of specialized software capabilities are available as add-on extensions to ArcGIS Desktop. Each extension enables user to add capabilities such as raster geoprocessing, 3D GIS, and network analysis.

List of Top 10 Sources of Free Remote Sensing Data

The requirement for high quality remote sensing data is skyrocketing with the surge in the application of remote sensing techniques and with the 'n' number of researches carried out each day. Every remote sensing analysis revolves around the term DATA with specified resolution, location, sensor and above all it should be FREE OF COST. Here I have listed some of the top players providing Remote sensing data free of cost.

1. GLOVIS

The USGS Global Visualization Viewer (GloVis) is one of the quick and easy online search and order tool for selected satellite and aerial data, especially for beginners. The instruction for downloading data can be found here. The products available for download are: Digital Orthophoto Quadrangle (DOQs), EO-1 ALI (Earth Observing-1 Advanced Land Imaging), EO-1 Hyperion (Earth Observing-1 Hyperion), Global Land Survey (GLS), Landsat 4-5 TM (L4-5 TM C1 Level-1), Landsat 7 ETM+ (L7 ETM+ C1 Level-1), Landsat 8 OLI/TIRS (L8 OLI/TIRS C1 Level-1), Sentinel-2, ISRO Resource SAT 1 and 2-AWIFS Sensor, ISRO ResourceSAT 1 and 2-LISS-3 Sensor, GeoEye's OrbView-3 (OrbView-3).

2. NASA Earth Observation (NEO)

NASA Earth Observation has more than 50 datasets on atmosphere, land, Ocean, energy, environment and much more on a daily, weekly and monthly frequency. The datasets are available in the form of JPEG, PNG, Google Earth and GeoTIFF.

3. USGS Earth Explorer

USGS Earth Explorer will stay the best portal for fetching Remote sensing data for a variety of reasons. Specially, a wide array of satellite and aerial images, a wide range of search criteria and the sequential arrangements of satellite imagery make the Earth Explorer a pro in terms of downloading imageries. USGS grants you full access to NASA's Land Data Products and Services such as Hyperion' s hyperspectral data, disperse Radar data and MODIS & AVHRR land surface reflectance.

4. ESA's Sentinel data

The Copernicus Open Access Hub (previously known as Sentinels Scientific Data Hub) provides complete, free and open access to Sentinel-1, Sentinel-2 and Sentinel-3 user products, starting from the In-Orbit Commissioning Review (IOCR). The ESA's sentinel data is chasing the USGS Earth Explorer with more bands and crisper resolution.

5. NASA Earth Data

With the retirement of the Reverb data search and discovery system on 1 January 2018, Earthdata Search will be the primary means for searching and discovering

NASA Earth observing data. The result will be faster data searches and more relevant search results for EOSDIS data users. Earthdata Search uses Client's natural language processing-enabled search tool to quickly narrow down to relevant collections as shown in the tutorial.

Similar to NASA Reverb, Earth Data communicates with a plethora of satellites such as NASA DC, GPS satellites, SMAP, JASON, METEOSAT, ALOS, TRMM, Aura, Aqua and much more.

6. NOAA Class

NOAA (National Oceanic and Atmospheric Administration) Class has a distinct online data library system, a pool of free top quality and valuable geographic data sets which set them apart. The Comprehensive Large Array- data Stewardship System (CLASS) is really in a class of its own with abundance of data accumulated from other rich and viable sources such as the US Department of Defense (DoD) Polar-orbiting Operational Environmental Satellite (POES), Environmental Satellite (GOES), NOAA's Geostationary, Operational), and other derived data. However when compared to USGS, NOAA Class is still amateurish.

7. NOAA Digital Coast

If Coastal data is your only requirement, there is no better portal to reach than NOAA's Digital Coast. Simply define your choice of interest and select from the range of free satellite imagery dataset such as infrared, radar and true colour composite to download. Apart from the coastal data you shall as well get imagery, land cover, elevation, socio-economic and benthic data.

8. IPPMUS Terra

IPUMS Terra integrates population census data from around the world with global environmental data, allowing users to obtain customized datasets that incorporate data from multiple sources in a single coherent structure. The country specific data can be obtained from Terraclip featuring MODIS data.

9. LANCE

The Land, Atmosphere Near real-time Capability for EOS (LANCE) supports application users interested in monitoring a wide variety of natural and man-made phenomena. Near Real-Time (NRT) data and imagery from the AIRS, AMSR2, MISR, MLS, MODIS, OMI and VIIRS instruments are available much quicker than routine processing allows. Most data products are available within 3 hours from satellite observation. NRT imagery are generally available 3-5 hours after observation.

10. VITO Vision

The VITO Vision provides coarse vegetation data from PROBA-V, SPOT-Vegetation and METOP. This coarse resolution satellite carves out vegetation patterns of the Earth's surface. The easy-to-use interface and delivers free low resolution satellite data. This type of data is a good for large-scale applications that doesn't need the finer details.

References

A Guide to the Global Positioning System (GPS). 2010. GPS Timeline. *Radio Shack. Archived from* the original *on February 13, 2010.* Retrieved January 14

Abel, J.S. and Chaffee, J.W., 1991. Existence and uniqueness of GPS solutions, IEEE Transactions on Aerospace and Electronic Systems, vol:26, no:6, p:748-53, Sept. 1991.

Advanced Very High Resolution Radiometer (AVHRR) Sensor Characteristics. Global Land 1-KM AVHRR Project. [Online] June 23, 2008. [Cited: September 19, 2013.] http://edc2.usgs.gov/1KM/avhrr_sensor.php.

AF Space Command Chronology. USAF Space Command. Archived from the original on August 17, 2011. Retrieved June 20, 2011.

Agarwal A and Narain S. 1997. Dying Wisdom: Rise, Fall and Potential of India's Traditional Water Harvesting Systems, Centre for Science and Environment, New Delhi, pp. 117-125.

Agnew, D.C. and Larson, K.M. 2007. Finding the repeat times of the GPS constellation. GPS Solutions. Springer. **11** (1): 71–76. doi:10.1007/s10291-006-0038-4. This article from author's web site Archived February 16, 2008, at the Wayback Machine., with minor correction.

Ahmed, S.A., Chandrashekarappa, K.N., Raj, S.K., Nischitha, V. and Kavitha, G. 2010. Evaluation of Morphometric ParametersDerived from ASTER and SRTM DEM - A study on Bandihole Sub-watershed Basin in Karnataka. Journal of Indian Social Remote Sensor 38: 227-238.

Air Force GPS Problem: Glitch Shows How Much U.S. Military Relies On GPS. Huffingtonpost.comm. June 1, 2010. Retrieved October 15, 2010.

Air Force Successfully Transmits an L5 Signal From GPS IIR-20(M) Satellite. LAAFB News Release. Archived from the original on May 21, 2011. Retrieved June 20, 2011.

Akhouri, A.P. 1996. Remote sensing approach for watershed based resource management in Sikkim Himalaya - A case study. Journal of Indian Society of Remote Sensing, 24: 69-83.

Alfred Kleusberg. 1994. Analytical GPS Navigation Solution, University of Stuttgart Research Compendium.

Amos, Jonathan. 2019. QE Engineering Prize lauds GPS pioneers. Archived *from the original on April 6, 2019*. Retrieved April 6, 2019 – *via www. bbc.co.uk.*

Anderson, J.R., Hardy, E.E., Roach, J.T., and Witmer, R.E. 1976. A Land Use and Land Cover Classification System for Use with Remote Sensor Data. U.S. Geological Survey Professional Paper 964, Reston, VA: U.S. Geological Survey.

Anonymous, 2007. losangeles.af.mil. *losangeles.af.mil. Archived from* the original *on May 11, 2011*. Retrieved October 15, 2010.

Anonymous. 1972. The USAF Central Inertial Guidance Test Facility (Holloman AFB) conducted developmental flight tests of four prototype GPS receivers in a Y configuration over White Sands Missile Range, using ground-based pseudo-satellites.

Anonymous. 1978. The first experimental Block-I GPS satellite was launched.

Anonymous. 1992. The 2nd Space Wing, which originally managed the system, was inactivated and replaced by the 50th Space Wing.

Anonymous. 1996. Recognizing the importance of GPS to civilian users as well as military users, U.S. President Bill Clinton issued a policy directive[47] declaring GPS a dual-use system and establishing an Interagency GPS Executive Board to manage it as a national asset.

Anonymous. 2011. United States Vice President Al Gore announced plans to upgrade GPS with two new civilian signals for enhanced user accuracy and reliability, particularly with respect to aviation safety and in 2000 the United States Congress authorized the effort, referring to it as GPS III.

Anonymous. 2017. United States President George W. Bush updated the national policy and replaced the executive board with the National Executive Committee for Space-Based Positioning, Navigation, and Timing.

Anonymous. 2018. The United States Government signed an agreement with the European Community establishing cooperation related to GPS and Europe's Galileo system.

Anonymous. 2019. the first modernized GPS satellite was launched and began transmitting a second civilian signal (L2C) for enhanced user performance.

Archived copy. Archived from the original on October 22, 2011. Retrieved 2011-10-27. Retrieved October 27, 2011

Arms Control Association.Missile Technology Control Regime Archived September 16, 2008, at the Wayback Machine.. Retrieved May 17, 2006.

Assisted-GPS Test Calls for 3G WCDMA Networks. 3g.co.uk. November 10, 2004. Retrieved November 24, 2010.

ASTER Overview. LP DAAC. [Online] August 19, 2013. [Cited: September 19, 2013.] https://lpdaac.usgs.gov/products/aster_overview.

Attewill, Fred. 2013. Vehicles that use GPS jammers are big threat to aircraft. Metro.co.uk. Retrieved on 2013-08-02.

Bakker KK and Higgins K.F. 2009. Planted grasslands and native sod prairie: equivalent habitat for grassland birds? Western North American Naturalist 69: 235–242.

Balakrishnan K and Saritha S. 2007. Groundwater Information Booklet of Kasaragod District, Kerala State. Central Ground Water Board, Ministry of Water Resources, Government of India, Trivandrum, pp. 1–22.

Balooni K, Kalro AH and Ambili KG. 2010. Sustainability of tunnel wells in a changing agrarian context: a case study from South India. Agric. Water Manage., **97**(5): 659-665.

Bancroft, S. 1985. "An Algebraic Solution of the GPS Equations". *IEEE Transactions on Aerospace and Electronic Systems*. AES-21 (1): 56–59.

Bancroft, S. January 1985. An Algebraic Solution of the GPS Equations. IEEE Transactions on Aerospace and Electronic Systems. AES-21: 56–59. Bibcode:1985ITAES..21.56B. doi:10.1109/TAES.1985.310538.

Basak P, Raghavendra Prasad PM and Sreedharan KE. 1997. Surangams - a traditional water harvesting system in North Malabar. Centre for Science and Environment, Thomson Press Limited,Faridabad, India, pp. 222–223.

Beidou satellite navigation system to cover whole world in 2020. Eng.chinamil.com.cn. Retrieved October 15, 2010.

Benvenuti, S. 2007. Weed seed movement and dispersal strategies in the agricultural environment. Weed Biol Manag 7:141–157. https://doi.org/10.1111/j.1445-6664.2007.00249.x

Between-Satellite Differencing. Gmat.unsw.edu.au. Archived from the original on March 6, 2011. Retrieved October 15, 2010.

Biswas, S.S .2014. Role of Human induced factors Soil erosion and Climatic variability in changing the fluvial system: A case study of the Barakar River Basin India Unpublished M Phil Dissertation. Jawaharlal Nehru University New Delhi.

Blegen, Carl. 1958. Troy 4: Settlements VIIa, VIIb and VIII. Princeton University Press. p. 76.

Bonsen, B., Pulles, R.J., Simons, S.W.H., Steinbuch, M., and Veenhuizen, P.A. (2005b). Implementation of a slip controlled CVT in a production vehicle. In Control pplications, 2005. CCA 2005. Proceedings of 2005 IEEE Conference on, 1212-1217.

Borre, Kai; M. Akos, Dennis; Bertelsen, Nicolaj; Rinder, Peter and Jensen Søren Holdt. 2007. A Software-Defined GPS and Galileo Receiver. A single-Frequency Approach. Springer. p. 18. ISBN 0-8176-4390-7.

Borre, Kai; M. Akos, Dennis; Bertelsen, Nicolaj; Rinder, Peter and Jensen, Søren Holdt. 2007. A Software-Defined GPS and Galileo Receiver. A single-Frequency Approach. *Springer. p. 18.* ISBN 978-0-8176-4390-4.

Burrough, P.A. 1986. Principles of Geographic Information Systems, 1st ed. Oxford University Press, New York 336 pp.

Butterly, Amelia. 2018. The woman who paved the way for GPS. Archived*from the original on February 13, 2019*. Retrieved January 17, 2019 – *via www.bbc.com.*

Cadastral Template - Field Data C4" (lists nations), CadastralTemplate.org, January 2008, webpage: CT-C4 Archived 2012-07-30 at the Wayback Machine: also has term "cadastral survey" and other land records.

Canadian Space Agency. Satellite Characteristics. Canadian Space Agency. [Online] January 21, 2011. [Cited: September 19, 2013.] http://www.asc-csa.gc.ca/eng/satellites/radarsat/radarsat-tableau.asp#r1.

Carter, J.R. 1988. Digital representation of topographic surfaces, Photogrammetric Engineering & Remote Sensing, 54(11):1577-1580.

Catherine Alexandrow. 2008. The Story of GPS. Archived from the original on February 24,2013.

Catherine Alexandrow. 2008. The Story of GPS. *Archived from* the original *on February 24, 2013.*

Chaffee, J. and Abel, J. 1994. On the Exact Solutions of Pseudorange Equations, IEEE Transactions on Aerospace and Electronic Systems, vol:30, no:4, pp: 1021–1030.

Chandrasekar, N. and Magesh .2014. GIS model-based morphometric evaluation of Tamiraparani sub basin Tirunelveli, India. Arab Journal Geo science 7: 131-141.

Charting a Course Toward Global Navigation. The Aerospace Corporation. Archived from the original on November 1, 2002. Retrieved October 14, 2013.

China Jamming US Forces' GPS. *September 26, 2016.* Archived *from the original on March 6, 2019*. Retrieved March 3, 2019.

Chowdhury, A., Jha, M.K., Chowdhury, V.M., Mal, B.C. 2009. Integrated remote sensing and GIS-based approach for assessing groundwater potential in West Mednapur district, West Bengal, India. Int. J. Rem. Sen. 30 (1), 231-250.

Clove Blog. January 10, 2012. Archived *from the original on March 10, 2016*. Retrieved October 29, 2016.

Coalition to Save Our GPS. Saveourgps.org. Archived from the original on October 24, 2011. Retrieved November 6, 2011.

Cohen. 1960. A coefficient of agreement for nominal scales Educ. Psychol. Meas., 20 (1960), pp. 37-46.

Common View GPS Time Transfer. nist.gov. Archived from the original on October 28, 2012. Retrieved July 23, 2011.

Contract Award for Next Generation GPS Control Segment Announced. Archived from the original on July 23, 2013. Retrieved December 14, 2012.

Cooke, R. U. and Doornkamp, J.C. 1990. Geomorphology in Environmental Management, Oxford Press.

Coursey, David. 2009. Air Force Responds to GPS Outage Concerns. ABC News. Retrieved May 22, 2009.

Coursey, David. 2009. Air Force Responds to GPS Outage Concerns. *ABC News.* Archived *from the original on May 23, 2009.* Retrieved May 22, 2009.

Crook D, Tripathi S and Jones RT. 2013. The sustainability of suranga irrigation in South Karnataka and northern Kerala, India. In First World Irrigation Forum, Conference Proceedings, Mardin, Turkey, pp. 50-55.

Crook D, Tripathi S and Jones RT. 2015. An investigation into the age and origin of suranga in the foothills of the Western Ghats of India. Water History, 7(3):253-270.

Crookshak H. 1963. Geology of southern Bastar and Jeypore from Bailadila range to the Eastern Ghat. Memoir Geol. Surv. India 87, pp. 149.

Crookshak H. 1963. Geology of southern Bastar and Jeypore from Bailadila range to the Eastern Ghat. Memoir Geol. Surv. India 87, pp. 149.

Crookshank, H. 1963. Geology of southern Bastar and Jeypore from the Bai-ladila range to Eastern Ghats. Geological Survey of India, Calcutta, India, Memoir 87, 1–150.

Daly, P. 1993. Navstar GPS and GLONASS: global satellite navigation systems. Electronics & Communication Engineering Journal. **5** (6): 349–357. doi:10.1049/ecej:19930069.

Dana, Peter H. 1996. GPS Orbital Planes (GIF).

Dana, Peter H. 1996. GPS Orbital Planes. *Archived from* the original (GIF) *on January 26, 2018.* Retrieved February 27, 2006.

Dana, Peter H. Geometric Dilution of Precision (GDOP) and Visibility. University of Colorado at Boulder. Retrieved July 7, 2008.

Danielle, Britni. 2018. Dr. Gladys West, Another 'Hidden Figure,' Inducted Into Air Force Hall Of Fame. *Essence. Archived from* the original *on December 22, 2018.* Retrieved December 24, 2018.

DARPA: 50 Years of Bridging the Gap. *April 2008. Archived from* the original *on May 6, 2011.*

Das, S., Behera, S.C., Kar, A., Narendra, P. and Guha, S., 1997. Hydrogeomor-phological mapping in groundwater exploration using remotely sensed data-a case study in Keonjhar District, Orissa. J Indian Soc Remote Sens 25: 247-259

Data Shows Disastrous GPS Jamming from FCC-Approved Broadcaster. gpsworld.com. February 1, 2011. Archived from the original on February 6, 2011. Retrieved February 10, 2011.

Dave, M. 2011. ASTER Global Digital Elevation Model Version 2-Summary of Validation Results. US Geological Survey, p. 28.

David W. Allan. 1997. The Science of Timekeeping (PDF). Hewlett Packard. Archived (PDF) from the original on October 12, 2012.

Dennis D. McCrady. The GPS Burst Detector W-Sensor (PDF). Sandia National Laboratories.

Dey, S. 2014. Delineation of ground water prospect zones using remote sensing, GIS techniques - a case study of Baghmundi development block of Puruliya district,

West Bengal. inter. J. Geol. Earth Env. Sci. 4 (2), 62–72. (ISSN: 2277-2081)(Online). (An open access, online international journal available at).)#http://www.cibtech.org/jgee.htm*#.

Dick, Steven and Launius, Roger. 2007. Societal Impact of Spaceflight (PDF). *Washington, DC: US Government Printing Office. p. 331*. ISBN 978-0-16-080190-7. Archived (PDF) *from the original on March 3, 2013*. Retrieved July 20, 2019.

Dietrich Schroeer and Mirco Elena (2000). Technology Transfer. Ashgate. p. 80. ISBN 0-7546-2045-X. Retrieved May 25, 2008.

DigitalGlobe. IKONOS - Data Sheet. DigitalGlobe. [Online] June 2013. [Cited: September 19, 2013.] http://www.digitalglobe.com/sites/default/files/DG_IKONOS_DS.pdf.

DigitalGlobe. QuickBird - Data Sheet. DigitalGlobe. [Online] [Cited: September 19, 2013.] http://www.digitalglobe.com/downloads/QuickBird-DS-QB-Web.pdf.

District Resource Map., 2010. Bastar District. Geological Survey of India, Chhattisgarh

Dora ML, Nair KKK and Shasidharan K. 2011. Occurrence of platinum group minerals in the Western Bastar Craton, Chandrapur District, and Maharashtra. Curr. Sci., **100**: 399-403.

Dora ML, Singh H, Kundu A, Shareef M, Randive KR and Joshi S. 2014. Tsumoite, (BiTe) and associated mineralization from Gondpipri mafic-ultramafic complex, Bastar Craton, Central India: Mineralogy and Genetic Significance. European Jour. Geosci., **6(4)**: 506-517.

Dora ML, Singh H, Kundu A, Shareef M, Randive KR and Joshi S. 2014. Tsumoite, (BiTe) and associated mineralization from Gondpipri mafic-ultramafic complex, Bastar Craton, Central India: Mineralogy and Genetic Significance. European Jour. Geosci., **6(4)**: 506-517.

Double differencing. Gmat.unsw.edu.au. Archived from the original on March 6, 2011. Retrieved October 15, 2010.

Dragut, L. and Blaschke, T. 2006. Automated classification of landform elements using object-based image analysis. Geomorphology, 81, pp. 330-344.

Dunning, D.J., Ross, Q.E. and Merkhofer, M.W., 2000. Multi-attribute utility analysis for addressing Section 316(b) of the Clean Water Act. Environ. Sci. Policy, v.3, pp.7-14.

E. Steitz, David. NATIONAL POSITIONING, NAVIGATION AND TIMING ADVISORY BOARD NAMED. Retrieved March 22, 2007.

E. Steitz, David. National Positioning, Navigation and Timing Advisory Board Named. Archived *from the original on January 13, 2010*. Retrieved March 22, 2007.

EADS Astrium. Astrium GEO-Information Services SPOT International Price List. EADS Astrium. [Online] 2013. [Cited: September 19, 2013.] http://www2.astrium-geo.com/files/pmedia/public/r146_9_pricelist_spot_en_ 2012.pdf.

Eastman, J. R. 1996. Multi-criteria evaluation and GIS. Geographical information systems, v.1, pp.493–502.

Editor (April 30, 2018). Russia Undermining World's Confidence in GPS. Archived*from the original on March 6, 2019*. Retrieved March 3, 2019.

Elachi, C. 1987. Introduction to the Physics and Techniques of Remote Sensing. Wiley Series in Remote Sensing, New York. http://www.ccrs.nrcan.gc.ca/ccrs/learn/tutorials/fundam/chapter1/chapter1_1_e.html

Embarrassing to defend: US general blasts Raytheon's GPS control system a 'disaster'. RT. December 9, 2015.

ESRI. 2010. What's new in ArcGIS 10, ArcGis Manual, Environmental System Research Institute (ESRI), Redlands, USA, p 177.

FactSheet: 2nd Space Operations Squadron. USAF Space Command. Archived from the original on June 11, 2011. Retrieved June 20, 2011.

Factsheets : GPS Advanced Control Segment (OCX). Losangeles.af.mil. October 25, 2011. Archived from the original on May 3, 2012. Retrieved November 6, 2011.

Factsheets : GPS Advanced Control Segment (OCX). *Losangeles.af.mil. October 25, 2011. Archived from* the original *on May 3, 2012*. Retrieved November 6, 2011.

Factsheets : GPS Advanced Control Segment (OCX)". Losangeles.af.mil. October 25, 2011. Archived from the original on May 3, 2012. Retrieved November 6, 2011.

Fang, B.T., Comments on Existence and uniqueness of GPS solutions by J.S. Abel and J.W. Chaffee, IEEE Transactions on Aerospace and Electronic Systems, vol. 28, no. 4, Oct. 1992.

Fashae, O.A., Tijani, M.N., Talabi, A.O., Adedeji, O.I., 2014. Delineation of groundwater potential zones in the crystalline basement terrain of SW-Nigeria: an integrated GIS and remote sensing approach. Appl. Wat. Sci. J. 4 (1), 19–38.

FCC Docket File Number: SATASG2001030200017, Mobile Satellite Ventures LLC Application for Assignment and Modification of Licenses and for Authority to Launch and Operate a Next-Generation Mobile Satellite System. FCC.gov. March 1, 2001. p. 9.

FCC Order permitting mobile satellite services providers to provide an ancillary terrestrial component (ATC) to their satellite systems (PDF). Federal Communications Commission. FCC.gov. February 10, 2003. Retrieved December 13, 2011.

FCC Order, Granted LightSquared Subsidiary LLC, a Mobile Satellite Service licensee in the L-Band, a conditional waiver of the Ancillary Terrestrial Component integrated service rule (PDF). Federal Communications Commission. FCC.Gov. January 26, 2011. Retrieved December 13, 2011.

FCC press release Spokesperson Statement on NTIA Letter – LightSquared and GPS. February 14, 2012. Accessed 2013-03-03.

Federal Communications Commission Fixed and Mobile Services in the Mobile Satellite Service. Federal Communications Commission. FCC.gov. July 15, 2010. Retrieved December 13, 2011. [3] Archived December 13, 2012, at the Wayback Machine.

Federal Communications Commission Fixed and Mobile Services in the Mobile Satellite Service. Federal Communications Commission. FCC.gov. July 15, 2010. Retrieved December 13, 2011.

Federal Communications Commission Presented Evidence of GPS Signal Interference. GPS World. Archived from the original on October 11, 2011. Retrieved November 6, 2011.

Federal Communications Commission Report and Order In the Matter of Fixed and Mobile Services in the Mobile Satellite Service Bands at 1525–1559 MHz and 1626.5–1660.5 MHz (PDF). FCC.gov. April 6, 2011. Retrieved December 13, 2011.

Federal Communications Commission Table of Frequency Allocations (PDF). FCC.gov. November 18, 2011. Retrieved December 13, 2011.

Fenta, A.A., Kifle, A., Gebreyohannes, T. and Hailu, G., 2015. Spatial analysis of groundwater potential using remote sensing and GIS-based multi-criteria evaluation in Raya Valley, northern Ethiopia. Hydrog. J. 23, 195–206. https://doi.org/10.1007/s10040-014-1198-x.

First Block 2F GPS Satellite Launched, Needed to Prevent System Failure. DailyTech. Retrieved May 30, 2010.

First Block 2F GPS Satellite Launched, Needed to Prevent System Failure. *DailyTech. Archived from* the original *on May 30, 2010*. Retrieved May 30, 2010.

Fix, R. and Burt, T. 1995. Global Positioning System: an effective way to map a small catchments, Earth Surface Processes and Landforms, 20,817-827.

Flug, M., Seitz, H. L. H. and Scott, J. F. 2000. Multi criteria decision analysis applied to Glen Canyon Dam. Jour. Water Resour. Plan. Managmt, v.126, no.5, pp.270–276.

French, David. 1998. Canhasan Sites I. British Institute of Archaeology at Ankara. ISBN 1-898249-09-1.

Frequently Asked Questions About Selective Availability. National Coordination Office for Space-Based Positioning, Navigation, and Timing (PNT). October 2001. Retrieved 2015-06-13. Selective Availability ended a few minutes past midnight EDT after the end of May 1, 2000. The change occurred simultaneously across the entire satellite constellation.

Full Operational Capability (FOC) was declared by Air Force Space Command (AFSPC) in April 1995, signifying full availability of the military's secure Precise Positioning Service (PPS).

Galileo navigation satellite system goes live. dw.com. Retrieved December 17, 2016. Beidou coverage Beidou satellite navigation system to cover whole world in 2020. Eng.chinamil.com.cn. Retrieved October 15, 2010.

Galileo navigation satellite system goes live. dw.com. Retrieved December 17, 2016.

Gallant, J.C. and Hutchinson, M.F. (1997). Scale dependence in terrain analysis, Mathematics and Computers in Simulation, 43:313-321.

Garg, N. K., and Hassan, Q. 2007. Alarming scarcity of water in India. Curr. Sci., v.93, pp.932–941.

GEODETIC EXPLORER-A Press Kit (PDF). NASA. October 29, 1965. Retrieved 20 October 2015.

GeoImage. Satellite Overview. GeoImage. [Online] 2012. [Cited: September 19, 2013.] http://www.geoimage.com.au/satellites/satellite-overview.

Georg zur Bonsen; Daniel Ammann; Michael Ammann; Etienne Favey; Pascal Flammant (April 1, 2005). Continuous Navigation Combining GPS with Sensor-Based Dead Reckoning. GPS World. Archived from the original on November 11, 2006.

George, M., Hamid, M., and Miller A. Gold Code Generators in Virtex Devices at the Internet ArchivePDF section 4 beginning on page 15 Geoffrey Blewitt: Basics of the GPS Technique.

George, M., Hamid, M., and Miller A. Gold Code Generators in Virtex Devices at the Internet ArchivePDF

Global Positioning System Standard Positioning Service Performance Standard: 4th Edition, September 2008 (PDF). Archived (PDF) *from the original on April 27, 2017*. Retrieved April 21, 2017.

Global Positioning System. Gps.gov. Archived from the original on July 30, 2010. Retrieved June 26, 2010.

Global Positioning System. *Gps.gov. Archived from* the original *on July 30, 2010*. Retrieved June 26, 2010.

GLOBAL POSITIONING SYSTEM: Updated Schedule Assessment Could Help Decision Makers Address Likely Delays Related to New Ground Control System (PDF). *US Government Accounting Office. May 2019.*

Global Positioning Systems (PDF). Archived from the original (PDF) on July 19, 2011. Retrieved October 15, 2010.

GNSS Positioning Approaches – GPS Satellite Surveying, Fourth Edition – Leick. Wiley Online Library. pp. 257–399. doi:10.1002/9781119018612.ch6.

Gossel, W., Ebraheem, A.M. and Wycisk, P., 2004. A very large scale GIS-based groundwater flow model for the Nubian sandstone aquifer in eastern Sahara (Egypt, northern Sudan and eastern Libya). Hydrog. J. 12 (6), 698–713.

GPS & Selective Availability Q&A (PDF). NOAA]. Archived from the original (PDF) on September 21, 2005. Retrieved May 28, 2010.

GPS Accuracy. *GPS.gov. GPS.gov.* Archived *from the original on April 16, 2015.* Retrieved May 4, 2015.

GPS Accuracy. GPS.gov. GPS.gov. Retrieved 4 May 2015.

GPS Almanacs, NANUS, and Ops Advisories (including archives). GPS Almanac Information. United States Coast Guard. Retrieved September 9, 2009.

GPS almanacs. *Navcen.uscg.gov.* Archived *from the original on September 23, 2010.* Retrieved October 15, 2010.

GPS almanacs. Navcen.uscg.gov. Retrieved October 15, 2010.

GPS and Relativity. Astronomy.ohio-state.edu. Retrieved November 6, 2011.

GPS Completes Next Generation Operational Control System PDR. Air Force Space Command News Service. September 14, 2011. Archived from the original on October 2, 2011.

GPS Constellation Status for 08/26/2015. Archived *from the original on September 5, 2015.* Retrieved August 26, 2015.

GPS III Operational Control Segment (OCX). GlobalSecurity.org.

GPS III Operational Control Segment (OCX). *GlobalSecurity.org.* Archived *from the original on December 31, 2006.* Retrieved January 3, 2007.

GPS jamming is a growing threat to satellite navigation, positioning, and precision timing. *www.militaryaerospace.com.* Archived *from the original on March 6, 2019.* Retrieved March 3, 2019.

GPS Overview from the NAVSTAR Joint Program Office Archived November 16, 2007, at the Wayback Machine. Retrieved December 15, 2006.

GPS Program Receives International Award. *GPS.gov. October 5, 2011. Archived from* the original *on May 13, 2017.* Retrieved December 24, 2018.

GPS Support Notes (PDF). January 19, 2007. Archived from the original (PDF) on March 27, 2009. Retrieved November 10, 2008.

GPS time accurate to 100 nanoseconds. Galleon. Retrieved October 12, 2012.

GPS will be accurate within one foot in some phones next year. *The Verge.* Archived *from the original on January 18, 2018.* Retrieved January 17, 2018.

GPS Wing Reaches GPS III IBR Milestone Archived May 23, 2013, at the Wayback Machine in Inside GNSS November 10, 2008.

GPS Wing Reaches GPS III IBR Milestone in Inside GNSS November 10, 2008 GPS CONSTELLATION STATUS FOR 08/26/2015

GPS.gov: GPS Accuracy. *www.gps.gov.* Archived *from the original on January 4, 2018.* Retrieved January 17, 2018.

GPS: Global Positioning System (or Navstar Global Positioning System) Wide Area Augmentation System (WAAS) Performance Standard, Section B.3, Abbreviations and Acronyms. [2]

GPS: Global Positioning System (or Navstar Global Positioning System) Wide Area Augmentation System (WAAS) Performance Standard, Section B.3, Abbreviations and Acronyms. [1] Archived April 27, 2017, at the Wayback Machine

Grafarend, Erik W. GPS Solutions: Closed Forms, Critical and Special Configurations of P4P. GPS Solutions. **5**: 29–41. doi:10.1007/PL00012897.

Greenemeier, Larry. GPS and the World's First Space War. Scientific American. Retrieved 2016-02-08.

Greenemeier, Larry. GPS and the World's First Space War. *Scientific American.* Archived *from the original on February 8, 2016.* Retrieved February 8, 2016.

Grewal, Mohinder S.; Weill, Lawrence R.; Andrews, Angus P. (2007). Global Positioning Systems, Inertial Navigation, and Integration (2nd ed.). John Wiley & Sons. pp. 92–93. ISBN 0-470-09971-2., https://books.google.com/books?id=6P7UNphJ1z8C &pg=PA92

Ground Water Year Book of Chhattisgarh. 2016. Ministry of water resources and Ganga Rejuvenation central ground water board. GOI, p:12.

Guier, William H.; Weiffenbach, George C. (1997). Genesis of Satellite Navigation (PDF). Johns Hopkins APL Technical Digest. **19** (1): 178–181.

Gupta, R.P. 2018. Remote sensing Geology. III ed. ISBN 978-3-662-55876-8. Springer, Heidekberger Platz 3, 14197 Berlin, Germany.

Halemane H (2007) Suranga a sustainable water resource. In National Seminar on Water and Culture, Hampi, Bellary, India, 2007, pp. 20-25.

Hammouri, N., El-Naqa, A., Barakat, M., 2012. An integrated approach to groundwater exploration using remote sensing and geographic information system. J. Wat. Res. Prot. 4, 717–724. IWM (Institute of Water Modeling), 2006. Groundwater Model Study for Deep Tubewell Installation Project in Barind Area. Final Report, Volume-I (Main Report).

Haralick, R.M. (1984). Digital step edges from zero crossing of second directional derivatives. IEEE Trans. PAMI 6 (1), 58–68.

Harinarayana, P., Gopalakrishna, G.S., Balasubramanian, A., 2000. Remote sensing data for groundwater development and management in Keralapura watersheds of Cauvery basin, Karnataka, India. Indian Mineral 34:11-17

Hegarty, Christopher J. and Chatre, Eric. 2008. Evolution of the Global Navigation SatelliteSystem (GNSS). Proceedings of the IEEE. **96**: 1902–1917. doi:10.1109/JPROC.2008.2006090.

Hegarty, Christopher J. and Chatre, Eric. 2008. Evolution of the Global Navigation SatelliteSystem (GNSS). Proceedings of the IEEE. **96** *(12): 1902–1917.* doi:10.1109/JPROC.2008.2006090.

Helen E. Worth and Mame Warren. 2009. Transit to Tomorrow. Fifty Years of Space Research at The Johns Hopkins University Applied Physics Laboratory (PDF).

Hinton, J.C. 1996. GIS and remote sensing integration for environmental applications. Int. J. Geographical Information Systems, Vol. 10, No.7, pp. 877-890

Horton, R.E .1932. Drainage basin characteristics Trans Am Geophysics Union. 13: 350-361.

Horton, R.E. 1945. Erosional development of streams and their drainage basins; hydrophysical approach to quantitative morphology: Geol. Soc. America Bull., Vol. 56. No. 3.p. 275-370.

Howell, Elizabeth. Navstar: GPS Satellite Network. *SPACE.com.* Archived *from the original on February 17, 2013*. Retrieved February 14, 2013.

Howell, Elizabeth. Navstar: GPS Satellite Network. SPACE.com. Retrieved February 14, 2013. http://harveycohen.net/crcss GPS Signal Science

Hussain MF, Mondol MEA, Ahmad T (2004) Geochemistry of basement gneissic enclaves from Bastar craton: geodynamic implications. Current Sci. 86:1543-1547.

ICAO Completes Fact-Finding Investigation. International Civil Aviation Organization. Archived from the original on May 17, 2008. Retrieved September 15, 2008.

IGIS. 2008. IGIS User Manual, Scanpoint Geomatics Limited (SGL), Ahmedabad, Gujarat, India and Government of India, Department of Space, Indian Space Research Organisation (ISRO), India., p 836.

Interface Specification IS-GPS-200, Revision D: Navstar GPS Space Segment/Navigation User Interfaces (PDF). Navstar GPS Joint Program Office. p. 103. Archived from the original (PDF) on September 8, 2012.

Interface Specification IS-GPS-200, Revision D: Navstar GPS Space Segment/Navigation User Interfaces (PDF). Navstar GPS Joint Program Office. p. 103. Archived from the original (PDF) on September 8, 2012.

ION Fellow - Mr. John A. Klobuchar. *www.ion.org.* Archived *from the original on October 4, 2017*. Retrieved June 17, 2017.

Isaaks, E. and Srivastava, R. 1989. Applied Geostatistics. Oxford University Press, 542 pp Jensen, J.R. (2005). Introductory digital image processing a remote sensing perspective, 3. Ed., Prentice Hall series of geographic information science.

Jaiswal, R.K., Mukherjee, S., Krishnamurthy, J. and Saxena, R. 2003. Role of remote sensing and GIS techniques for generation of groundwater prospect zone towards rural development: an approach. Inter. J. Rem. Sen. 24 (5), 993-1008.

Javad Ashjaee GPS World webinar. gpsworld.com. December 8, 2011. Archived from the original on November 26, 2011. Retrieved December 13, 2011.

Jeff Carlisle (June 23, 2011). Testimony of Jeff Carlisle, LightSquared Executive Vice President of Regulatory Affairs and Public Policy to U.S. House Subcommittee on Aviation and Subcommittee on Coast Guard and Maritime Transportation (PDF). Archived from the original (PDF) on September 29, 2011. Retrieved December 13, 2011.

Jensen, J. R. 1996. Introductory digital image processing: a remote sensing perspective. Prentice Hall, Upper Saddle River.

Jenson, S.K. and Domingue, J.O. 1988. Extracting Topographic Structure from Digital Elevation Data for Geographical Information System Analysis, Photogrammetric Engineering & Remote Sensing, 54(11): 1593-1600.

Jenssen, L.L. and Middelkoop, F.H. 1992. Knowledge-basecrop classification of Landsat Thermatic Mapper image, International Journal of Remote Sensing, 13, pp 2827-2837.

Jerry Proc. Omega. *Jproc.ca.* Archived *from the original on January 5, 2010*. Retrieved December 8, 2009.

Jha, V.C. 1996. Himalayan Geomorphology Study of Himalayan Ramganga Basin Jaipur and New Delhi: Rawat Publication.

John A Klobuchar. 2003. ION Fellow http://harveycohen.net/crcss GPS Signal Science

John Deere StarFire. 3000. Operator Manual (PDF). 2011 John Deere. Archived from the original (PDF) on January 5, 2012. Retrieved November 13, 2011.

John Pike. 2009. GPS III Operational Control Segment (OCX). Globalsecurity. org. Retrieved December 8, 2009.

John Pike. GPS III Operational Control Segment (OCX). *Globalsecurity.org.* Archived *from the original on September 7, 2009*. Retrieved December 8, 2009.

Johnson S. 2010. Where good ideas come from, the natural history of innovation, New York: Riverhead Books

Johnson, Bobbie. 2009. GPS system 'close to breakdown'. The Guardian. London. Retrieved December 8, 2009.

Jon .2012. "GLONASS the future for all smartphones?". *Clove Blog*. Archived from the original on March 10, 2016. Retrieved October 29, 2016.

Joseph, G. 1996. Imaging Sensors. Remote Sensing Reviews, 13: 257-342.

Julius Genachowski. 2011. FCC Chairman Genachowski Letter to Senator Charles Grassley (PDF). Archived from the original (PDF) on January 13, 2012. Retrieved December 13, 2011.

Jury, H.L. 1973. Application of Kalman Filter to Real-Time Navigation using Synchronous Satellites, Proceeding of the 10th International Symposium on Space Technology and Science, Tokyo, 945–952.

Kale, V.S. and Gupta, A .2010. Introduction to Geomorphology (First impression edition). Hyderabad: University Press.

Katyal, J. C., Narayana Reddy, M. and Virmani, S. M., 1996. "A case study on the spatial and temporal dynamic of area and productivity of sorghum and pigeonpea in India through GIS", The world Bank-NARP Report on "Resource Characterization of Rain fed Farming Systems in Peninsular India", Hyderabad, India: CRIDA.

Khetarpaul, S., Chauhan, R., Gupta, S. K., Subramaniam, L. V. and Nambiar, U. 2011. Mining GPS data to determine interesting locations. Proceedings of the 8th International Workshop on Information Integration on the Web.

Knighton, D .1998. Fluvial Forms and Processes: A New Perspective London: Arnold.

Kriening and Torsten (January 23, 2019). Japan Prepares for GPS Failure with Quasi-Zenith Satellites. *SpaceWatch.Global*. Retrieved August 10, 2019.

Kumar A. 2009. Response of glacier to climate change a case study of Indrawati River Basin Kullu (Himachal Pradesh) Unpublished M Phil Dissertation. Jawaharlal Nehru University New Delhi.

Landsat 8. [Online] 2013. [Cited: September 19, 2013.] http://pubs.usgs.gov/fs/2013/3060/pdf/fs2013-3060.pdf.

Leopold, L.B., Wolman, M.G. and Miller, J.P. 1964. Fluvial Processes in Geomorphology New York: Dover Publication Magesh.

Levin, Dan. 2009. Chinese Square Off With Europe in Space. The New York Times. China. Retrieved November 6, 2011.

LightSquared Tests Confirm GPS Jamming. Aviation Week. Archived from the original on August 12, 2011. Retrieved June 20, 2011.

Lillesand, T.M. and Kiefer, R.1993. Remote Sensing and Image Interpretation. Third Edition John Villey, New York.

Lodwick, W.A., Monson, W. and Svoboda, L. 1990. Attribute error and sensitivity analysis of map operations in geographical information systems: suitability analysis. Inter. J. Geog. Info. Sys. 4 (4), 413-428.

Machiwal, D., Jha, M.K. and Mal, B.C. 2011. Assessment of groundwater potential in a semiarid region of India using remote sensing, GIS and MCDM techniques. Wat. Res. Manag. 25 (5), 1359-1386.

Magesh, N.S., Jitheshlal, K.V., Chandrasekar, N. and Jini, K.V. 2012. GIS based morphometric evaluation of Chimmini and Mupily watersheds parts of Western Ghats Thrissur, India. Earth Science Informatics, 5: 111-121.

Magesh, N.S., Jitheshlal, K.V., Chandrasekar, N. and Jini, K.V.2013. Geographical information system-based morphometric analysis of Bharathapuzha river basin Kerala, India. Applied Water Science 3: 467-477.

Mark, D.M. 1984. Automatic detection of drainage networks from digital elevation models. Cartographica 21, 168-178.

Martz, L.W. and Garbrecht. J. 1995. Automated recognition of valley lines and drainage networks from grid elevation models: A review and new method-Comment. Journal of Hydrology, 167:393-96

Massatt, Paul and Wayne Brady Summer. 2002. Optimizing performance through constellation management (PDF). Crosslink: 17–21. Archived from the original on January 25, 2012.

McNamara, Joel. 2008. GPS For Dummies. John Wiley & Sons. p. 59. ISBN 0-470-45785-6., https://books.google.com/books?id=Hbz4LYIrvu MC&pg= PA59

MDA. Geospatial Services International. MDA Essential Information Solutions. [Online] 2012. [Cited: September 19, 2013.] http://gs.mdacorporation.com/

Mellaart, James.1967. Çatal Hüyük: A Neolithic Town in Anatolia. Thames & Hudson. ISBN 0-07-041462-9.

Michael Russell Rip and James M. Hasik. 2002. The Precision Revolution: GPS and the Future of Aerial Warfare. Naval Institute Press. p. 65. ISBN 1-55750-973-5. Retrieved January 14, 2010.

Michael Russell Rip and James M. Hasik. 2002. The Precision Revolution: GPS and the Future of Aerial Warfare. Naval Institute Press. ISBN 1-55750-973-5. Retrieved May 25, 2008.

Michael Russell Rip and James M. Hasik. 2002. The Precision Revolution: GPS and the Future of Aerial Warfare. *Naval Institute Press. p. 65.* ISBN 978-1-55750-973-4. Retrieved January 14, 2010.

Michael Russell Rip and James M. Hasik. 2002. The Precision Revolution: GPS and the Future of Aerial Warfare. *Naval Institute Press.* ISBN 978-1-55750-973-4. Retrieved May 25, 2008.

Mishra A, Singh V and Desai V. 2009. Drought characterization: a probabilistic approach. Stochastic Environ. Res. Risk Assessm, 23 (1):41-55.

Mishra VP, Dutta NK, Kanchan VK, Vasta US and Guha K. 1984. Archaean granulite and granite gneiss complexes area, Bastar district, M.P. Record Geol. Surv. India, 113, part 6, pp150-158.

Mishra, V.P., Dutta, N.K., Guha, K.K., Kumaran, K. and Ramachandra, H.M. 1981. Geology of Pakahanjur area, Bastar and Rajnandgaon dis-trict, Madhya Pradesh, Raipur, India. Geological Survey of India (unpub. report) 76.

Mishra, V.P., Dutta, N.K., Kanchan, V.K., Vasta, U.S. and Guha, K. 1984. Archaean granulite and granite gneiss complexes of Kondagaon area, Bastar District, M.P. Records of Geological Survey of India 113(6), 150–158.

Mishra, V.P., P. Singh and Dutta, N.K. 1988. Stratigraphy, structure and metamorphic history of Bastar Craton. Records of Geological Survey of India 117(3–5), 1–26.

Misra, Pratap and Enge, Per. 2006. Global Positioning System. Signals, Measurements and Performance (2nd ed.). Ganga-Jamuna Press. p. 115. ISBN 0-9709544-1-7. Retrieved August 16, 2013.

Misra, Pratap and Enge, Per. 2006. Global Positioning System. Signals, Measurements and Performance *(2nd ed.). Ganga-Jamuna Press. p. 115.* ISBN 978-0-9709544-1-1. Retrieved August 16, 2013.

Mizokami, Kyle. 2016. North Korea Is Jamming GPS Signals. *Popular Mechanics.* Archived *from the original on March 6, 2019.* Retrieved March 3, 2019.

Moore, I.D., Grayson, R.B. and Ladson, A.R. 1991. Digital terrain modeling: A review of hydrological, geomorphological, and ecological applications. Hydrological Processes, 5:3–30.

Nag, S.K. and Chakraborty, S. 2003. Influence of rock types and structures in the development of drainage network in hard rock area. Journal of the Indian Society of Remote Sensing 31: 25-35.

Nair GU. 2016. Traditional wisdom in harvesting water. J. Tradit. Folk Pract., 4(1):50-53.

Napolitano, P. and Fabbri, A.G., 1996. Single parameter sensitivity analysis for aquifer vulnerability assessment using DRASTIC and SINTACS. In: Kovar, K., Nachtnebel, H.P. (Eds.), Proc. Hydro. GIS: application of geographical information systems in hydrology and water resources management, IAHS Publ. 235. IAHS, Wallingford, UK, pp. 559-566.

Narasimha, K.N.P., Janardhan, A.S. and Mishra, V.P. 1996. Granulites of Bhopalpatnam and Kondagaon Belts, Bastar Craton, M.P. Petrological and Fluid inclusion studies. Journal of South East Asian Earth Sciences 14, 221–229.

NASA. Aster. NASA Jet Propulsion Laboratory. [Online] July 9, 2004. [Cited: September 19, 2013.] http://asterweb.jpl.nasa.gov/eos.asp.

NASA. Overview of the GOES Mission. GOES I-M DataBook. 1st Revision. Greenbelt : NASA, 1996.

NASA. Specifications. MODIS Web. [Online] [Cited: September 19, 2013.] http://modis.gsfc.nasa.gov/about/specifications.php.

NASA. Technical Details. Landsat Science. [Online] September 18, 2013. [Cited: September 19, 2013.] http://landsat.gsfc.nasa.gov/?p=5081.

National Archives and Records Administration. U.S. Global Positioning System Policy. March 29, 1996.

National Archives and Records Administration. U.S. Global Positioning System PolicyArchived April 6, 2006, at the Wayback Machine. March 29, 1996.

National Executive Committee for Space-Based Positioning, Navigation, and Timing. Pnt.gov. Archived from the original on May 28, 2010. Retrieved October 15, 2010.

National Research Council (U.S.). Committee on the Future of the Global Positioning System; National Academy of Public Administration (1995). The global positioning system: a shared national asset: recommendations for technical improvements and enhancements. National Academies Press. p. 16. ISBN 0-309-05283-1. Retrieved August 16, 2013., https://books.google.com/books?id=FAHk65slfY4C&pg=PA16

NAVSTAR GPS User Equipment Introduction (PDF). Section 1.2.2

NAVSTAR GPS User Equipment Introduction (PDF). United States Government. Chapter 7

NAVSTAR GPS User Equipment Introduction (PDF). *United States Government.* Archived (PDF) *from the original on September 10, 2008*. Retrieved August 22, 2008.Chapter 7

Nayak N.C. 2001. Study on age old non-conventional adit/tunnel wells in the lateritic terrain of Kasaragod district, Kerala. Central Ground Water Board, Trivandrum, pp.1-20.

Nazimuddin M and Kokkal K. 2002. Studies on development of surangams as a nonconventional water resource in the Kanhangad block panchayat, Kasaragod district, Kerala. Groundwater Division, Centre for Water Resources Development and Management, Kunnamangalam, Kozhikode, Kerala, India, pp. 1-50.

Nellis, M.D., Lulla, K. and Jensen, J.R. 1990. Interfacing geographic information systems and remote sensing for rural land-use analysis, Photogrammetric Engineering & Remote Sensing, 56:329-331.

NOAA. Advanced Very High Resolution Radiometer - AVHRR. NOAA Satellite Information System. [Online] March 28, 2013. [Cited: September 19, 2013.] http://noaasis.noaa.gov/NOAASIS/ml/avhrr.html.

NOAA. GOES - Introduction. NOAA CLASS. [Online] [Cited: September 19, 2013.] http://www.class.ngdc.noaa.gov/data_available/goes/index.htm.

Notice Advisory to Navstar Users (NANU) 2016069. GPS Operations Center. Archived from the original on May 25, 2017. Retrieved June 25, 2017.

Notice Advisory to Navstar Users (NANU) 2016069. GPS Operations Center. Archived from the original on May 25, 2017. Retrieved June 25, 2017.

November 2004, Qualcomm announced successful tests of assisted GPS for mobile phones.

O'Callaghan, J.F. and Mark, D.M. 1984. The Extraction of Drainage Networks From Digital Elevation Data, Computer Vision, Graphics and Image Processing, 28: 328-344

O'Leary, Beth Laura and Darrin, Ann Garrison. 2009. Handbook of Space Engineering, Archaeology, and Heritage. Hoboken: CRC Press. pp. 239–240. ISBN 9781420084320.

O'Leary, Beth Laura and Darrin, Ann Garrison. 2009. Handbook of Space Engineering, Archaeology, and Heritage. Hoboken: CRC Press. pp. 239–240. ISBN 978-1-4200-8432-0.

Obi Reddy, G.P., Chandra Mouli, K., Srivastav, S.K., Srinivas, C.V. and Maji, A.K. 2000. Evaluation of groundwater potential zones using remote sensing data - a case study of Gaimukh watershed, Bhandara district, Maharashtra. J Indian Soc Remote Sens 28(1):19-32

On February 25, 2010, the U.S. Air Force awarded the contract to develop the GPS Next Generation Operational Control System (OCX) to improve accuracy and availability of GPS navigation signals, and serve as a critical part of GPS modernization.

ORDER ON RECONSIDERATION (PDF). Jul 3, 2003. Retrieved October 20, 2015.

Origin of Global Positioning System (GPS). *Rewire Security.* Archived *from the original on February 11, 2017*. Retrieved February 9, 2017.

Oszczak, B., New Algorithm for GNSS Positioning Using System of Linear Equations, Proceedings of the 26th International Technical Meeting of The Satellite Division of the Institute of Navigation (ION GNSS+ 2013), Nashville, TN, September 2013, pp. 3560–3563.

Padre S. 2008. Farming without pumps. Leisa India, AME Foundation, Bangalore, India, pp.34-35.

Panwar S. and Chakrapani GJ. 2013. Climate change and its influence on groundwater resources. Curr. Sci., 105:37-46

Patel, P.P. and Sarkar, A. 2010. Terrain Characterization using SRTM Data. Journal of Indian Social Remote Sensor 38: 11-24.

Paul Riegler, FBT. FCC Bars Light Squared Broadband Network Plan. February 14, 2012. Retrieved February 14, 2012.

PCI. 2009. Geomatica Version 10.2. Richmond Hill, Ontario, Canada.

Penttinen, Jyrki T. J. The Telecommunications Handbook: Engineering Guidelines for Fixed, Mobile and Satellite Systems. John Wiley & Sons. ISBN 9781119944881.

Penttinen, Jyrki T.J. 2015. The Telecommunications Handbook: Engineering Guidelines for Fixed, Mobile & Satellite Systems. *John Wiley & Sons*. ISBN 978-1-119-94488-1.

Peter Dale and John McLaughlin. 2000. *Land Administration*, Oxford University Press, 186 pages.

Peter H. Dana. 2013. GPS Week Number Rollover Issues. *Archived from* the original *on February 25, 2013*. Retrieved August 12, 2013.

Peter H. Dana. 2013. GPS Week Number Rollover Issues. Retrieved August 12, 2013.

Peter H. Dana. Receiver Position, Velocity, and Time. University of Colorado at Boulder. Retrieved July 7, 2008.

Pradhan A, Patil SK, Marothia DK, Chandrakar T, Nag SK and Mukherjee SC. 2019. Effect of Catchment and Hydrology of Ancient Dalpatsagar Reservoir on Water Resources of Jagdalpur City, Bastar, India. Int.J.Curr. Microbiol. App. Sci. 8(01): 1797-1812. doi: https://doi.org/10.20546/ijcmas.2019.801.191 (1) CO_2; (2) Well (3) Blockmaking; (4) Meterology.

Prasad PMR, Jayakumar NS. and Basalt P. 1991. Surangams of Kasargod - an unconventional water harvesting mechanism. Centre for Water Resources Development and Management, Kunnamangalam, Kozhikode, Kerala, pp. 40-45.

Pratap, K., Ravindran, K.V. and Prabakaran, B. 2000. Groundwater prospect zoning using remote sensing and geographical information system: a case study in Dala-Renukoot Area, Sonbhadra District Uttar Pradesh. J Indian Soc Remote Sens 28(4):249–263

Press release: First Modernized GPS Satellite Built by Lockheed Martin Launched Successfully by the U.S. Air Force - Sep 26, 2005. Lockheed Martin.

Press release: First Modernized GPS Satellite Built by Lockheed Martin Launched Successfully by the U.S. Air Force - Sep 26, 2005. *Lockheed Martin*. Archived *from the original on August 10, 2017*. Retrieved August 9, 2017.

Preview of Root Finding. Books.google.com. 2007. ISBN 978-0-521-88068-8. Retrieved October 15, 2010.

Publications and Standards from the National Marine Electronics Association (NMEA). *National Marine Electronics Association. Archived from* the original *on August 4, 2009*. Retrieved June 27, 2008.

Publications and Standards from the National Marine Electronics Association (NMEA). National Marine Electronics Association. Retrieved June 27, 2008.

Rahman, A.T.M.S., Jahan, C.S., Mazumder, Q.H., Kamruzzaman, M., Hossain, A., 2016. Evaluation of spatio-temporal dynamics of water table in NW Bangladesh - an integrated approach of GIS and statistics. J. Sust. Water Res. Manag. 2 (3), 297–312. https://doi.org/10.1007/s40899-016-0057-4.

Rai, P.K., Mohan K., Mishra S., Ahmad A. and Mishra, V.N. 2014. A GIS-based approach in drainage morphometric analysis of Kanhar River Basin India. Applied Water Science.

Ramachandra, H. M., Roy, A., Mishra, V.P. and Dutta, N.K. 2001. A critical review of the tectonothermal evolution of the Bastar Craton. Proceeding M.S. Krishnan Centenary Commemorative National Seminar. Geological Survey of India, Special Publications: Calcutta, India 55, 161–180.

Recap story: Three Atlas 5 launch successes in one month. Archived *from the original on November 1, 2015*. Retrieved October 31, 2015.

Recap story: Three Atlas 5 launch successes in one month. GPS almanacs. Navcen.uscg.gov. Retrieved October 15, 2010.

Reddy, G.P.O. and Maji, A.K. 2003. Delineation and Characterization of Geomorphological features in a part of Lower Maharahstra Metamorphic Plateau, using IRS-ID LISS-III data, Journal of the Indian Society of Remote Sensing, 31 (4), 241-250

Reddy, G.P.O., Nagaraju. M.S.S., Ramteke, I.K. and Sarkar, D. 2012. Terrain characterization for soil resource mapping using IRS-P6 data and GIS - A case study from Basaltic terrain of Central India, Journal of the Indian Society of Remote Sensing (in press).

Reddy, Obi G.P., Kumar, N. and Sarkar, D. 2012. Training manual on GIS and digital image processing. NBSS & LUP Publ. 153:155-156.

Relativistische Zeitdilatation eines künstlichen Satelliten (Relativistic time dilation of an artificial satellite. *Astronautica Acta II (in German) (25). Retrieved 19 October 2014*. Archived *from the original on July 3, 2014*. Retrieved October 20, 2014.

Richharia, Madhavendra and Westbrook, Leslie David. 2011. Satellite Systems for Personal Applications: Concepts and Technology. John Wiley & Sons. p. 443. ISBN 1-119-95610-2.

Richharia, Madhavendra and Westbrook, Leslie David. 2011. Satellite Systems for Personal Applications: Concepts and Technology. *John Wiley & Sons. p. 443.* ISBN 978-1-119-95610-5. Archived *from the original on July 4, 2014*. Retrieved February 28, 2017.

Rose, R.S. and Krishnan, N. 2009. Spatial analysis of groundwater potential using remote sensing and GIS in the Kanyakumari and Nambiyar basins, India. J. Ind. Soc. Rem. Sen. 37 (4): 681–692.

Rumerman, Judy A. 2009. NASA Historical Data Book, Volume VII (PDF). NASA. p. 136.

Rumerman, Judy A. 2009. NASA Historical Data Book, Volume VII (PDF). *NASA. p. 136.* Archived (PDF) *from the original on December 25, 2017*. Retrieved July 12, 2017.

Russia Launches Three More GLONASS-M Space Vehicles. Inside GNSS. *Archived from* the original *on February 6, 2009*. Retrieved December 26, 2008.

Russia Launches Three More GLONASS-M Space Vehicles". *Inside GNSS*. Archived from the original on February 6, 2009. Retrieved December 26, 2008.

Saaty, T.L. 1980. The Analytic Hierarchy Process. McGraw-Hill, New York, pp. 278.

Sabins, F. F. 1987. Remote Sensing: Principles and Interpretation. NY: W.H. Freeman and Company.

Sabins, F.F. 1997. Remote Sensing and Principles and Image Interpretation. WH Freeman, New York.

Samama, Nel. 2008. Global Positioning: Technologies and Performance. John Wiley & Sons. p. 65. ISBN 0-470-24190-X., https://books.google.com/books?id=EyFrcnSRFFgC&pg=PA65

Sandia National Laboratory's Nonproliferation programs and arms control technologyArchived September 28, 2006, at the Wayback Machine.

Santosh, M., Yokoyama, K. and Acharya, S.K. 2004. Geochronology of tec-tonic evolution of Karimnagar–Bhopalpatnam granulite belts, Central India. Gondwana Research 7(2), 501–518.

Sarkar G. Gupta S.N. and Bishui P.K. 1994. New Rb-Sr isotope ages and geochemistry of granitic gneisses from southern Bastar: implications for crustal evolution. Indian minerals, 48: 7-12

Satellite Imaging Corporation. QuickBird Satellite Imagery and Satellite System Specifications. Satellite Imaging Corporation. [Online] 2013. [Cited: September 19, 2013.] http://www.satimagingcorp.com/satellite-sensors/quickbird.html.

Satellite message format. *Gpsinformation.net.* Archived *from the original on November 1, 2010*. Retrieved October 15, 2010.

Schumm, S.A .1956. The evolution of drainage system and slopes in badlands at Perth Amboy, New Jersey. Geological Sicence America Bull 67: 597-646.

SECOR Chronology. Mark Wade's Encyclopedia Astronautica. Archived from the original on January 16, 2010. Retrieved January 19, 2010.

Section 4 beginning on page 15 GEOFFREY BLEWITT: BASICS OF THE GPS TECHNIQUE

Sen, P.K .1993. Geomorphological analysis of drainage basins Burdwan: The University of Burdwan.

Sener, E., Davraz, A. and Ozcelik, M. 2005. An integration of GIS and remote sensing in groundwater investigations: a case study in Burdur, Turkey. Hydrog. J. 13 (5–6), 826–834.

Shreve, R.L. 1966. Statistical law of stream numbers. Journal of Geology, 74, 17–37.

Singh R.L. India: A Regional Geography Varanasi: National geographical Society of India 1971.

Singh, P. K., Rathore, L. S., Mali, P. and Singh, K. K., 2009, "Spatial Analysis of Mandal-wise rainfall Variability for Drought in Anantapur District of Andhra Pradesh in India", International Journal of Meteorology, July, 34, 339, 147-154.

Sinha, Vandana. 2003. Commanders and Soldiers' GPS-receivers. Gcn.com. Retrieved October 13, 2009.

Sirola, Niilo. 2010. Closed-form algorithms in mobile positioning: Myths and misconceptions. 7th Workshop on Positioning Navigation and Communication. WPNC 2010. pp. 38–44. doi:10.1109/WPNC.2010.5653789.

Space Segment. *GPS.gov.* Archived *from the original on July 18, 2019*. Retrieved July 27, 2019.

Space Technology Hall of Fame, Inducted Technology: Global Positioning System (GPS). Archived from the original on June 12, 2012.

Spotlight GPS pet locator. *Spotlightgps.com. Archived from* the original *on October 16, 2015*. Retrieved October 15, 2010.

Sreedevi, P.D., Srinivasulu, S. and Raju, K.K. 2001. Hydrogeomorphological and groundwater prospects of the Pageru river basin by using remote sensing data. Environ Geol 40:1919-1924

Srivastava R.K., Hall R.P., Verma R. and Singh R.K. 1996. Contrasting precabrian mafic dykes of the Bastar craton, central India: petrological and geochemical characteristics. J. Geol. Soc. India, 48, 537-546.

Srivastava, Ishan. 2014. How Kargil spurred India to design own GPS. The Times of India. Retrieved 9 December 2014.

Srivastava, Ishan. 2014. How Kargil spurred India to design own GPS. The Times of India. Archived *from the original on December 15, 2016*. Retrieved December 9, 2014.

Srivastava, P.K. and Bhattacharya, A.K. 2006. Groundwater assessment through an integrated approach using remote sensing, GIS and resistivity techniques: a case study from a hard rock terrain. Int J Remote Sens 27(20):4599-4620

Statement of Julius P. Knapp, Chief, Office of Engineering and Technology, Federal Communications Commission (PDF). gps.gov. September 15, 2011. p. 3. Retrieved December 13, 2011.

Strahler A.N. 1964. Quantitative geomorphology of drainage basins and channel networks In V T Chow Edition. Handbook of Applied Hydrology pp: 439-476.

Strahler, A. N. (1957). Quantitative analysis of watershed geomorphology: Am. Geophys. Union Trans, Vol. 38, No. 6, p.013-020.

Strahler, A.N .1952. Dynamic basis of geomorphology Bull. Geological Science America, 63: 923-938.

Superaccurate GPS Chips Coming to Smartphones in 2018. *IEEE Spectrum: Technology, Engineering, and Science News. September 21, 2017*. Archived *from the original on January 18, 2018*. Retrieved January 17, 2018.

Tarboton, D.G. 1997. A new method for the determination of flow direction and contributing areas in grid digital elevation models, Water Resource Research 33(2):309-319.

Technical Information about the SPOT Satellites. EADS Astrium. [Online] 2013. [Cited: September 19, 2013.] http://www.astrium-geo.com/en/191-spot-technical-information.

Tessler, Joelle. 2011. Internet network may jam GPS in cars, jets. The Sun News. Archived from the original on May 1, 2011. Retrieved April 7, 2011.

TextGenerator Version 2.0. United States Nuclear Detonation Detection System (USNDS). Fas.org. Archived from the original on October 10, 2011. Retrieved November 6, 2011.

The Global Positioning System Assessing National Policies, by Scott Pace, Gerald P. Frost, Irving Lachow, David R. Frelinger, Donna Fossum, Don Wassem, Monica M. Pinto, Rand Corporation, 1995, Appendix B, GPS History, Chronology, and Budgets

The Global Positioning System Assessing National Policies, by Scott Pace, Gerald P. Frost, Irving Lachow, David R. Frelinger, Donna Fossum, Don Wassem, Monica M. Pinto, Rand Corporation, 1995,Appendix B Archived March 4, 2016, at the Wayback Machine, GPS History, Chronology, and Budgets

The Global Positioning System: Assessing National Policies Archived December 30, 2015, at the Wayback Machine, p.245. RAND corporation

The Global Positioning System: Assessing National Policies, p.245. RAND corporation

The Navstar Global Positioning System, hereafter referred to as GPS, is a space-based radio navigation system owned by the United States Government (USG) and operated by the United States Air Force (USAF). [1]

The Pacific Northwest Geodetic Array. *cwu.edu*. Archived *from the original on September 11, 2014*. Retrieved October 10, 2014.

The Role of GPS in Precise Time and Frequency Dissemination (PDF). GPSworld. July–August 1990. Retrieved April 27, 2014.

The USA's GPS-III Satellites. *Defense Industry Daily. October 13, 2011*. Archived *from the original on October 18, 2011*. Retrieved October 27, 2011.

The Use of GPS Tracking Technology in Australian Football. Archived *from the original on September 27, 2016*. Retrieved September 25, 2016.

The Use of GPS Tracking Technology in Australian Football. Retrieved 2016-09-25.

Thomas, B.C., Kuriakose, S.L. and Jaydev, S.K. 2009. A method for groundwater prospects zonation in data poor areas using remote sensing and GIS: a case study in Kalikavu Panchayth of Malappuram district, Kerala, India. Int. J. Dig. Earth 2 (2), 155–170.

Thomas, J., Joseph, S., Thrivikramji, K.P. and Abe, G. (2011). Morphometric analysis of the drainage system and its hydrological implications in the rain shadow regions, Kerala, India. J. Geogr. Sci., 21(6): 1077-1088 (12 pages).

Thomassen, Keith. 2014. How GPS Works. avionicswest.com. Archived from the original on March 30, 2016. Retrieved April 22, 2014.

Three Classes of Orbit. NASA Earth Observatory. [Online] [Cited: September 19, 2013.] http://earthobservatory.nasa.gov/Features/OrbitsCatalog/page2.php.

Three Classes of Orbit. NASA Earth Observatory. [Online] [Cited: September 19, 2013.] http://earthobservatory.nasa.gov/Features/OrbitsCatalog/page2.php.[3] Archived December 13, 2012, at the Wayback Machine.

Tobler W. 1970. A computer movie simulating urban growth in the Detroit region. Economic Geography, 46(2): 234-240.

Townshend, J.R.G. 1981. Terrain Analysis and Remote Sensing. Allen & Unwin. Verstappen, H.T., van Zuidam, R.A. (1968). ITC system of geomorphological survey. ITC Publ. 7,3-49. (Ed.)

Triple differencing. Gmat.unsw.edu.au. Archived from the original on March 6, 2011. Retrieved October 15, 2010. chapter on root finding and nonlinear sets of equations Preview of Root Finding. Books.google.com. 2007. ISBN 978-0-521-88068-8. Retrieved October 15, 2010.

Trueller, P. T. 1996. "Rangeland management", The remote sensing core curriculum, Applications in Remote Sensing, vol 4, on the internet at http://www.asrps.org, 1996.

U.S. GPS Industry Council Petition to the FCC to adopt OOBE limits jointly proposed by MSV and the Industry Council. FCC.gov. September 4, 2003. Retrieved December 13, 2011.

UNDP (United Nations Development Programme), 1992. Groundwater Survey, The Hydrogeological Condition of Bangladesh, United Nations Development Project Technical Report, Prepared for the Govt. of the People's Republic of Bangladesh.

United Launch Alliance Successfully Launches GPS IIF-12 Satellite for U.S. Air Force. *Www.ulalaunch.com.* Archived *from the original on February 28, 2018*. Retrieved February 27, 2018.

United States Coast Guard General GPS News 9–9–05

United States Department of the Interior. AVHRR. National Atlas. [Online] January 14, 2013. [Cited: September 19, 2013.] http://nationalatlas.gov/articles/mapping/a_avhrr.html.

United States Naval Research Laboratory. National Medal of Technology for GPSArchived October 11, 2007, at the Wayback Machine. November 21, 2005

United States Updates Global Positioning System Technology. America.gov. February 3, 2006.

United States Updates Global Positioning System Technology. *America.gov. February 3, 2006. Archived from* the original *on October 9, 2013*. Retrieved June 17, 2019.

US Air Force Eyes Changes To National Security Satellite Programs. *Aviationweek.com. January 18, 2013*. Archived *from the original on September 22, 2013*. Retrieved September 28, 2013.

USCG Navcen: GPS Frequently Asked Questions. Archived *from the original on April 30, 2011*. Retrieved January 31, 2007.

USGS, 2012. Global data explorer, http://gdex.cr.usgs.gov/(accessed 11.12.12).

USGS. Frequently Asked Questions about the Landsat Missions. USGS Landsat Missions. [Online] August 29, 2013. [Cited: September 19, 2013.] http://landsat.usgs.gov/tools_faq.php.

USGS/NASA. ASTER Data Access Policies. LP DAAC. [Online] August 19, 2013. [Cited: September 19, 2013.] https://lpdaac.usgs.gov/products/aster_policies.

USGS/NASA. MODIS Overview. LP DAAC. [Online] August 19, 2013. [Cited: September 19, 2013.] https://lpdaac.usgs.gov/products/modis_overview.

Using GPS to improve tropical cyclone forecasts. *ucar.edu*. Archived *from the original on May 28, 2015*. Retrieved May 28, 2015.

USNO NAVSTAR Global Positioning System Archived February 8, 2006, at the Wayback Machine. Retrieved May 14, 2006.

USNO NAVSTAR Global Positioning System. Retrieved May 14, 2006.

USNO NAVSTAR Global Positioning System. *U. S. Naval Observatory. Archived from* the original *on January 26, 2011*. Retrieved January 7, 2011.

Van Westen CJ (1993) Application of geographic information systems to landslide hazard zonation. Ph.D. dissertation. ITC publ. no. 15. ITC, Enschede, p 245.

Vansutre, S., Hari, K.R. 2010. Granulite belts of Central India with special reference to the Bhopalpatnam Granulite Belt: Significance in crustal evolution and implications for Columbia Supercontinent. Journal of Asian Earth Sciences. DOI: 10.1016/jsaeas.2010.06.004.

Vittala, S.S., Govindaiah S, Gowda HH .2004. Morphometric analysis of subwatersheds in the pavagada area of Tumkur district South India using remote sensing and gis techniques. Journal of the Indian Society of Remote Sensing 32: 351-362.

Waikar, M.L. and Nilawar, A.P., 2014. Identification of groundwater potential zone using remote sensing and GIS technique. Inter. J. Inn. Res. Sci. Engr. Tech. 3, 12164–12174 (ISSN: 2319–8753).

Weng, Q. 2001. A remote sensing-GIS evaluation of urban expansion and its impact on surface temperature in the Zhujiang delta, Southern China. Int. J. Remote Sens. 22 (10), 1999–2014.

What is a GPS?. Archived *from the original on January 31, 2018*. Retrieved January 28, 2018.

What the Global Positioning System Tells Us about Relativity Archived January 4, 2007, at the Wayback Machine.. Retrieved January 2, 2007.

Why Did the Department of Defense Develop GPS?. Trimble Navigation Ltd. Archived from the original on October 18, 2007. Retrieved January 13, 2010.

Why Did the Department of Defense Develop GPS?. *Trimble Navigation Ltd. Archived from* the original *on October 18, 2007*. Retrieved January 13, 2010.

Winterberg, Friedwardt (1956). Relativistische Zeitdiiatation eines künstlichen Satelliten (Relativistic time dilation of an artificial satellite). Astronautica Acta II (in German) (25). Retrieved 19 October 2014.

XM982 Excalibur Precision Guided Extended Range Artillery Projectile. GlobalSecurity.org. May 29, 2007. Retrieved September 26, 2007. (Registration required (help)).

XM982 Excalibur Precision Guided Extended Range Artillery Projectile. *GlobalSecurity.org. May 29, 2007*. Archived *from the original on September 4, 2006*. Retrieved September 26, 2007.

XM982 Excalibur Precision Guided Extended Range Artillery Projectile. GlobalSecurity.org. May 29, 2007. Retrieved September 26, 2007. (Registration required (help)).

Yellappa T., Chetty T R., Santosh, M. 2011. Tectonic framework of southern Bastar Craton, Central India: A study based on different spatial information data sets. Geological Journal Geol. J. Published online in Wiley Online Library (wileyonlinelibrary.com). DOI: 10.1002/gj.1333.

Annexure: Projection Details

Projection	Type	Properties	Creator	Notes
Equirectangular =equidistant cylindrical = rectangular = la carte parallélogrammatique	Cylindrical	Equidistant	Marinus of Tyre	Simplest geometry; distances along meridians are conserved Plate carrée: special case having the equator as the standard parallel.
Cassini-Cassini Soldner	Cylindrical	Equidistant	César-François Cassini de Thury	Transverse of equidistant projection; distances along central meridian are conserved. Distances perpendicular to central meridian are preserved.
Mercator = Wright	Cylindrical	Conformal	Gerardus Mercator	Lines of constant bearing (rhumb lines) are straight, aiding navigation. Areas inflate with latitude, becoming so extreme that the map cannot show the poles.
Web Mercator	Cylindrical	Compromise	Google	A variation of the Mercator projection, ignoring the ellipticity of Earth for faster computation. The de facto standard for web mapping applications, used by Google Maps, Bing Maps, Mapquest, Mapbox, Open Street Map and others.
Gauss Krüger = Gauss conformal = (Ellipsoidal) Transverse Mercator	Cylindrical	Conformal	Carl Friedrich Gauss Johann Heinrich Louis Krüger	This transverse,ellipsoidal form of the Mercator is finite, unlike the equatorial Mercator.forms the basis of the Universal Transverse Mercator coordinate system.

Gall stereographic similar to Braun	Cylindrical	Compromise	James Gall	Intended to resemble the Mercator while also displaying the poles. Standard parallels at 45°N/S. Braun is horizontally stretched version with scale correct at equator.
Miller = Miller cylindrical	Cylindrical	Compromise	Osborn Maitland Miller	Intended to resemble the Mercator while also displaying the poles.
Lambert cylindrical equal-area	Cylindrical	Equal-area	Johann Heinrich Lambert	Standard parallel at the equator. Aspect ratio of p(3.14). Base projection of the cylindrical equal-area family.
Behrmann	Cylindrical	Equal-area	Walter Behrmann	Horizontally compressed version of the Lambert equal-area. Has standard parallels at 30°N/S and an aspect ratio of 2.36.
Hobo–Dyer	Cylindrical	Equal-area	Mick Dyer	Horizontally compressed version of the Lambert equal-area. Very similar are Trystan Edwards and Smyth equal surface (= Craster rectangular) projections with standard parallels at around 37°N/S. Aspect r atio of ~2.0.
Gall–Peters = Gall orthographic = Peters	Cylindrical	Equal-area	James Gall (Arno Peters)	Horizontally compressed version of the Lambert equal-area. Standard parallels at 45°N/S. Aspect ratio of ~1.6. Similar is Balthasart projection with standard parallels at 50°N/S.
Central cylindrical	Cylindrical	Perspective	(unknown)	Practically unused in cartography because of severe polar distortion, but popular in panoramic photography, especially for architectural scenes.
Sinusoidal = Sanson Flamsteed = Mercator	Pseudoc ylindrical 1	Equal-area	(Several; first is unknown)	Meridians are sinusoids; parallels are equally

equalarea				spaced. Aspect ratio of 2:1. Distances along parallels are conserved.
Mollweide = elliptical = Babinet = homolo-graphic	Pseudoc ylindrical	Equal-area	Karl Brandan Mollweide	Meridians are ellipses.
Eckert II	Pseudoc ylindrical	Equal-area	Max Eckert-Greifendorff	Max Eckert-Greifendorff
Eckert IV	Pseudocylindrical		Equal-area	Parallels are unequal in spacing and scale; outer meridians are semicircles; other meridians are semiellipses.
Eckert VI	Pseudoc ylindrical	Equal-area	Max Eckert-Greifendorff	Parallels are unequal in spacing and scale; meridians are half-period sinusoids.
Ortelius oval	Pseudoc ylindrical	Compromise	Battista Agnese	Meridians are circular.[1]
Goode homolosine	Pseudoc ylindrical	Equal-area	John Paul Goode	Hybrid of Sinusoidal and Mollweide projections. Usually used in interrupted form.
Kavrayskiy VII	Pseudoc ylindrical	Compromise	Vladimir V. Kavrayskiy	Evenly spaced parallels. Equivalent to Wagner VI horizontally compressed by a factor of. 3/2
Robinson	Pseudoc ylindrical	Compromise	Arthur H. Robinson	Computed by interpola-tion of tabulated values. Used by Rand McNally since inception and used by NGS 1988–98.
Natural Earth	Pseudoc ylindrical	Compromise	Tom Patterson	Computed by interpola tion of tabulated values.
Tobler hyperelliptical	Pseudocy-lindrical	Equal-area	Waldo R. Tobler	A family of map projections that includes as special cases Mollweide projection, Collignon projection, and the various cylindrical equal-area projections.
Wagner VI	Pseudocy-lindrical	Compromise	K.H. Wagner	Equivalent to Kavrayskiy VII vertically compressed by a factor of $\sqrt{3/2}$
Collignon	Pseudocy-lindrical	Equal-area	Édouard Collignon	Depending on configuration, the

				projection also may map the sphere to a single diamond or a pair of squares.
HEALPix	Pseudocy-lindrical	Equal-area	Krzyszt of M. Górski	Hybrid of Collignon + Lambert cylindrical equal-area
Boggs eumorphic	Pseudocyl-indrical	Equal-area	Samuel Whittemore Boggs	The equal-area projection that results from average of sinusoidal and Mollweide *y*-coordinates and thereby constraining the *x* coordinate.
Craster parabolic =Putnins P4	Pseudocy-lindrical	Equal-area	John Craster	Meridians are parabolas. Standard parallels at 36°462N/S; parallels are unequal in spacing and scale; 2:1 Aspect.
Flat-polar quartic = McBryde- Thomas #4	Pseudocy-lindrical	Equal-area	Felix W. Mc Bryde, Paul Thomas	Standard parallels at 33°452N/S; parallels are unequal in spacing and scale; meridians are fourth-order curves. Distortion-free only where the standard parallels intersect the central meridian.
Quartic authalic	Pseudocy-lindrical	Equal-area	Karl Siemon Oscar Adams	Parallels are unequal in spacing and scale. No distortion along the equator. Meridians are fourth-order curves.
The Times	Pseudocy-lindrical	Compromise	John Muir	Standard parallels 45°N/S. Parallels based on Gall orthographic, but with curved meridians. Developed for Bartholomew Ltd., The Times Atlas.
Loximuthal	Pseudocy-lindrical	Compromise	Karl Siemon, Waldo Tobler	From the designated centre, lines of constant bearing (rhumb lines/loxodromes) are straight and have the correct length. Generally asymmetric about the equator.
Aitoff	Pseudoazi-muthal	Compromise	David A. Aitoff	Stretching of modified equatorial azimuthal equidistant map.

				Boundary is 2:1 ellipse. Largely superseded by Hammer.
Hammer =Hammer-Aitoff variations: Briesemeister;	Pseudoazi-muthal	Equal-area	Ernst Hammer	Modified from azimuthal equal-area equatorial map. Boundary is 2:1 ellipse. Variants are oblique versions, centred on 45°N.
Nordic				
Winkel tripel	Pseudoazi-muthal	Compromise	Oswald Winkel	Arithmetic mean of the equirectangular projection and the Aitoff projection. Standard world projection for the NGS 1998–present.
Van der Grinten	Other	Compromise	Alphons J. van der Grinten	Boundary is a circle. All parallels and meridians are circular arcs. Usually clipped near 80°N/S. Standard world projection of the NGS1922–88.
Equidistant conic projection =simple conic	Conic	Equidistant	Based on Ptolemy's 1st Projection	Distances along meridians are conserved, as is distance along one or two standard parallels[2]
Lambert conformal conic	Conic	Conformal	Johann Heinrich Lambert	
Albers conic	Conic	Equal-area	Heinrich C. Albers	Two standard parallels with low distortion between them.
Werner	Pseudoco-nical	Equal-area	Johannes Stabius	Distances from the North Pole are correct as are the curved distances along parallels.
Bonne	Pseudoco-nical, cordiform	Equal-area	Bernardus Sylvanus	Parallels are equally spaced circular arcs and standard lines. Appearance depends on reference parallel. General case of both Werner and sinusoidal
Bottomley	Pseudoco-nical	Equal-area	Henry Bottomley	Alternative to the Bonne projection with simpler overall shape Parallels are elliptical arcs

				Appearance depends on reference parallel.
American polyconic	Pseudoconical	Pseudoconical	Ferdinand Rudolph Hassler	Distances along the parallels are preserved as are distances along the central meridian.
Azimuthal equidistant =Postel zenithal equidistant	Azimuthal	Equidistant	Abk Rayhan al-Biruni	Used by the USGS in the National Atlas of the United States of America. Distances from centre are conserved. Used as the emblem of the United Nations, extending to 60° S.
Gnomonic	Azimuthal	Gnomonic	Thales(possibly)	All great circles map to straight lines. Extreme distortion far from the center. Shows less than one hemisphere.
Lambert azimuthal equal-area	Azimuthal	Equal-area	Johann Heinrich Lambert	The straight-line distance between the central point on the map to any other point is the same as the straight-line 3D distance through the globe between the two points.
Stereographic	Azimuthal	Conformal	Hipparchos (deployed)	Map is infinite in extent with outer hemisphere inflating severely, so it is often used as two hemispheres. Maps all small circles to circles, which is useful for planetary mapping to preserve the shapes of craters.
Orthographic	Azimuthal	Perspective	Hipparchos (deployed)	View from an infinite distance.
Vertical perspective	Azimuthal	Perspective	Matthias Seutter (deployed)	View from a finite distance. Can only display less than a hemisphere.
Two-point equidistant	Azimuthal	Equidistant	Hans Maurer	Two "control points" can be almost arbitrarily chosen. The two straight-line distances from any point on the map to the two control points are correct.

Peirce quincuncial	Other	Conformal	Charles Sanders Peirce	-
Guyou hemisphere-in-a-square projection	Other	Conformal	Émile Guyou	-
Adams hemisphere-in-a-square projection	Other	Conformal	Oscar Sherman Adams	-
Octant projection	Polyhedral	Compro-mise	Leonardo da Vinci	Projects the globe onto eight octants (Reuleaux triangles) with no meridians and no parallels.
Cahill's Butterfly Map	Polyhedral	Compro-mise	Bernard Joseph Stanislaus Cahill	Projects the globe onto an octahedron with symmetrical components & contiguous landmasses that may be displayed in various arrangements
Cahill–Keyes projection	Polyhedral	Compro-mise	Gene Keyes	Projects the globe onto a truncated octahedron with symmetrical components and contiguous land masses
Waterman butterfly projection	Polyhedral	Compro-mise	Steve Waterman	Projects the globe onto a truncated octahedron with symmetrical components and contiguous land masses that may be displayed in various arrangements
Quadrilateralized spherical cube	Polyhedral	Equal-area	F. Kenneth Chan, E. M. O' Neill	-
Dymaxion map	Polyhedral	Compro-mise	Buckminster Fuller	Also known as a Fuller Projection.
Myriahedral projections	Polyhedral	Compro-mise	Jarke J. van Wijk	Projects the globe onto a myriahedron: a polyhedron with a very large number of faces.[3][4]
Craig retroazimuthal =Mecca		Retroazi-muthal	James Ireland Craig	-
Hammer retroazimuthal, front hemisphere		Retroazi-muthal	Ernst Hammer	-
Hammer retroazimuthal, back hemisphere		Retroazi-muthal	Ernst Hammer	-

Littrow		Retroazi-muthal	Joseph Johann Littrow	Also conformal
Armadillo	Other	Compro-mise	Erwin Raisz	-
GS50	Other	Conformal	John P. Snyder	Designed specifically to minimize distortion when used to display all 50U.S. states.